MAXIMILIAN VOLOSHIN AND THE RUSSIAN LITERARY CIRCLE

Maximilian Voloshin and the Russian Literary Circle

Culture and Survival
in Revolutionary Times

BARBARA WALKER

Indiana University Press
Bloomington and Indianapolis

This book is a publication of

Indiana University Press
601 North Morton Street
Bloomington, IN 47404-3797 USA

http://iupress.indiana.edu

Telephone orders   800-842-6796
Fax orders   812-855-7931
Orders by e-mail   iuporder@indiana.edu

The paper used in this publication meets the minimum requirements
of American National Standard for Information Sciences—
Permanence of Paper for Printed Library Materials, ANSI Z39.48-
1984.

MANUFACTURED IN THE UNITED STATES OF AMERICA

Library of Congress Cataloging-in-Publication Data

Walker, Barbara, date
   Maximilian Voloshin and the Russian literary circle : culture and
survival in revolutionary times / Barbara Walker.
      p. cm.
   Includes bibliographical references and index.
   ISBN 0-253-34431-X (cloth : alk. paper)
   1. Voloshin, Maksimilian Aleksandrovich, 1877–1932—Friends and
associates. 2. Russian literature—Societies, etc. 3. Intellectuals—
Russia—History—20th century. 4. Intellectuals—Soviet Union—
History. 5. Literature and state—Russia. 6. Literature and state—
Soviet Union. I. Title.
   PG3470.V68Z9 2004
   891.71'3—dc22

2004004470

1 2 3 4 5 10 09 08 07 06 05

To my parents,
Irma and Mack Walker

Ah, but a man's reach should exceed his grasp,
or what's a Heaven for?

—Robert Browning, "Andrea del Sarto"

CONTENTS

ILLUSTRATIONS

ACKNOWLEDGMENTS

There are those who argue that acknowledgments have grown too long and serve to locate the author in a network of professional ties rather than to express his or her appreciation for the aid of others. No doubt there is something to that. But even so I wish to acknowledge my simple and deep gratitude to those many institutions and individuals who helped me to bring this project to fruition. Any errors of fact or interpretation are, of course, my own.

Among the institutions are the International Research Exchange; American Council for Teachers of Russian; University of Michigan, Department of History, Rackham School of Graduate Studies, and Center for the Education of Women; Hoover Institution on War, Revolution, and Peace; John and Marie Noble Endowment for Historical Scholarship of the University of Nevada, Reno, Department of History; and University of Nevada, Reno Office for the Vice President of Research.

I have had the opportunity to present material or ideas and to gain feedback through the University of Michigan, Department of History; Cornell University Peace Studies Program; University of Nevada, Reno, Department of History, Faculty Research Colloquium; American Association for the Advancement of Slavic Studies; Social Science History Association; the conference organized by Gyorgy Peteri on "Patronage under Social-Democracy and State Socialism: A Comparative Study of Postwar Academic and Artistic Life in Scandinavia and Eastern Europe" at the Norwegian University of Technology and Science; the conference organized by Choi Chatterjee and Karen Petrone on "Inventing the Soviet Union: Language, Power, and Representation, 1917–1945," at Indiana University, Bloomington; and the Giessen-Berkeley Workshop organized by Jan Plamper on "Personality Cults in Stalinism: Practices, Experience, Meanings" (special thanks to Viktor Zhivov for his illuminating commentary at that conference!).

Among the individuals who read part or all of the manuscript and commented on it at various stages are my advisor and Doktormutter Jane Burbank, Michael Makin, Valerie Kivelson, Ruth Behar, Patricia Turner, Rosamund Bartlett, Walter Pintner, Choi Chatterjee, Douglas Weiner, Mack Walker, Douglas Jones, Aleksandr Shaposhnikov, Janet Rabinowitch, Jane Lyle, Rebecca Tolen, Rita Bernhard, Dawn Ollila, and two helpful anonymous readers at Indiana University Press. Particular thanks to Irina Paperno for her generous intellectual engagement in this project. And many thanks as well to Katerina Clark, who was the first to introduce me and many others to the ideas of anthropologist Victor Turner in her groundbreaking work on Soviet literature and society, *The Soviet Novel: History as Ritual.* Those who helped me to gather the research material for this project are also many, and I do not know all their names; I can only emphasize my appreciation for the kindness and good organization of the archivists and administrators at the Dom-Muzei Maksimiliana Voloshina, Gosudarstvennyi Arkhiv Russkoi Federatsii, Gosudarstvennyi Literaturnyi Muzei, Institut Mirovoi Literatury, Arkhiv Gor'kogo, Institut Russkoi Literatury Pushkinskii dom, Rossiiskii Gosudarstvennyi Arkhiv Literatury i Iskusstva, and Rossiiskii Arkhiv Sotsial'no-Politicheskoi Istorii. Several private archives were made available to me, including those of Mikhail Polonskii and others mentioned below. Thanks to those many I interviewed for this project, including Ida Nappelbaum, Mikhail Polivanov, Anastasiia Polivanova, Mirel Shaginian, Andrei Borisovich Trukhachev, and Anastasiia Tsvetaeva, for their generous contribution of thought and time. Individuals who gave me interviews I do not cite, whose reflections nevertheless made a powerful impression on me, were Nina Berberova, Lidiia Libidinskaia, Lev Levin, Lev Gornung, Vera Artisevich, Nina Fedina, and Iudis Kogan. Konstantin Polivanov and his wife, Olga Polivanova, know how much they helped me every step of the way—from inviting me as a lonely and hungry graduate student into their home, to giving me a copy of Konstantin Polivanov's grandfather's unpublished memoir of Voloshin, to enabling me to acquire the photographs that make this book a visual as well as intellectual experience.

More than anyone, however, I owe a debt of gratitude to the late Vladimir Kupchenko and his wife Roza Khruleva. The foremost Russian scholar on Maximilian Voloshin, Vladimir Kupchenko uncovered, prepared, and published many if not most of the materials on Maximilian Voloshin and his life that made this book possible; and he personally provided me with materials both written and visual, both published and unpublished, along with invaluable guidance.

Doug and Delia, you are the joy of my life. How could I ever thank you enough?

MAXIMILIAN VOLOSHIN AND THE RUSSIAN LITERARY CIRCLE

An Introduction
in Three Parts

MAXIMILIAN VOLOSHIN
AND HIS CIRCLE

All day long you see a trickle of pilgrims clambering up and down the hill about a mile outside of town, the tiny black figures moving and pausing, dividing and reuniting in uneven rhythm. Take the trail yourself and you find yourself stepping along behind them, up toward the grave of the Russian poet, artist, and cult figure Maximilian Voloshin. The hillside is sprinkled with wildflowers, short yellow hollyhocks and endless varieties of tiny blue and purple flowers along the bald grassy knolls; but if you look closely you can see the broken stems where many of them have been seized and torn up. The last steps are by far the steepest, and you stop to rest and look out over the blue glaze of the Black Sea, across at the reddish Karadag mountains, and then down into the little coastal town of Koktebel', where you can make out the rooftop of Voloshin's home—itself a shrine for dozens of visitors every day. At the top you find a small scattering of bemused individuals wandering along the narrow ridge: a group of young girls snapping soulful photographs of one another by the great rock that marks both Voloshin's grave and his wife's; a couple in neon sports clothing— blazing red, yellow, orange; and a grandmother with her granddaughter, the grandmother in a dowdy ruffled housedress and cheap white cardboard sandals, her companion tomboy lean in simple shirt and shorts.

"So this is what you dreamed of!" says the neon-shirted young man to his companion. He lays a yellow hollyhock on the gravestone, on top of a scattering of dried hillside vegetation. They both stand for a moment and then walk away to explore the precarious ridge. Small black and white birds soar above them. The grandmother beckons to her granddaughter to rest for a moment on the stone bench just below the grave, and then they begin the narrow descent, the grandmother teetering aside from the path every so often to gather up the scented greenery she finds along the way. From the valley far below the strains of half-a-dozen competing beach discotheques wend their way up—*aiiii, Macarena!* A few drops of rain fall. As you begin your own descent the rain picks up, turning the path into a bed of mud that cakes the shoes of the pilgrims in thick black slabs. "*Kakaia romantika* [how romantic]"—laughs one of the young girls, scraping her shoes against a rock. And then all at once they all vanish among the knolls and crags near the bottom of the hill, taking any of a number of separate paths down toward the sea.

Though the pilgrims may smile behind their hands—a reflection of the post-Soviet cynicism that has overtaken them—still they come. The man who arranged this experience for them was Maximilian Voloshin himself, when he requested that his body be carried up that steep hill to be buried where he had loved to stand, looking out over the sea. Did he expect this endless little parade? Quite possibly, or at least he had hoped for it, for though by the end of his life he surely knew that he had not lived up to his childhood reputation as a "second Pushkin," he had pressed energetically to implant himself in the memory of his time, place, and social group: the Russian intelligentsia of the twentieth century. And he was successful, despite the recalcitrance of the Soviet government, which sought to prevent the spread of his renown after his death in 1932. It was a long slow process which began to gather strength in the 1950s, with a small trickle of stories, questions, readings, and gallery shows among the Russian intelligentsia of the Thaw generation, and by the mid-1980s had developed into a veritable rushing stream of books and articles, even one pop song by folk singer Alla Pugacheva. By the early 1990s familiarity with his life—and with his circle of intellectual friends—was widespread.

If he is little known outside Russia, even among intellectuals and scholars familiar with the region, that is because we outsiders do not really understand his world. Our attention to the Russian intelligentsia—that passionate and rebellious social group, with its rich endowment of talent in literature, politics, the sciences, music, and fine arts—tends to concentrate on its intellectual, creative, and political contribution to history. Maximilian Voloshin, though he was a minor poet and artist in his own right, is not widely recognized for these things.[1] Rather, he is known and loved among members of the Russian educated elite for reasons that remain hidden from the uninitiated, above all for his contribution to the internal cultural history of the Russian intelligentsia at a vital moment in its development: that is, to the organization, values, and self-conception of a social group that has struggled mightily with those aspects of its history over the past two hundred years, never more so than during the years of transition from the Imperial polity to the Soviet one.[2] Only by grasping this central fact can we understand why those people straggle endlessly up the hillside to his grave. The tale of Voloshin's cult is inextricably bound up with the historical formation of his remarkable social class, particularly with one segment of it: the literary intelligentsia, those who produced the literary tradition that has been a source of great national pride as well as intense political concern in the nineteenth and twentieth centuries.[3]

Thus this book is as much about the culture and society of the Russian intelligentsia, with a particular focus on the literary intelligentsia, as it is about Voloshin himself. That its narrative structure is determined by the events of a single life might lead the reader to see it as a biography, perhaps, and given that it is about a poet, a literary biography. But it is not.[4] Rather, it addresses a set of interlinked questions pertaining to the culture and society of the literary intelligentsia—questions, above all, about social organization—through the prism of a life history. It seeks thereby to place the individual at the heart of the historical process, not through the traditional "great man" approach, in which historical developments are ascribed primarily to the actions of powerful leaders but rather in a newly problematized fashion that is informed by the impact of the social sciences, anthropology in particular, on the field of professional history. This approach makes it possible to trace a single cultural theme as it weaves its way in and out of a lifetime of personal experience with a multitude of permutations and implications (and contradictions) over time. The fruits of this approach are worthwhile: new insights into the history of the Russian literary intelligentsia which may be best obtained from the perspective of the individual experience, and new possibilities for thinking and writing about the place of the individual in history, both as subject to cultural and historical forces and as agent in their transformation.[5]

Maximilian Voloshin as a distinctive historical individual and personality is particularly appropriate for such a study. He was keenly attuned to his milieu, quick to absorb the lessons it taught him. At the same time he came to be a remarkable social creator after his own fashion, a wily and skillful manipulator of his culture, a master of its microdynamics of power. These personal qualities enabled him to touch the very cultural pulse of his world. That pulse, the focus of inquiry in this book, is what may be called *"kruzhok* culture": a distinctive pattern of Russian intelligentsia behavior and thinking associated with participation in the intelligentsia *kruzhok*, or circle, as a form of social organization.

The *kruzhok* was a central phenomenon of Russian intellectual life from the late eighteenth century well into Soviet history, as members of the Russian educated elite gathered themselves throughout this period into small groups dedicated to the pursuit of intellectual and educational development and high culture. A sociologically precise description of the intelligentsia circle can be difficult to pin down: intelligentsia circles have varied widely in shape and purpose, from informal schoolboy or student gatherings to elite aristocratic salons to professional and scientific circles to many others, including the literary circles with which this book is primarily concerned. Even groups apparently similar in purpose and structure could vary greatly; for a fundamental quality of *kruzhok* culture was the sheer idiosyncrasy of each circle insofar as it was made up of unique individuals bound together by personal ties. And yet there were some significant common themes among them, certain anxieties, yearnings, patterns of thought and behavior, appearing here and there over time and space, sometimes in concert and sometimes disjointedly, which link them as a social and historical phenomenon worthy of study.

Voloshin entered the story of this culture by establishing a circle of his own early in the twentieth century, on the Crimean Peninsula at the fringes of the Russian Empire. The site of his circle was the village of Koktebel', a formerly Bulgar settlement which at this time was rapidly becoming a favorite seaside vacation spot for a new Russian educated elite. In creating his circle, Voloshin drew on his powerful sensitivity to the meanings and potentials of *kruzhok* culture—both positive and negative—as he had grasped them first as a child and then in his early adulthood among the Russian avant-garde circles of the fin de siècle. During summertime gatherings in Koktebel' he offered a vital emotional and intellectual haven from the prevailing avant-garde literary scene of the period, the Symbolist movement, and helped to nurture a new, more eclectic post-Symbolist generation. This new generation included some of the liveliest figures in twentieth-century Russian literary history, such as Marina Tsvetaeva, Vladislav Khodasevich, and Osip Mandelshtam, as well as a variety of other intellectuals, professionals, and artists, from ballerinas to engineers. In the prerevolutionary period his circle was vibrantly successful, offering its participants summers of intellectual play, of literary and theatrical as well as emotional engagement under protected circumstances, where identities and bonds were shaped that would endure through the winters back in Moscow and Petersburg. By the time of the revolution, the reputation of Voloshin's circle was well established. But its contribution to intelligentsia history was not yet complete. What was to anchor it even more powerfully into the consciousness and the history of the intelligentsia was the way that Voloshin managed to carry the spirit of his circle across the two revolutions of 1917, through the terrifying years of the civil war (which had a devastating impact on the Crimea as the last outpost of the White Army), and then to resurrect that spirit in the Soviet period.

During the early years of Soviet state formation, Voloshin built upon the popularity of his prerevolutionary circle to create something that would have real impact on the future of the intelligentsia under Soviet power. He invited growing numbers of Soviet writers, professionals, and other intellectuals into his home for summer vacations in the early 1920s, continuing the traditions of intellectual engagement that had been the source of its popularity in the prerevolutionary period. But these intellectuals were poor, often ill, heavily hit by the stresses of war and economic collapse, and putting them up was expensive. In order to ensure the economic survival of his circle—as well as his own survival—he set out to integrate it into the emerging Soviet system of bureaucratized welfare and privilege for the elite by proposing that his home serve as an official vacation haven for Russian intellectuals whose visits were to be paid for by the Soviet state. He succeeded. His house became a kind of early version of the *dom otdykha*, the House of Rest, an institution that would soon be sponsored by the Soviet Writers' Union as a standard type of vacation resort for literary folk.[6] The emergence of the *dom otdykha* was symptomatic of a significant historical change that was taking place in the relationship between Russian writers and the Russian state. By the end of Stalin's rule, the vacation in a *dom otdykha* or other similar vacation colony had become one of a great carrot chain of social services and privileges for Russian writers that would bind them to the Soviet state perhaps as much as the whip of censorship and fear.[7] In return for these privileges, writers owed the state loyalty, obedience, and support. This relationship was to have a considerable impact on the fate of Russian letters under Soviet rule.

That Voloshin's circle, a haven to some of the most spirited literary creators of Russian twentieth-century literature, might have played a role in this process is an irony of Russian intelligentsia history, painful perhaps to consider. Such a development was not intended, however, nor was Voloshin alone responsible for it. Others, too, among the Russian literary intelligentsia were busily tying the circle formation into the growing bureaucracy of the state during this period, unaware of the ultimate consequences of their actions: that the state would, with the literary circle firmly in its grip, eliminate it as an organizational form by a decree against circles in 1932 and the establishment, in 1934, of the Soviet Writers' Union as the sole institution of Russian literary life.[8] These intellectuals were simply following the logic of *kruzhok* culture under the pressures of time and forces beyond their control: they tried to achieve the best possible deal for themselves and their colleagues under the new conditions offered by the state, using the cultural tools familiar to them.

But their actions do raise the question of agency. To witness the energetic struggles of these writers for a place in the Soviet system is to gain an unexpectedly strong impression of the power of writers to control their own destiny under Soviet rule in its early years, despite a long tradition in memoirs and scholarship of viewing the Russian literary world as helpless in the face of state oppression during this formative period of Soviet power.[9] And it brought them benefits. Beyond the actual material advantages of this system of privilege and welfare, the deal they achieved also, to some extent, enabled them to retain certain familiar qualities of *kruzhok* culture, as this book will demonstrate. Voloshin carried the intellectual and spiritual values of his circle into the very heart of the Soviet system, where they would work upon a new generation of intellectuals in the 1950s, 1960s, and 1970s—the Thaw generation that would ultimately bring down the Soviet state. To grasp the meaning of this tale one must begin with *kruzhok* culture itself.

THE CULTURE OF THE RUSSIAN LITERARY CIRCLE BETWEEN STRUCTURE AND ANTI-STRUCTURE

One of the most important themes of *kruzhok* culture is a constant and lively interplay between the identity of the Russian intelligentsia circle as an idealistic, antimaterialistic, antihierarchical form of human association and its simultaneous potential to serve the far more practical purposes of professional and economic advancement, both individual and institutional. This interplay between the two tendencies sometimes took the form of tension, and sometimes mutual reinforcement, but it dogged the phenomenon of the circle almost from its beginnings until its ultimate demise in the Soviet period.

To understand this interplay we must consider the original context of the intelligentsia circle in a widespread Russian social and economic culture of tough and wiry personalized political and economic ties, firmly established patronage chains, and intricate but pervasive social networks of mutual obligation and responsibility. The behavior contributing to this kind of social order was a significant component of Russian elite culture, at least from the medieval period on, and in varying forms it was also to be found in many other parts of Russian society. Profoundly pragmatic, this social order involved the cultivation of human personal ties for the sake of physical survival and economic advancement. Today sociologists and economists sometimes dismiss this kind of culture as "corrupt." But it made up the very texture of early modern and Imperial Russian political and economic relations, especially relations between the Russian state and the society it sought to govern. What gave it such power and made it distinctive were its deep roots in Russian traditions of family and household structure, of patriarchal power, and of clan relations among the governing elite.[10] It was also closely linked to a very particular culture of collective responsibility, which bound medieval and early modern Russians into circles and chains of mutual assistance and responsibility.[11] Throughout early Russian history, political issues of obligation, entitlement, control, and balance all were touched by this family- and collective-based culture of networking and patronage, despite strenuous efforts on the part of some in the Russian state to move toward a system of more impersonal merit by the early eighteenth century.

Russian secular intellectual life was first instigated and nurtured by the Russian state and, in its early stages, was greatly influenced by these inter-dependent relations between the state and society—especially between the state and elite society. This was in part because those whom the autocracy trusted enough to offer the opportunity of education came from the elite. Peter the Great began the autocratic practice of sending some of the sons of the Russian gentry to Western Europe for Western education. He was also the first Russian ruler to sponsor the emergence of early, sparse institutions of scholarship and education. He pursued these policies largely in order to strengthen the workings of his new imperial state by increasing the pool of well-qualified and competent state personnel, both military and civilian. By the same token he tried to enhance the importance of merit, as opposed to patronage and family ties, in the structures of state governance. That was the significance of his Table of Ranks, his new system for controlling the advance of members of the military and civil bureaucracies through a de-tailed list of qualifications. But just as eighteenth-century Russian historian Brenda Meehan-Waters found the upper levels of the Table of Ranks in 1730 to be dominated by certain elite families and clans presumably re-gardless of merit, so the new world of an educated elite was also greatly in-fluenced by more traditional relations.[12] Close to the sources of political power in eighteenth-century Russia, early educational and intellectual in-stitutions as well as activities could be greatly affected by the network and patronage politics of court and clan circles.[13]

Under the influence of the cultural, intellectual, and political ambi-tions of Catherine the Great, the late eighteenth century saw the emer-gence of a lively new literary and intellectual realm.[14] Catherine had a de-gree of critical mass as she continued and expanded the Petrine practice of Westernizing the Russian elite, pushing them to read books, to attend liter-ary salons, and to frequent the theater. Establishing the conditions for a rel-atively free press in 1783, and offering considerable patronage herself, she did much to expand the development of presses, journals, and other types of literary activity.[15] While she encouraged the importation of the ideas of the Western Enlightenment into this growing new world of Russian publi-cation, however, she grew increasingly less willing to tolerate the public ap-plication of those ideals to Russian politics and society. Especially after 1790, she kept a relatively tight grip on the literary and intellectual realm through autocratic control and censorship, as well as through the power of patronage.

Out of these pressures and contradictions, and fortified by the growing numbers of educated people, a new spirit arose toward the end of the century among Russian intellectuals, a spirit usually associated with the emergence of the so-called oppositional Russian intelligentsia as a social group highly critical of the Russian state and its social order. It was a mixture of resistance and idealism, a rejection of what were seen as materialistic, self-interested, indeed exploitative traditional values and social hierarchies, in the interest of egalitarianism, of social justice, of yearning for brotherhood among men. Those infected by this spirit sought new independence from the Russian state and court, from its control over their thoughts and behavior, and new means of self-expression.

Fundamental to this new mood of resistance was opposition to the hierarchy of serfdom, first openly criticized by Alexander Radishchev in his famous book, *A Journey from St. Petersburg to Moscow*, published in 1790.[16] But it had an impact as well on the social organization of the literary and intellectual scene early in the nineteenth century. As Russian intellectual life began to gain increasing independence from the state through a variety of new organizations such as secret societies, a novel social formation began to reveal itself that was in many ways a focal point for the new feelings, discourses, and ambitions.[17] The bonds among participants in this new social formation were very different from the pragmatic, self-interested, and servile bonds of networking and patronage, better reflecting the new spirit of brotherhood. These bonds in their ideal state were egalitarian rather than hierarchical, mutually supportive rather than mutually exploitative, communal in a spiritual as opposed to an economic sense. This new form of association manifested itself in what people now picture when they think of the Russian intelligentsia circle or *kruzhok*: gatherings of educated, often young folk drawn together by a mutual fervor for ideas, frequently for literature, for impassioned discourse over existential topics. Not all the circles of this period in the early to mid-nineteenth century possessed these qualities; to some extent one could argue that both circles and circle ideals were as much a fashion as they were a reality among an educated gentry elite. But some did exist, and their spirit was infectious.

One such circle was the Friendly Literary Society of 1801, analyzed in detail by Marc Raeff, the renowned U.S. scholar of the Russian intelligentsia during this renowned period, in his article, "Russian Youth on the Eve of Romanticism: Andrei Turgenev and his Circle." Imbued with a powerful desire to serve their country and their people, Raeff writes, Andrei Turgenev and a small group of his friends rejected not only the dull bureaucratic service that the Russian state desired of them but also the dry, unemotional values of the rational Enlightenment, upon whose principles they saw that bureaucracy as having been built. Seeking new social identities, new ways to contribute to their society, they drew themselves together into a circle of masculine friendships characterized by intense emotional and intellectual openness, a self-sacrificial commitment, and an almost (but not quite) sexual love toward one another, as they communicated daily by letter if not in person. In pursuit of self-understanding, self-criticism, and self-transformation, they established a literary circle in which they gathered almost weekly for about six months to discuss topics and writings of concern to them.[18] Despite its short life, the experience of this circle had a powerful impact on its participants, who communicated with one another for years thereafter.

Raeff sees in this circle the expression of the values of Romanticism as they were absorbed by the Russian intellectual elite of the time; he also sees in it the emergence of a new spirit that would be fundamental to the intelligentsia identity until 1917, as well as the roots of that identity in the circle formation. Unquestionably these values of intensive mutual commitment to self-understanding and self-transformation were central to some of the paradigmatic circles of later intelligentsia history as well, such as those of Alexander Herzen with his friend Nikolai Ogarev, and the circle of Nikolai Stankevich.[19] But the circle as an institution lasted more than a century after the demise of the Friendly Literary Society, and it underwent considerable buffeting throughout that period. Furthermore, the values revealed in those circles are unique neither to the time period nor indeed to the Russian intelligentsia. To better understand the historical meaning of the intelligentsia circle it is useful to turn to a cultural model drawn from comparative anthropological research, that of Victor Turner's anti-structural communitas.

The *communitas*, as Turner describes it in his book, *The Ritual Process: Structure and Anti-Structure,* is a widespread form of human association that takes shape outside of and in opposition to traditional social order, offering its participants a temporary retreat from "law, custom, convention, and ceremony" for the sake of the self-transformation of its participants and ultimately, perhaps, of the transformation of the traditional order from which it is a haven as well. Communitas is antithetical to institutional structure, to hierarchy and all its manifestations in material evidence of wealth and status, fostering instead a spirit of humble egalitarianism among its members, who are bound together by intensely personal, spontaneous, unmediated ties, formed in mutual pursuit of a goal more ineffable than pragmatic. Turner characterizes these ties by drawing on Martin Buber's theory of the I-Thou relationship; rather than being "segmentalized into roles and statuses," individuals in a state of communitas associate with one another in a "direct, immediate, and total confrontation of human identities."[20]

From the perspective of the traditional social order, which is both its context and its antithesis, communitas is often viewed as magical, sometimes as dangerous, with the potential to disrupt or pollute the regular order.[21] The role of communitas is closely linked with the holy fool, the king's jester who can "speak truth to power," and the artist and prophet who reveal to us the deeper truths and meanings of existence.[22] Turner's conception of this social phenomenon is broad. According to *The Ritual Process*, the communitas experience has a variety of manifestations ranging from the installation rites of a chief elect in the Ndembu tribe of Zambia, to millenarian groups on the fringes of society, to early Franciscan monks with their vows of poverty, and even to the American hippy communes of the 1960s.[23]

Although Turner does not specifically mention the Russian literary circle as one possible expression of communitas, the degree to which his model helps to explain certain aspects of the circle phenomenon is striking. The nineteenth- and early-twentieth-century Russian intelligentsia literary *kruzhok*—like the intelligentsia itself, in fact, which never fit into the traditional estate, or *soslovie*, hierarchy of Imperial Russia[24]—flourished at the fluid interstices of the regular order of society and a state that in many ways sought to prevent intelligentsia activity from impinging upon a formally recognized sphere.[25] In this liminal realm, outside the traditional hierarchies of Russian society, ideal *kruzhki* were characterized by intense emotional ties, by a strong spirit of personal equality among members, and by an overwhelming sense of what Turner has described as "sacred outsiderhood."[26] Thus the circle provided the social foundations for the kind of idealistic and antimaterialistic fervor that lay at the heart of the intelligentsia commitment to intellectual, and especially literary, life.

Respect for the life of the mind, the power of ideas, the beauty of high cultural production lay at the spiritual core of the literary *kruzhok* as being of far greater importance than any sort of material or professional advancement. All these things were to enable its participants to fulfill one of the central roles of communitas: to scrutinize and criticize the values of the traditional hierarchical culture by which they were surrounded, ideally from the point of view of what Turner calls "humankindness."[27] As in communitas, ritual theatricality within the intelligentsia circle could aid in the self-transformation of its members, as they played out the multiple crises of identity involved in seeking to find their places in their world as a social group and as individuals.[28] This activity was to become particularly significant in the late nineteenth and early twentieth centuries, and in Voloshin's circle. All these characteristics—though by no means did they reveal themselves uniformly in every circle and, indeed, for many they were more of an aspiration than a reality—made the intelligentsia circle and the intelligentsia itself objects of fascination and admiration both inside and outside Russia.

But, as Turner tells us, communitas is fleeting, sometimes more a dream than reality. It emerges from the context of structure, of the traditional social system that is its very reason for being, and it can resist the insistent influence of structure only briefly.[29] Either communitas fades rapidly and its participants return transformed to the traditional system—the chief-elect, having undergone the liminal rituals of transformation, takes his ruling position, the millenarian returns to daily life, and the hippy becomes the yuppie—or communitas itself begins to change, taking on the characteristics of the structure that is both its context and its antithesis. So it was with the intelligentsia circle.

Even in the early days of the circle, there were signs of interplay between the forces of anti-structure and those of structure. For example, the self-interested networking and patronage relations that were, in this social context, the antithesis of the intimate, idealistic communitas bond clearly manifested themselves in many early- to mid-nineteenth-century circles, as they became vehicles for social climbing as well as for making valuable intellectual and professional connections in a small and sparse intellectual world.[30] This was a way in which traditional networking culture could intervene to weaken the culture of antimaterialistic and egalitarian communitas. But there were other ways in which structure intruded upon communitas that were not necessarily so antipathetic to it. For example, the anticommercial ethos of a gentry elite, bound up though it was in a tradition of hierarchy according to birth, meshed curiously well with the antimaterialistic mood of communitas, and helped to perpetuate it. It is easier to be devoted to the spiritual bond as opposed to the material if one is independently wealthy, as were most participants in the circles of the first decades of the nineteenth century.

The interplay between structure and anti-structure in the literary circle became more complex as time went on, and must be understood in the context of the broader history of the Russian intelligentsia as a social group. After the mid-nineteenth century, following Russia's loss of the Crimean War, the Great Reforms led to a significant transformation of Russian society and hierarchy. From the point of view of educated and intellectual life, the most important of those reforms was the opening of the doors of higher education to non-gentry students, who had previously been barred from that opportunity by Nicholas I. This step greatly expanded the ranks of the Russian educated elite. Sons of clergy, Jews, peasants, and many others began to find their way into the system of higher education alongside those of the upper classes, and into the ranks of the educated elite.[31] These new folk had many new needs and desires, eager as they were to achieve success. Perhaps what they most needed were new institutions of professional and intellectual life. So tiny had the elite been, and so closely controlled by the autocracy, that relatively few such institutions existed at mid-century. But now, in ever growing numbers, scientists needed laboratories, musicians needed conservatories, engineers needed professional organizations, artists needed museums, galleries, and shows, and, of course, with a growing literate community to address, writers needed journals, publishing houses, and other literary outlets as they increasingly sought to shape Russian national discourse.

From the perspective of Turner's model of anti-structure and structure, this might have been a good time for the circle as communitas to fade away, having served its transformative role, and to allow members of the educated elite to reintegrate themselves into the traditional order. And, in a way, something like this did happen. In pursuit of professional opportunity, many educated people began to form personal bonds that were essentially pragmatic, not idealistic; calculated, not unmediated; self-interested, rather than self-sacrificial—bonds that drew in many ways on the longstanding Russian elite tradition of network and patronage relations. These personal associations often coalesced into small social groups that, despite a resemblance to the earlier circles of communitas, were actually something rather different: as essential focal points for professional and intellectual networking, they were network nodes, as the scholarship on networking calls them.[32] These circles were vital to the institutionalization process under way. It was often in these circles as network nodes that institutional needs were first discussed, that plans were made and action organized. Network circles lay at the foundations of professional educational facilities, of scientific laboratories, engineering associations, of publications and publishing houses, and of many other institutions of educated life.[33]

Given its more traditional, structural function, the circle as network node quickly manifested a number of the more traditional elements of Russian elite networking and patronage culture, above all that of leadership, which could be seen as a leading edge of hierarchical structure into anti-structure.[34] There had been spiritual leaders of intellectual circles in the past, individuals who were lauded and loved for the inspiration they offered in epitomizing the ineffable spirit of communitas: Andrei Turgenev and Nikolai Stankevich had been such individuals, and after their deaths they were adored for it by their fellow circle members. But now something else was needed in the growing world of institutionalizing circles: people with the talent and energy to obtain, or to offer, organizational and material support for establishing the new institutions of educated and professional life.

And so a new type of circle leader began to emerge, somewhat more like a traditional patron figure than the spiritual leader of communitas: a more practical kind of mentor to this new educated milieu.

The mid- to late-nineteenth-century history of Russia's educated elite is heavily populated by such mentors and institution builders, from the Rubinshtein brothers, who established the Moscow and Petersburg musical conservatories, for example, to Aleksandr Stoletov and his physics laboratories, to Alexander Herzen and Nikolai Chernyshevskii and their journals, to the merchant Savva Mamontov, who did much to support the visual and dramatic arts at his estate, Abramtsevo. In a slightly later period, such figures as Valerii Briusov and Maxim Gorky would demonstrate considerable energy in creating publishing opportunities for aspirants to print in journals, publishing houses, and other literary venues, and Sergei Diaghilev would generate a historic opportunity for Russia to have an impact on the European art scene through his organizational influence on the World of Art movement, to name only a few. These institution builders opened up opportunities for the expanding new educated elite as never before, and were urgently needed in a rapidly changing Russia.

Not all of them sponsored network circles of their own—but many did, because it helped inordinately in their task. For mentors had to do more than just establish institutions; they also had to populate them effectively. The network circle proved an ideal base from which to seek out, organize, and acculturate the personnel they needed for their institutional endeavors. Many mentors facilitated the formation of such circles in their homes, where they encouraged the development of intellectual discourse, the exchange of ideas, and debates in the interest of professional engagement and development. They also facilitated professional networking among circle members, enabling young people to meet one another, to size one another up for future plans, and to encounter older, more powerful figures in the field. And mentors often nurtured both physically and emotionally as well, sometimes simply feeding their visitors, offering personal support and advice on matters ranging from professional behavior to appropriate dress, and generally aiding these often upwardly mobile clients in their attempts to build new ways of living. It is a striking feature of these networking circles that they may have done as much to facilitate self-transformation among their younger participants as any manifestation of communitas did.

That the circle as network node generally met in the household, often the household of a mentor figure, was to have a real impact on its history— as well as on the history of *kruzhok* culture and of the Russian intelligentsia more broadly—for the domestic sphere had its own traditional structures. Of greatest significance was the tradition of patriarchal order, with a dominant male figure in formal possession of the domestic sphere, a less powerful but still important female figure providing many other benefits, from food and drink to emotional support, and a "younger generation" of sorts, clients who owed a certain degree of respect, if not submission, to the patriarch, and, to a lesser extent, to the female figure. The traditional potency of these relations in the domestic sphere did a great deal to enhance the power of the mentorship figure in the institutionalization process.

It might be assumed that the literary circle as communitas was indeed on the way out, at least among the professional writers who sought to gain professionally from their circles of association, and that "structure" had taken over entirely. Yet this was not the case. By the early twentieth century many literary circles were indeed committed to establishing and running formal outlets for literary production such as journals and publishing houses. But among Realists and Symbolists, the two main literary groupings of the time, many of the qualities of communitas still lingered. Literary *kruzhki* continued to be a focus of intense, intimate I-Thou-type relations, of the will to self-transformation, of a kind of self-sacrificial devotion to particular literary and other causes. Yet at the same time the impact of the traditional organization of the circle as network node on these literary circles manifested itself clearly. Of greatest importance were the structures of patriarchy as they were located in the domestic sphere, and of mentorship as it built upon patriarchy, for these literary circles, too, met primarily in people's homes. The two seemingly opposite cultures—of structure and of anti-structure—were indeed closely interlocked, seeming almost to feed off each other in a sort of cultural chemistry that was to have a profound impact on the history of Russian letters.

Exactly why the spirit of communitas persisted with such tenacity is not entirely clear. Perhaps it had something to do with the nature of literature itself as many Russians seem to have experienced it—demanding of its readers and writers a kind of openness to self-exploration and self-transformation that took them into a realm beyond the everyday struggles for survival.[35] Perhaps it was intensified by the continued "sacred outsider" status experienced by literati and many other intellectuals, as the autocracy continued to demonstrate its reluctance to share power in the late Imperial period, and to hold them firmly outside the traditional caste or *soslovie* system.[36]

And there may also have been another reason: while late Imperial literati, true to the spirit of communitas, were indeed deeply concerned about exploitative and hierarchical relationships, the manifestation of exploitation that worried them was not so much that of network and patronage ties as that of capitalist market relations. To some extent, this may have represented the persistence of the anticommercial ethos of the gentry intellectuals of an earlier time. By the end of the nineteenth century, that anticommercial ethos was greatly enhanced by the growth of a variety of revolutionary movements and outlooks that expressed discomfort with or out-right opposition to market relations. Anticapitalist sentiment among many Russian intellectuals was founded upon deep cultural feelings as well as on political argumentation.[37] It was not the possibility of hierarchical, ex-ploitative relations among themselves that most worried writers but, rather, the possibility of exploiting literature itself, as well as their readers, through market relations.

This anxiety found explicit expression in a strong resistance to produc-ing literature for material gain rather than out of a spirit of deep commit-ment. Many argued against the notion of writing for material gain: "Why do you need money, or stupid literary fame? It's better to write something good with conviction and passion," wrote gentry novelist Lev Tolstoy.[38] "Lit-erature should not earn one's daily bread. One should earn that in some other fashion," wrote N. V. Shelgunov.[39] Realist author Maxim Gorky re-ferred to writers who made money by catering to popular taste as "specula-tors in popularity, adventurers, those who look on authorship as easy sea-sonal labor."[40] An anonymous writer complained of the practice of selling one particular genre of literary expression, namely, memoirs, for financial profit: "Now memoirs are a form of money speculation."[41] Condemnation of the pursuit of material self-interest in publishing one's work, as opposed to self-sacrificial commitment to the enlightenment of one's readers, could be vociferous in the nineteenth and early twentieth centuries.[42]

Against the background of a perceived opposition between self-sacrifi-cial commitment, on the one hand, and self-interested exploitation in a capitalist market sense, on the other, traditional power structures, expressed in networking and patronage relations, may in many ways have seemed rel-atively compatible with the I-Thou bonds of communitas. Network ties in particular—which have a long history of mutual as opposed to hierarchical exploitation in Russian history—may have seemed less competitive, more intimate, closer to those idealistic bonds that may be characterized as the bonds of communitas. This hybrid social form made a certain kind of emo-tional and cultural sense. Moreover, it seemed to be working: these circles were central to the institutionalization process among literati.

THE TROUBLE WITH LITERARY CIRCLES
AND EFFORTS TO FIND A SOLUTION
THROUGH LEADERSHIP

Literary circles were vital indeed to literary institutionalization, but they did not necessarily work very well. Many of them were structurally frail, tending toward disharmony, factionalism, and disintegration, which made them a dangerous foundation for institutions for professional development.

When a literary circle fell apart, as they often did, a whole project could fall apart as well, to the detriment of the literary community and its ambitions for contributing to the national discourse. One reason for this frailty might be sought precisely in the hybrid nature of the social formation.[43] The intense, totalizing, I-Thou bonds of communitas were not necessarily compatible with the more pragmatic ties of networking and patronage, and the effort to integrate them was not always successful. Some intellectuals of the mid- to late nineteenth century began to ponder the frailty of the circle, focusing on the question of more and less effective circle relationships and, in the process, implicitly proposing and developing a theory of what many of them viewed as a potential solution to the problem of circle instability: successful circle leadership.

The discourse that developed over this issue took place, or at least was reflected, in an intelligentsia memoir tradition that may be called the "contemporaries" memoir genre, as these memoirs were often called "memoirs of contemporaries about so-and-so" or "so-and-so in the memoirs of contemporaries."[44] Often nostalgic tales about circles of the past, "contemporaries" memoirs provided the opportunity for mulling over the weaknesses as well as the strengths of the circle formation. One author who participated in the memoir discourse over circle relationships with great insight was the Russian chronicler of the circles of the 1840s, P. V. Annenkov. His memoir, *The Extraordinary Decade*, offers a thoughtful analysis of the potential of the intelligentsia circle to accomplish programmatic goals, especially from the point of view of the personal bonds among group participants, and with a particular focus on the bonds formed by a group leader with his followers.[45]

Of greatest interest to Annenkov were the liberal, Westernizing circles of the 1840s, and the leadership figure upon whom he focused was Vissarion Belinsky. Belinsky was a man of considerable influence among the literary intellectuals of his time who laid the foundations of the Utilitarian movement in Russian literature. As more of a spiritual than an institutional leader, he was committed to absolute integrity in his relationships, even at the cost of friendship and of circle harmony and effectiveness, certainly of institutional effectiveness. This, in a way, was the source of his attraction to other members of his circle: "It is common knowledge," wrote Annenkov, "that the morality underlying all of Belinsky's ideas and all his works was exactly the power of attraction that rallied ardent friends and supporters around him. His, so to speak, fanatical quest for truth and verity in life did not leave him even when, for a time, he departed from the truth."[46] This quest of his, however, could lead him to break entirely with his friends. If he could not establish an utterly principled, "concrete and total," form of association (to use Turner's description of the personal bond of communitas) with them, compatible with the integrity of his own spiritual search, he refused to interact with them at all.[47]

Annenkov analyzed the impact of this kind of purity of association on circle politics. As he saw it, Belinsky's obsession with pure, uncompromising association was to have a major impact on the survival of Belinsky's circle. "Belinsky [was] . . . to contribute so much toward effecting a dissolution of the [Westernizer] circle into its component parts, toward a delimitation and definition of factions which issued from it," Annenkov wrote, expressing a certain admiration for the intellectual commitment that went into finding and expanding the factional rifts among allies.[48] Mulling over the consequences of this approach for Belinsky's friends, partisans, and supporters as participants in mutual endeavor, however, he expressed doubt. Comparing Belinsky's circle to its ideological opponent, the Slavophile circle, he balanced the benefits of absolutely principled relationships among Slavophile members against the cost of the damage they caused: "[At first t]he Slavic party . . . undertook to wash its dirty linen and to square accounts with its own members," he wrote, "but it immediately relinquished the attempt, probably finding that the small size of its family required extreme caution and consideration in the mutual dealings among its members. Only on the condition of reciprocal support could the party retain its integrity and keep all its personnel, needed for the struggle, intact." But Belinsky did not care about this. "There was never any place in Belinsky's mind for such considerations and calculations, and they never could have stopped him."[49] This was why harmony was more difficult to maintain among the participants in Belinsky's Westernizer circle than among the Slavophiles, according to Annenkov's reasoning.

This narrative posed a quandary: the same quality that drew people to Belinsky—his moral and spiritual authority—threatened the potential programmatic or institutional goals of the circle. And yet the value of spiritual leadership in drawing people together was self-evident. Was it really necessary to give that up? Could it not be harnessed in some way? What might the most effective balance be between spiritual and pragmatic leadership? Were there other leadership skills that might mediate or moderate some of the tensions inherent in this social formation? Annenkov did not provide an answer; he just presented the problem. This problem of how to achieve circle unity and success through suitable circle bonds and leadership continued to draw the attention of memoirists, however, and over time some of them began to offer the outlines of an answer that made a kind of internal cultural sense.

Early expressions of this answer manifested themselves in mid-nineteenth-century memoirs about the rebellious gentry Decembrist circles, whose leaders had initiated the 1825 palace coup against the autocracy (sacred outsiders indeed). Despite the obvious failure of this coup from an organizational point of view, memoirists sought to provide examples and models for successful social relationships and leadership through their admiring, almost hyperbolic writings about the Decembrists. An important leadership quality was to be found, they hinted, in the capacity for personal engagement with the individual feelings and sensibilities of followers — charm, it was sometimes called, the source of a simple but useful skill in managing social relations. One memoirist wrote of the Decembrist Ryleev: "I've never known another person as attractive as Ryleev. Of middle height, well-built, with an intelligent, serious face, from the first glance he inspired in you something like a premonition of that charm to which, with closer acquaintance, you had to submit."[50] Another Decembrist was characterized as being charming and an effective peacemaker, as well as a successful father figure in the domestic context: "In his family they all adored him, and called him a *genie bienfaisance*, he always reconciled everything and everyone, gave good advice; his younger sisters called him their second father."[51]

The discourse about what made for an attractive and successful leader quickly expanded beyond memoirs about the Decembrists. Writing of his friend, Nikolai Ogarev, the center of a Westernizing circle of the 1840s, Alexander Herzen wrote: "Ogarev . . . was endowed with a peculiar magnetism, a feminine quality of attraction. For no apparent reason others are drawn to such people and cling to them; they warm, unite and soothe them, they are like an open table at which everyone sits down, renews his powers, rests, grows calmer and more stout-hearted, and goes away a friend."[52] Individuals with the emotional sensitivity to make others feel comfortable and harmonious around them were invaluable to the potentially volatile circle formation.

Such people were more important to the successful functioning of circle life than the cleverest and most dashing, even the intellectually successful, among them. In her nostalgic memoir about the Pushkin circle of the 1830s Anna Kern wrote: "In that young circle kindness and playful, free gaiety reigned, inexhaustible cleverness shone, the highest practitioner of which was Pushkin." Yet cleverness was not necessarily the most valuable quality to Russian intellectual life, as we see when Kern goes on to praise with even greater enthusiasm another figure in the circle altogether: "But the soul of that happy family of poets was Del'vig, in whose house they generally gathered."[53] As Kern explained, the personal characteristics that made Del'vig the "soul" of his circle were his kindness, his delicacy, and his ability to joke without hurting anyone's feelings, an ability Pushkin apparently possessed to a far lesser degree, if at all. This personal talent for community building was essential to the smooth functioning of the circle (although note as well the reference to Del'vig's role as master of the domestic sphere in which the circle gathers).

It was in those who had the personal talent to build and maintain effective intellectual community—whether communitas or goal-oriented institution—through sensitive and humane consideration of their followers that the memoirists found their most attractive models for appropriate intelligentsia behavior and leadership. In the discourse about such model figures they established a powerful definition of intelligentsia identity as it could be controlled through recommendations of appropriate behavior. Such figures could quickly become the objects of cult adoration in the intelligentsia memoir literature. Hyperbolic, hagiographic praise for their personal and social skills reveals the importance of the topic to memoirists as they strove to outdo one another in honoring those whom they considered great intelligentsia social leaders, usually circle leaders, of the past. It is quite probable that, in an effort to mark out such qualities as worthy of imitation, memoirists attributed them to certain individuals in greater degree or quality than they in fact existed.

This "contemporaries" memoir tradition, as noted elsewhere, is indeed at times notably untrustworthy as a historical source in the simplest sense.[54] Not only is it marked by the tendency toward exaggeration, but it also reveals the repeated reliance of memoirists on an oral intelligentsia tradition of gossip and storytelling. Use of this oral tradition took the form of inserting into the text gossipy sketches about personalities and their interactions, called *anekdoty*, without alerting the reader or providing any reference to the fact that the information provided did not stem from first-person experience. It may be argued that the "contemporaries" tradition is itself a kind of written offshoot of the oral storytelling tradition among the Russian intelligentsia, serving the dual purpose of network building and alliance building among them as much as giving factual insight into the past. The tendencies toward hagiographic exaggeration and repetition of gossip are both reasons for caution in using such documents as historical sources.

It has been particularly important to be aware of the peculiarities of these memoirs in researching the subject of this book, for such memoirs make up a significant part of the material documenting the life of Maximilian Voloshin. The influence of the tradition of the hyperbolic discourse about circle leadership manifests itself strongly in these documents. Voloshin is depicted in the "contemporaries" memoirs written about him as having ideal social skills; he is often described in highly emotional terms as a veritable master in the formation and maintenance of successful intellectual community through a variety of leadership skills. Descriptions of these skills draw on many of the specific leadership qualities mulled over by earlier memoirists. His mastery is often described in terms of his ability to provide inspirational leadership, for example, reminiscent of the successful spiritual leaders of the communitas literary circles of the past. Thus circle member Marina Tsvetaeva wrote of Voloshin's skills in drawing people about him in pursuit of a common spiritual goal: "Max belonged to another set of laws than the human ones, and when we fell into his orbit we invariably fell under his set of laws. Max himself was the planet. And when we revolved around him we were revolving in some other large circle together with him around a luminary that we did not know."[55]

Voloshin is also praised in terms that reflect the activities of the more traditional leader of the circle as network node, that is, as a mentor. Above all Marina Tsvetaeva, the most famous beneficiary of his mentorship, sees him in this way: "I owe Maximilian Voloshin my first self-conception as a poet."[56] Furthermore, he is seen as peculiarly capable of fulfilling one of the roles of a mentor by facilitating network formation among those around him: "One of Max's vocations in life was to bring people together, to create encounters and destinies."[57] What is less a focus of fatuous admiration but nevertheless comes through clearly in the memoirs (and is supported by other documentation) is that Voloshin was also a master at mobilizing the material resources needed to maintain circle life through personal networking, a skill of the traditional patron and mentor that was also vital to his persona.

He is described, too, as possessing that personal sensitivity to those around him that had become a focus of memoirists: "Maximilian Aleksandrovich approached everyone with a gentle and attentive word. He could bring the best and most valuable to the surface, which sometimes hides deep within a person . . . Voloshin was the center to whom all were drawn. He could accept everything and understand everything."[58] He is also described as a peacemaker in the troubled world of circles, superbly skilled at easing the tensions of those around him and providing the foundations for emotional harmony among those engaged in programmatic activities. Wrote Andrei Bely: "Voloshin was essential to Moscow in those years: without him, the smoother of sharp corners, I don't know how the sharpening of opinions would have ended up between 'us' and our malevolent mockers; in Symbolist demonstrations he was precisely a placard with the inscription 'angel of peace.'"[59] In a new but intriguing development of the discourse over leadership, he is also depicted as being skilled in creating and cementing community in another way: through storytelling and mythmaking. "Max would tell stories about events the way a people tells them."[60]

In the memorialized figure of Voloshin, in other words, we have a kind of coalescence of many of the themes of leadership in the context of circle life, representing a balance between spiritual and pragmatic leadership, a talent for managing human relations and group harmony through the exceptional appreciation of human feelings and interactions in a variety of ways. Whether Voloshin actually possessed these qualities is not always clear. There is evidence that at times he was indeed a gifted leadership figure, but there are also indications that his talents have been exaggerated. But that is not entirely the point. The very hyperbole of these memoirs, the intensity of attention given to the problem of effective community leadership, reveals the pervasive concern of these memoir-writing intellectuals about the problems of community cohesion and identity.

This concern for community leadership had a very real foundation. During the period when Voloshin was most active, and also later when the memoirs were being written, writers and other intellectuals were under a great deal of pressure with regard to both social organization and identity. In the prerevolutionary period members of the intelligentsia were confronted by ever more varied possibilities for defining their identity and determining their economic and social behavior.[61] This was a great challenge to a group that only recently had been relatively homogeneous in social terms, consisting largely of members of the gentry. The growing anxiety about the role and the appropriate identity and behavior of the educated elite in Russian society is also reflected in such vigorous ideological struggles as those of the famous collection of intelligentsia debate and dissent over the role of the intelligentsia in Imperial Russian society, *Signposts.*[62] Fractures and fissures seemed to be opening up at every turn in educated life in late Imperial Russia, and these were both reflected in and caused additional cracks within the fundamental social organization of the literary intelligentsia, namely, the circle. Indeed the circle itself seems to have contributed to the problem through its own potential to function in the outside world as itself an ideological network, given to struggle against still other circles or factions.

Anxiety about the intelligentsia community and its identity was also embedded in a more widespread anxiety about national community, as Russia itself demonstrated increasing fragmentation as a traditional society experiencing the pressures of growing modernity under the leadership of Tsar Nicholas II, whose ability to lead was widely questioned. Contemporary scholars of the period such as Leopold Haimson, John Bushnell, and Geoffrey Hosking have pieced together a panorama of a society intensely at odds with itself, one suffering deep and intractable conflicts of culture, interests, and political conviction both within and between the populace, the elites, and the state.[63] The Revolution of 1905, which involved many writers, was but one manifestation of the growing tensions in a polity soon to disintegrate. Faith in the very existence of Imperial Russia as a unified body politic was eroding well before the internal convulsions brought on by World War I ultimately destroyed it.

The memoir discourse described above reflected a yearning among the literary community for an answer to the problems of disharmony and disintegration through a kind of leadership that was inspired and pragmatic, sensitive and effective. But as the events in the years following 1917 would demonstrate, this longing for harmony was in many ways treacherous. The literary community would step by step follow its leaders into a condition of servitude to the state. Thus literati would finally and fully negate the original impetus of communitas (completing the cycle of what Turner calls the "ritual process") by integrating themselves into the most powerful traditional structure in Russian history, namely, that of the state as it was interpenetrated by the traditional personal ties of networking and patronage. It was the faith of the literary community in its leaders, to whom they perhaps attributed, and thus offered, too much power—or too many different kinds of power—that led them to this pass.

As we pursue the themes of structure and anti-structure in this study of circle formation through the prism of Voloshin's life, we will first discover the traditional context of networking and patronage relations from the domestic sphere to the state that Voloshin experienced in his childhood and early youth; we will watch as he undergoes a painful encounter with a strange intermixture of the compelling spirit of communitas, on the one hand, and the power of patriarchal mentorship, on the other, in Symbolist social organization; we will then see his own communitas-style rebellion against the traditional structures of Symbolist circle life through his mentorship of a social group new to the literary scene: women poets. This may be seen as his first expression of agency, as he seeks to have a serious impact on the culture within which he lives and functions.

We will then trace his consolidation of that original rebellious impulse through the establishment of his own communitas-style circle in 1911, permeated by the spirit of self-transformation through theatricality among his largely adolescent visitors. As his circle matures in the teens of the twentieth century, we will observe the mellowing of the intense original 1911 spirit of communitas into a kind of group mythology of identity in self-transformative communitas through gossip and storytelling among its members. Then we will leave the theme of communitas behind for a time as we witness Voloshin's struggles to survive the civil war by implementing his skills in establishing traditional networking and patronage ties; on the basis of those same skills, he revives his circle and integrates it into the Soviet state privilege and welfare bureaucracy for writers and other intellectuals. In the context of similar activities on the part of several other leaders in the literary community, the tale of Voloshin's agency in this matter helps to show how literati were integrated into the structure of the young state one step at a time in the early Soviet period, beginning with their pursuit of the mentorship/patronage of such familiar and beloved leaders.

Turning to an exploration of Voloshin's revived Soviet circle, we will examine the persistence and transformation of two familiar forms of traditional structure, as well as the quiet preservation of communitas, in the form of a growing Soviet-made model for ideal intelligentsia behavior and identity that was built up around the person of Voloshin. And finally we will witness the collapse of his particular patronage network within the state during the turmoil of Stalin's rise to power in the late 1920s and early 1930s, as the literary community found itself at last fully consolidated into the structure of the state under the patronage, as well as the spiritual leadership, of a single figure, Stalin himself.

This tale is in many ways a tragic one, although it does have moments of hope. But above all it offers new insights into a topic of great importance in the history of Russian literary life: the cultural sources of social and political power in the literary circle between structure and anti-structure, and the ways that certain individuals could draw on those sources, sometimes to the advantage, sometimes to the detriment, of those they led.

ONE

Voloshin's Social
and Cultural Origins

A BRIEF NARRATIVE OF VOLOSHIN'S
EARLY YEARS; INTRODUCING SOME
CHARACTERS AND SOME THEMES

Approach Maximilian Voloshin from almost any direction at all and you will find a woman in your path. The first, of course, is his mother, Elena Ottobal'dovna Glaser, born to a Russian family of German heritage whose ancestors had made the eastward journey in the eighteenth century but still maintained a quiet sense of German ethnic identity. We see the Glasers in a photographic family portrait of the 1860s: five adults and four children, with Elena Ottobal'dovna's mother at the center, her dark hair drawn tightly back, gazing sternly at a point to the right of the camera. Her father, a sturdy balding man with spectacles and a walrus mustache, sits with the child Elena balanced against his shoulder on the far right of the picture. Showing promise of the unusual beauty she would possess in a few years time, Elena's fine brows, full lips, and small rounded chin are set against a broad, almost square face, giving an impression of grace and considerable self-possession.[1]

Elena Ottobal'dovna's father, the sturdy-looking Ottobal'd Glaser, was an engineer who worked for the Russian state telegraph department. The man Elena would marry at the age of sixteen, Alexander Kirienko-Voloshin, was a jurist and a member of the criminal and civil court of Kiev. Thus the two men who determined the milieu in which Elena Ottobal'dovna lived and into which Maximilian Voloshin would soon be born were mid-level professionals at a time when there were relatively few of them, as well as early members of what Voloshin himself would later describe as the "middle circles of the liberal intelligentsia."[2] Although generalizations about such "middle circles" must be made with caution, it is fair to say that there was among them an enormous respect for education and the opportunities it offered, as well as a certain degree of uncertainty and concern about the place of such a new educated class of people in the nation and in history. Many in these circles also demonstrated an intense and self-conscious love of high culture, including literature, music, and theater; they nurtured this love among themselves and in their children in the domestic sphere with passion, engaging in poetry recitations and musical and theatrical evenings, among other activities.

Elena Ottobal'dovna, with her grace, self-possession, and what was emerging as a lively personality, early revealed a particular flair for theatrical masquerade much in the self-transformative spirit of communitas. Soon after her marriage, she would occasionally costume herself in boy's clothing—much like Nadezhda Durova, the "cavalry maiden" who had ridden with the tsar's troops and whose memoirs had been published in the 1830s, and long before modernist Zinaida Gippius donned her trousers in an erotic, Decadent statement. In a classic intelligentsia *anekdot*, one of those gossipy narratives of personality of the "contemporaries" memoir genre, Marina Tsvetaeva passes on to us this image of Elena: dressed in her worst trousers and shirt and white-washing the ballroom ceiling on a ladder, when a friend of her husband's arrived and mistook her for his friend's son rather than wife. Astonished to find her in a skirt later at a social event, he stammered, "Well, do forgive me, where were my eyes?" "That's all right, they were where they should have been," came Elena's punch line, revealing the wit and power of her personality.[3]

In an unusual step that further indicates her strong will, Elena Ottobal'dovna left her husband after thirteen years of marriage, two years after Max was born.[4] Max's father died two years later, in 1881. It is not entirely clear how Elena Ottobal'dovna supported herself after the separation. Marina Tsvetaeva believes that she worked in a telegraph office. This is possible, considering Elena's father's association with the Russian telegraph system. Apparently her own family continued to help and support her after the separation from her husband. But Elena Ottobal'dovna's financial situation was never again as good as it had been during her marriage; for the rest of her life money was to be a nagging problem, although not catastrophic. In the early years after her separation, she seems to have handled the financial pressure, and perhaps also the isolation—for she never remarried—by living in the homes of friends. Upon departing from her husband, Elena Ottobal'dovna first went to live with a woman friend in the Crimean city of Sevastopol. Through this woman, she made friends with Elena Dmitrievna Viazemskaia, the wife of another engineer. In 1883 the Viazemskii family invited her and her six-year-old son, Max, to live with them in the Moscow suburbs, where the mother and son were quickly drawn into the family circle of a sprawling elite household.

Our earliest eyewitness glimpse of Elena Ottobal'dovna—as well as of the young Max—comes from a daughter of the Viazemskii family, Valentina Viazemskaia, who was twelve when Max and his mother came to live with them. She remembers Elena as lively and articulate with a strong sense of humor, often debating and joking vigorously with Valentina's maternal uncle. Elena was just as lively in her dealings with Max: it was "terribly funny" to listen to her humorous replies to Max's demands as a child, Viazemskaia recalls, although it may not have been quite so funny for Max as Elena Ottobal'dovna was a very strict mother.[5] Thus Valentina Viazemskaia observed the early stages of what was to develop as an intensely close but also difficult relationship between mother and son—a relationship that would lie at the core of Voloshin's circle in later years. All their lives they were to maintain intimate contact with each other either by living together or by maintaining a prolific correspondence. Each depended on the other both emotionally and economically. Yet discontent and tension troubled the association. Voloshin's first wife, Margarita Sabashnikova, described it in this way: "The mother passionately loved the son, and at the same time something about him constantly irritated her, which made his life with her very difficult."[6]

Tsvetaeva, who believed that Elena Ottobal'dovna left her husband owing to grief over the death of her dearly beloved four-year-old daughter, explained the tension between mother and son in terms of the anxieties about sexuality and gender roles that troubled the Russian cultural intelligentsia of the period.[7] "They were an inseparable pair," she tells us, "and not at all a friendly pair. All the masculinity, given for two, went to the mother; all the femininity—to the son, for there was no elementary masculinity ever in Max, just as in E. O. there was no elementary femininity. . . . The warrior was never in him, which fact particularly galled the warrior woman in body and soul—Elena Ottobal'dovna. 'Just look at Serezha, Max, there you are—a real man.[8] If there's a war—he fights. And you? What do you do, Max?'—'Mama, I can't crawl into a shirt with epaulettes and shoot at live people only because they think differently than I do.' 'They think. They think. There are times, Max, when you must not think but act. Act—without thinking.' 'Mama, animals always have times like that—it's called bestial instinct.'"[9]

Even as a child Max was quickly developing a strong personality and will of his own. Valentina Viazemskaia describes all the precocity and cleverness of an intelligentsia child one might expect to find in a "contemporaries" memoir, a child who read widely, memorized poetry, and passed youthful judgment on the classics of Russian literature. He loved to declaim poetry and was able to recite long passages from the works of Pushkin and Nekrasov. Viazemskaia also comments on two other qualities that dis-

Maximilian
Voloshin as a child
with his mother,
Elena Ottobal'dovna
Kirienko-Voloshina.
Date unknown.
*Courtesy of Vladimir
Kupchenko.*

tinguished Max early on. For one thing, he rarely cared about what others thought of him. He found others' comments about him "interesting," but he did not react as his critics might have expected. Even criticizing him to his face did not upset him, Viazemskaia tells us.[10] This quality of serene unflappability was to prove invaluable later in his life among the high-spirited, often quarrelsome Russian intelligentsia. The other characteristic he early revealed was a strong inclination toward playful masquerade and theatricality, like that of his mother. Max loved what Russians of the time called the *"mistifikatsiia,"* or joke involving deception either simple or elaborate, sometimes mere word play, sometimes costumes and role playing. His mother encouraged him in this, the two playing many jokes on each other or together playing jokes on others. Just as his essential calm would aid him in the future, so this theatrical skill—especially as it touched on the role of appearance in self-transformation—would later give Voloshin access to some of the most intimate levers of Russian intelligentsia identity, especially among the avant-garde circles he would later join.

But as Max approached his adolescence and left his tutor behind, it became clear that he was not yet prepared to make his mark in the great world, at least not in the competitive world of Moscow education. First he was enrolled in the prestigious private Polivanov Gymnasium, where many of the Russian educated elite formed personal ties that would last them the rest of their lives; in his second year, however, he was removed and enrolled in a state school. He later had to repeat his third year (grade 7). In 1893 Elena Ottobal'dovna decided to return with him to the Crimea. Voloshin greeted this decision with joy, as it offered him the hope of a new beginning after several years of academic struggle.

As it turned out, the new beginning came even before they left for the Crimea. Elena and her son were obliged to welcome new tenants into their Moscow apartment before the Crimean arrangements had been finalized, and so they shared their living quarters for three months with another family, the Dosekins. Nikolai Dosekin was a landscape artist from Kharkov, and during the time the two families lived under one roof he introduced Max to a new world of acquaintances from the Moscow artistic and literary scene, people who came to visit him in their shared home. Many of these individuals were drawn together by a mutual love of the Russian poet Afanasii Fet, whom they recited and discussed at length. Along with several artists, this group included a number of journalists, many associated with the *Moscow Gazette*. Philosopher Vladimir Solovev and artist Konstantin Korovin of the Moscow School and future World of Art were also known to appear at the Dosekins' home.

The opportunity to witness and perhaps take part in the lively discourse in Dosekin's circle had a considerable impact on Voloshin. "For me," he wrote many years later, "having grown up exclusively among the middle circles of the liberal intelligentsia, all these artistic discussions and opinions were a novelty, and had a decidedly favorable impact on my outlook on the world."[11] This glimpse of an intellectual milieu above and beyond the "middle circles" of his earlier childhood was his first encounter with what many Russians of the time described as the "cultural intelligentsia": those among the tiny educated elite of Russia who sought energetically to shape Russian identity and discourse through art, literature, music, theater, and philosophy.

When Elena Ottobal'dovna at last succeeded in completing the move to the Crimea, she sent Max to a new gymnasium—by now he was in his fifth year (grade 9)—in Theodosia, while she settled nearby in the tiny village of Koktebel' on the coast of the Black Sea. The arduous move paid off: unlike Moscow, Theodosia, on the fringe of the Russian Empire and of elite society, proved a secure and supportive community in which Max could develop his talents and make close friends, one of them to become a lifelong friend and intellectual associate. As he passed through his middle teens, he became ever more involved in the kinds of activities associated with the intelligentsia identity: reading, memorizing, writing, and translating poetry; giving public readings first of Alexander Pushkin's poetry and later his own; taking lively part in home theatricals; and so on. The poetry he was writing earned much praise and encouragement in Theodosia, gaining him a youthful reputation (which, although not fulfilled, would remain precious to him for the rest of his life) as a "future Pushkin."[12]

The respect for the written word that was being imbued in Voloshin during this time, a respect for literacy, literature, and literary culture that bordered on the idolatrous, was symptomatic of what those aspects of life meant in a society where a relatively small proportion of the country was literate and where very few were interested in literature at all.[13] One letter Max wrote to his mother reflects this intelligentsia fixation on literature as a source of prestige as well as identity, with an attendant scorn of those less fixated. Max was participating in a carnival theatrical in the Theodosia home of a local artist. The man himself was out of town, and so when Max, alone in the house, "somehow was in his study," he took the opportunity to look into his folders of drawings and generally to look around: "By the way, an interesting and characteristic detail: among the drawing materials on his desk is only one book, and that with the superb title . . . 'List of highest-ranking officials in the Russian Empire!!!' Not only that, but I saw a mass of very interesting French and German books—covered with dust, tossed into various boxes which have evidently gone untouched by a human hand for many years."[14] That this supposedly "cultured" artist ignored his French and German books in favor of a kind of "Who's Who" of Russian officialdom apparently gave Voloshin a pleasant sense of superiority. Note, too, the scorn Voloshin felt for the excessive interest in structural hierarchy taken by this artist.

In the fall of 1897 Max left the Crimea and returned to Moscow to study at the Law Faculty of Moscow University, urged on by his mother to follow his father's professional path. His expectations were high as he returned to the second largest city in the country. As he wrote his Theodosian friend, Aleksandra Petrova, he had imagined from reading contemporary novels that an intense political spirit would prevail among Moscow students. But he was disappointed at first by the lack of heroism among his peers. Struggling like others in the Russian educational system for a sense of place and direction in Russian history at the turn of the century, he wrote: "I understand why our youth is so shallow and cheerless. It knows neither its past nor its present. And how can it know, when all is well and truly hidden from it. We all live in a kind of artificially created hothouse from which all external impressions and fresh currents are excluded. When we want to know what is going on over on the other side of the wall, they (the censored journals) tell us that there's nothing good out there, and that should we look out the window, the wolf will get us."[15]

Initially Max identified with what he saw and described as the "personalities" of the generation of the 1870s ("*semidesiatniki*") because of their seriousness of purpose in seeking to change Russia for the better of "the people." It was their heroism that he wanted to find among his own generation of students, but could not. Soon he discovered a broader spectrum of intelligentsia identities. Building on his earlier ties with the well-connected Dosekin family and establishing new bonds with some of his fellow students, and frequenting the editorial offices of the journal *Russian Thought*, he began increasingly to engage with intelligentsia society, attending the theater, lectures, and private gatherings. Soon he began to recognize a whole variety of intelligentsia "personalities" shaped by the rapidly changing times in late Imperial Russia, and to develop a more complex system of classifying intelligentsia individuals and groups according to their place in time. "It is interesting to trace back the waves of Russian generations," Voloshin wrote, "the sixties generation—logical intellect, a passion for learning, rejection of feelings; the seventies generation—the 'dictatorship of the heart,' a passion for the people, a willingness to sacrifice oneself entirely for their sakes; the eighties generation—the tsardom of Lev Tolstoi, self-analysis, immersion in the self, questions of conscience; the nineties generation—the absence of activity, a passion for Marx, scientific materialism, everything is explained in terms of economic factors. Will we, the first generation of the twentieth century, finally have something to say? What? At this point I still feel as if I were in the situation of a speaker at a ceremonial dinner, raising his wineglass from the table in order to give a speech but without any idea of where to begin. There is a mass of topics, but he doesn't know which one to choose."[16]

Voloshin was being drawn into a broader intelligentsia discourse about its identity through history. He identified a very small part of Russian society (even of the Russian intelligentsia itself) with Russians in general; he exuded a strong sense of rapidly changing times; and he demonstrated an overpowering impression that the personalities of individuals are profoundly influenced by their circumstances, by their positions in time and place and among specific groups of people. A sense of destiny also revealed itself here: Voloshin believed (or wanted to believe) that he was an important participant in this process.

Voloshin continued to write poetry and to pursue other literary interests, especially the translation of poetry. This work, too, often reflected his fledgling political concerns. Surely it was no accident that, around the time he discovered that he was under police suspicion, he was translating Heinrich Heine's bitter poem against the Prussian state, "Germany: A Winter Fairytale."[17] He gradually became more and more engaged in the student disturbances of the turn of the century.[18] Already under police suspicion during his first year at the university, in the second he was suspended for one year for "agitation" during a Russia-wide student strike. He was sent back to Theodosia. He and his mother took the opportunity to go abroad in the fall of 1899, traveling in Italy, Switzerland, France, and Germany, where Max audited some lectures at the University of Berlin. Returning to Moscow University in February 1900, he resumed his studies and also became involved in student literary publications. But in August 1900 he was arrested, jailed for two weeks, and again sent to the Crimea.

There he embarked on a trip to Central Asia. While in Central Asia, during the fall of 1900, he decided that he would not return to the university, telling his concerned mother that it was pointless for him to continue his education in law since he did not intend to enter government service. Dissatisfied with his father's profession and the "middle circles" of his early milieu, and building on his youthful experience of literature and other aspects of high culture, he aspired to what he viewed as more elevated and perhaps more prestigious goals, goals resembling those of the Dosekin circle and the "cultural intelligentsia." By April 1901 he was in Paris.

MAX AND THE MEANS OF
EXCHANGE IN LATE IMPERIAL RUSSIA

At the same time that Voloshin was struggling with these loftier questions of intelligentsia and national destiny, family financial concerns were pulling him back to earth. His attempts to resolve these financial issues reflect the complex nature of Russia's system of economic exchange in the late Imperial period. Money was the primary means of exchange in this modernizing economy, yet it was not the only means. It was not necessarily even the most favored means: money, because it facilitated cold, impersonal, and supposedly exploitative market relations, engendered a certain anxiety among some elements of the Russian intelligentsia. Voloshin's youthful experiences with money, especially in his relations with his mother, both reflected and shaped that anxiety in him and also revealed to him an important alternative to direct monetary exchange: economic networking through personal relationships.

Many of the letters that passed between Elena Ottobal'dovna and her son while Max was in school, at the university, and during his early years abroad indicate a shortage of funds and a struggle to make them last. On his father's death, Max had received an inheritance of twelve thousand rubles; much of that capital (forty rubles a month in the early years and later increasingly smaller amounts) paid for his schooling.[19] But this amount was not enough to prevent financial strain, or the consequent tension and discomfort between mother and son over the issue. In early 1896, while still attending the Theodosia gymnasium, Max wrote a letter to his mother containing a long explanation about lost galoshes and a Christmas present costing two and a half rubles for the maid at his lodgings in Theodosia: "Will you count that toward my expenses?" he asked delicately. Then he went on to explain that the tutoring job he had found had fallen through yet again, because his student had caught pneumonia.[20] Tutoring was a common means of financial support at this time among the less wealthy of Russia's ambitious students.

Writing to his mother in November 1897 as a new university student in Moscow, where he was lodging with his grandmother, he announced: "I got your letter and money today. The latter I did not expect to receive at all and would never have asked for it: Babushka [Grandma] wrote without my consent."[21] Presumably Babushka, though unauthorized, had let his mother know about financial strains that he would have preferred to keep to himself. Max had paid his rent to Babushka up to the end of November by taking out a temporary loan, he continued in his letter, which would have to be repaid in full by January. Regarding December's rent, he hoped to have obtained some tutoring work by then, or at least some other way to make money.

Then he launched into his new plan: he was going to sell translations of poetry to such journals as *Vestnik innostrannoi literatury* (Herald of foreign literature). This, he told his mother enthusiastically, "would be much more profitable and convenient than tutoring." He went on to explain his analysis of the market forces involved: "All the students tutor in Moscow, but only a few translate poetry, and though the demand for tutoring is far greater than the demand for translations, it nevertheless seems to me that in the final analysis the chances of getting work are far greater, if my translations really are good, as Dosekin told you they are. To go back to my present financial situation, . . ."[22] Nikolai Dosekin, the landscape artist who had first introduced Voloshin to the world of the cultural intelligentsia, was already exerting a significant influence on Voloshin's economic as well as intellectual aspirations.

But Elena Ottobal'dovna was not generally impressed by Max's notions of practicality, as is revealed by their correspondence after he decided to abandon jurisprudence and travel to Western Europe. In response to her son's request for money after he arrived in Paris in 1901, she wrote: "Dear Max, I got your letter of the 26th of October with the request for money yesterday, and will send you a small sum sometime after November 1st: I don't know how much I'll be able to send after paying the carpenter. Is it really impossible to find work in Paris, despite the mass of acquaintances you have? You can't live on forty rubles a month. This means that you need money one way or another."

Turning to comment more broadly on what she saw as his lack of discipline in financial matters, she continued in a tone of increasing impatience: "I do not agree with you that it is possible to borrow money in good conscience . . . and that it is impermissible only when you don't know how you are going to pay the money back; it's much more conscientious for a young, healthy, strong person to find a way of living from his own labors[;] obviously you have been on your own feet for some time now . . . you ought to study and work like a real person and not like a dilettante desiring [the word *brat'*, *to borrow*, is crossed out here] and searching only for those pleasures (scholarly though they may be) which can be obtained without labor, hardship, and the sacrifice of many of the pleasures of life. Even weak, sick girls like Zoya attain that sort of independence through labor; besides studying at the gymnasium, she is tutoring, not wishing to live at someone else's expense."[23]

Thus Elena Ottobal'dovna sternly attempted to imbue her son with the most stringent of what might be called bourgeois economic values, linked as they are with money as the means of exchange: hard work, delay of gratification, and economic independence. She did not hesitate to drive her point home by employing a means that Marina Tsvetaeva would have recognized immediately—by linking money and manhood, and impugning his masculinity with her reference to the virtuous "Zoya." Given her long experience with financial stress first as a wife separated from her husband and then as a widow, Elena Ottobal'dovna had occasion for particular respect for money and for financial self-discipline, and she clearly considered it important to pass that respect on to her son.

While Voloshin did not struggle openly (at least in the documents I have seen) against the rather shiftless image of himself that his mother reflected back at him, his letters to her are notably more focused on money issues than those, for example, to his friend Aleksandra Petrova. He wanted his mother to know that he was economically competent. But economic competence in the turn-of-the-century world of which Voloshin was becoming a part did not consist exclusively of mastery of the classic bourgeois values that Elena Ottobal'dovna espoused. There were other economic skills that were at least as important, and Voloshin grasped this early on. In that 1897 letter to his mother, in which he considered the market possibilities of translating poetry, he continued: "The only thing is, it seems that it's difficult to get into a journal at all without patronage [*protektsia*], and

I just had this thought: why not revive the acquaintance with Turkin [Viazemskii family tutor]—maybe it would be possible to arrange something with him or through him."[24]

Voloshin thus revealed his growing attention to an important characteristic of the intellectual economy of late Imperial Russia. The stringent bourgeois values of his mother, the principles of merit, determination, and self-sufficiency (as even she seemed to admit when she referred somewhat scornfully to the "masses of acquaintances" in Paris who should have been able to find Voloshin a job) were not enough for making one's way among the cultural intelligentsia. Personal ties were needed, and not just the ties of emotional or intellectual empathy but those of economic and professional value. In Voloshin's words about "*protektsia*," therefore, we see the birth of a networking star. He had quickly recognized a central force in the economic culture of the realm to which he aspired. Networking for the sake of patronage and other types of professional advantage was critical in the literary world.

But networking had its rules, its habits, and its traditions of power and control; one could not simply make one's demands and expect to gain one's desires. Good networking involved an understanding of where and when to do it, and with whom, and how to frame one's request for help, as well as a myriad of other cultural complexities which I hope to illuminate in this book. Voloshin had been learning about this reality since his childhood, as it was a vital element of the culture he grew up in, and it was to have an impact on his life and the lives of many others that he would prove uncommonly attuned to that reality.

LEARNING TO NETWORK
FROM THE HOUSEHOLD TO THE STATE

Networking took place at many levels in late Imperial Russian society, with locality and the familiarity built up through mutual experience of locality as a key to its impetus. One of the most important localities for networking, and the place where many educated Russians first experienced it, was the household, that protective "nest" of elite Russian identity and power. This had many implications for the way networking operated and its impact on Russian society and history. First, it meant that even children had a chance to watch, test, and develop networking skills. It also meant that children often already had a collection of useful personal ties by the time they left home to go out into the world.

Voloshin lived in a number of households during his childhood and adolescence, and thus he had many opportunities to discover what it meant to form domestic ties of mutual toleration and interest in the locality of the household. He also had the opportunity to explore a range of household structures, many reflecting a broad pattern of Russian elite household formation in which members of the extended as well as the nuclear family and indeed entirely unrelated members, such as servants (including tutors and governesses), boarders (sometimes), and long- and short-term visitors, might all interact with one another with some degree of regularity. Turn-of-the-century statistics on household composition in Moscow and Petersburg—centers of the educated elite—show that only 52 percent and 53 percent of the population, respectively, living in "family" households (as opposed to those living in workers' barracks or as "solitaries") were actually family members. Of this population in these two cities, 48 percent and 47 percent, respectively, was made up of boarders, servants, and other resident employees. The average household size was just over eight members in Moscow and just under eight members in Petersburg.[25] The frequent presence of friends and distant relatives, whether they actually lived in the household for a time or were merely repeated guests at the table, was also likely, given the longstanding culture of elite hospitality rooted in the patterns of Russian intelligentsia social life.[26] In such households the enforced familiarity among individuals, both related and unrelated by blood, brought about by living together or even just visiting, building a history of interaction based on mutual toleration and interest, provided an ideal atmosphere for nurturing the formation of extensive networks. The personal ties established in such group living situations could develop not only emotional content but also economic significance, both within the context of the household and potentially beyond its boundaries.

The structure of the Viazemskii household in the Moscow suburbs, where Voloshin lived for a number of years with his mother, fit the typical Moscow and Petersburg household pattern of combining family members with a large percentage of nonfamily members under a single roof. The household consisted for a time not only of the Viazemskii nuclear family and the broken Voloshin nuclear family (who may technically have been boarders) but also of the Viazemskii mother's brother and a children's tutor.[27] In this household Voloshin interacted intimately not only with members of the Viazemskii nuclear and extended family but also with its employees, for example, with Turkin, the Viazemskii tutor.

This was the very same Turkin, now no longer a tutor but a successful journalist, with whom Max had suggested reviving relations for the sake of *protektsia* in the letter to his mother cited above. Thus when Voloshin first raised the issue of literary patronage, he immediately proposed drawing on a personal tie formed during his childhood household experience. Another name that had come up in Voloshin's letters to his mother about his early literary ambitions was, of course, Nikolai Dosekin, with whom Voloshin had also formed a personal tie in the household context, when they had all lived together in one apartment in Moscow before Voloshin's move to the Crimea.

Such household-based ties could serve pragmatic purposes well beyond the borders of the immediate household, as shown in these two cases. But such ties may also be seen as a natural extension of the ways in which living or interacting together in a household could in itself represent a notable mingling of personal and economic forms of association. Voloshin experienced this in many ways not only as a child and youth but also as he got older. While living in the Theodosia Gymnasium dormitory, for example, he made friends with a boy, Sasha Peshkovskii, who was to become the closest companion of his youth. Soon he and Peshkovskii agreed to move out of the dormitory together and to board with the Petrov family household, a decision that was both personally and economically significant. Here the two became not only economically associated with this household, since they paid board, but they also became close personal friends with the granddaughter of the household, Aleksandra Petrova. In Moscow, as a university student, Voloshin crossed kinship and economic relations and began to board with his grandmother. In all these domestic situations Voloshin experienced that blend of personal and material association with his domestic companions that is central to the network bond.

The household, despite its formative influence, was not the only locality to serve as a context for building up personal ties. While attending Moscow University Voloshin discovered a type of association established on the basis of a broader locality, the student *zemliachestvo*, a university organization typically based on the common geographical (sometimes educational) origins of its members. He joined the Moscow University *zemliachestvo* for students from the Crimea. The *zemliachestvo* provided its members with companionship and a way to meet new people; at the same time it offered significant material support. It had its own bank, or mutual assistance fund, and Voloshin's first mention of his *zemliachestvo* involvement is to tell his mother in a letter that he had borrowed money from that fund to pay the rent.[28] Other *zemliachestvo* amenities were group libraries and *kruzhki samorazvitiia* (circles for self-development), where students could prepare for classes together, read one another's papers, and so on. The *zemliachestvo* could also make petitions and proclamations, and maintained lists of addresses. Officially these organizations were illegal, but the need, especially the material need, of students across the Russian Empire for these well-organized personal networks based on regional affiliation was recognized as being so great that university administrators looked the other way.[29]

When Voloshin decided to travel to Central Asia after being suspended from the university a second time, he again turned to one of his earlier household contacts: the Viazemskii family. Through Valerian Viazemskii, now an engineer with the state railway, Voloshin acquired a job with surveyors of the Tashkent-Orenburg railroad line in Central Asia. The job was undemanding and gave him the delightful privilege of traveling certain routes in Central Asia by train without having to pay for his tickets. Thus we find in his personal archive in Petersburg a state identity paper, or *udostoverenie*, confirming his privilege of free train travel from Tashkent to Krasnovodsk, with stopovers in Ashkhabad and Samarkand.[30] This *udostoverenie* was an early indication of how the state would become drawn into private network relations in Voloshin's life: through a personal tie he had gained free train tickets, courtesy of the state. The document foreshadows the means by which Voloshin would revive his circle in the Soviet period.

Suffering travel difficulties in Tashkent, Voloshin experienced another way in which locality played a role in network relations, and saw how personal contacts could become entangled with and even subvert state action, far away from central power, on the weakly governed fringe of the empire. Voloshin's problem was this: his passport had been confiscated upon his second arrest and exile to the Crimea;[31] if state authorities caught him in Tashkent without this form of identity, and figured out who he was, they could make considerable trouble for him (since he was officially supposed to be in the Crimea, not Tashkent). But soon after arriving in Tashkent, he wrote to his mother: "My affairs are perfectly in order or, in other words, they remain entirely unordered. I think I already wrote to you about Geyer —a *znatok* [expert; literally, one who knows] of Turkestan, editor of the newspaper *Russian Turkestan*, and one-time exile. A man whom I met on the ferry sent me to him. No matter what, I would have come to know him, because without him none of the surveyors in Tashkent can take a single step. When I explained my problem to him and asked his advice, he advised me not to appear before anyone [i.e., the police or other official figures] and not to ask anybody anything, as long as nobody [official] has received any information about me. And any [such] information would have to go through his hands since he works for the oblast' government." Thus Geyer could warn him in advance of any impending difficulties. Geyer also told Voloshin that he could remain out on the steppe as long as he pleased without passport or any other kind of identification, because no one would be interested in him out there. If a problem came up in town while Voloshin was on the steppe, Geyer would resolve it without him.[32]

Geyer, a *znatok,* as Voloshin identified him, knew the local situation well, having gained familiarity with his small part of the world, Tashkent and Turkestan, through proximity over time. Though originally a political exile, he had been integrated into the local system. He had gained some control over local networks and means of power. Not only did he understand how the police operated but he also had access to the flow of information among state bureaucratic and police entities. However, he did not use his state-based bureaucratic power to exercise impersonal, rational control in the interest of the state. Rather, the impact and influence of proximity, such as that due to his personal encounter with Voloshin, led Geyer instead to frustrate the government's attempts at control by advising Voloshin to move out of reach on the steppe. Both an outsider and an insider, Geyer was invaluable not only to Voloshin but also to the surveyors, also outsiders in Tashkent. As a fellow outsider, Geyer took their interests to heart; but as an insider, he was familiar with and had influence over local conditions in a way that no outsider could. It is probably not entirely coincidental that Geyer had another source of power as editor of a local newspaper. Voloshin's budding journalistic career found one of its earliest outlets in that newspaper, *Russian Turkestan*.[33]

This particular experience of network and local power was not explicitly economic but, rather, was primarily bureaucratic, though one could surely argue that one's whereabouts directly influenced one's economic situation, and that the state, in exiling Voloshin, was imposing itself not only on his social life but also on his economic life. Certainly it demonstrates the kind of personal power that could accrue from access to bureaucratic control. Personal power had long been an important component of the Russian system of bureaucratized control, despite much official struggle against it since the days of Peter the Great.[34] Moreover, for a variety of reasons, it appears that the significance of personal power in the Russian bureaucracy was increasing in the late Imperial period.[35] In any case, Voloshin's experience was a portent of what was to come after the Revolution of 1917, when the state bureaucracy would become both explicitly and integrally involved in Russian economic relations. At the turn of the century in Central Asia, Geyer was a local patron; Voloshin, like the surveyors, was, for a time, his client. After the 1917 revolution, Voloshin, also on the fringe of empire in the Crimea, would become a local *znatok* and patron himself.

Voloshin's early networking experiences offer a narrow but detailed glimpse of everyday network and patronage relations among the late Imperial Russian educated elite. This web of personalized economic ties found its origins in proximity and familiarity, and could extend from the most intimate of domestic personal associations to the official, yet also potentially personal, encounter of the private individual with the state. In order to gain access to this network and to its benefits, one needed the personal skills to find the individual who could provide assistance, and to convince that person to offer it. Those who possessed such skills could put them to very good use indeed, both within the literary world and outside it. These were the skills Voloshin was acquiring in his early years; this was the "structure," to use Turner's terminology, of the economic system to which Voloshin was being acculturated.

TWO

The Russian Symbolists
and Their Circles

THE WELCOME GUEST

Back from his travels abroad by the early 1900s Voloshin soon began to network his way into what seemed to him the liveliest literary milieu in town—that of the Russian Symbolists. In Paris he had made some influential friends, among them the mistress of a French-Russian salon, Madame Gol'shtein, and the Symbolist poet Konstantin Bal'mont. From these friends he obtained letters of introduction to, among others, Valerii Briusov, one of the most effective organizers in the Symbolist movement and also the editor of the Symbolist journal *Vesy*.[1] Through Briusov, Voloshin gained access to Symbolist affairs as well as to journalistic work as the Paris correspondent for *Vesy*. Voloshin soon became a popular figure among this crowd, in Moscow especially, if perhaps less so in Petersburg.[2]

The modernist cultural movement into which Voloshin was making his way consisted of a great variety of overlapping and ever changing circles of association.[3] What these groups shared above all was an aggressive resistance to Russian Realism, with its utilitarian focus on literature as a means of transforming society. "Art for art's sake," not society's, was the Symbolist cry, and from this fundamental point of agreement the members of this movement took a number of different paths that were reflected in its various interconnected associational webs. These ranged from the early Decadent movement, to the theatrical World of Art group of Aleksandr Benois and Sergei Diaghilev, to the circle around Briusov's *Vesy*, to the Religious-Philosophical Circle of Zinaida Giuppus and Dmitrii Merezhkovskii, to Andrei Bely's playful Argonauts, to Viacheslav Ivanov's "Tower" group, to name only a few of its more formal or self-conscious organizations. Numerous less formal circles spun into and out of these organizations in a swirl of changing personal and professional ties.

Maximilian Voloshin,
Paris, 1905.
*Courtesy of Vladimir
Kupchenko.*

Despite a sense of common cause among many in the Symbolist move-ment, it was a community with considerable potential for struggle and disharmony. The wide variety of its circles, the passionate commitment of many of its participants to their ideas, and the idiosyncrasies of the person-alities involved, all could contribute to personal tension. A central source of stress was the potentially hybrid nature of the Russian literary circle, as de-scribed in the introduction. Like many such groupings of the period, Sym-bolist circles mingled the anti-structural relations of communitas with the opposed tendency toward traditional hierarchical power relations in a way that could greatly exacerbate group tensions—as the second section of this chapter will vividly demonstrate.

It was against this background of tension and personal stress that Volo-shin quickly began to shape an identity that would serve him well among literary circles: he emerged—or so the memoirs tell us—as an individual with that vital quality of humaneness, of sensitivity to the feelings of those around him, that was so lauded in the "contemporaries" memoir celebra-tion of great intelligentsia social leaders. This talent lay at the heart of his growing skill in facilitating harmony within the potentially fraught circle formation, a skill that would in many ways lie at the heart of his cult. For when a circle leader lacked the quality of humaneness and, like Vissarion Belinsky, pursued idealistic goals without consideration for the feelings of those around him, both individuals and social webs could suffer great damage. Voloshin demonstrated this quality most significantly in the domestic sphere, where Symbolist circles and their offshoots generally gathered. Above all he attuned himself to the needs and anxieties of the weakest members of this domestically based world of intellectual networks, namely women and children, who would come to be his most significant circle constituency and the most important source of his social influence.

One of the puzzles this book addresses is the extent to which the often hagiographic memoirs about Voloshin reflect historical reality; this question must certainly be raised about the memoir characterizations of Voloshin's social sensitivity and skill. Was he really such a thoughtful fellow, or was he endowed with those qualities only in retrospect? Yet, curiously, the first sign of his social skill comes not in the memoirs but in more trustworthy documents: in letters between Voloshin and a close friend during the former's university years. These letters reveal Voloshin's attempt to resolve a quarrel between the two closest friends of his youth—not, coincidentally, between those very friends with whom he had recently shared a household: Aleksandra Petrova and Sasha Peshkovskii. In examining the tale of Voloshin's attempt to heal this rift, we gain a deeper understanding of what appears to have been his genuine growing talent for managing human relations.

At the beginning of 1898, while Voloshin was still at Moscow University, Aleksandra Petrova (living at home in Theodosia) and Sasha Peshkovskii (now with Voloshin at the university) had fallen into strife. Aleksandra Petrova was angry with Sasha, and Sasha, perplexed as to the cause of this anger, had turned to Voloshin for help and support. Seeking to alleviate the tension, Voloshin wrote to Petrova: "This is my plea: please explain to me how Sasha offended you. Why do you consider the insult impossible to forgive? Write me everything that you feel, keeping in mind that I have only a dim understanding of the circumstances. I repeat: if it is too hard for you to write, don't write. Whether you write or not—*nothing will change* my relationship to you. My goal: to clear away confusion. I consider it my duty as your friend and Peshkovskii's."[4]

Petrova was embarrassed. In order to show her how far the Theodosia gossips would go, Sasha had joked to her about a rumor that she and Sasha were to be married. She had reacted with alarm. Voloshin replied in his letter to her: "You write that you long for the 'old Peshkovskii.' Isn't he still the same Peshkovskii? Can that 'Peshkovskii' that you knew really have changed?

Didn't that Peshkovskii also suffer from an absence of manners every now and then? . . . How could you have attributed to 'that Peshkovskii' 'such' thoughts?" He went on to quote a segment of Sasha's letter to him about the quarrel in order to show her that Peshkovskii was bewildered and embarrassed about the cause of the quarrel. Voloshin concluded somewhat briskly that the vulgar and stupid Peshkovskii that she was imagining did not exist, only a "sensitive, good, modest, refined, deep, thoughtful, and talented Peshkovskii, whom everyone loved the more, the better they got to know him."[5]

Voloshin's reassurance about the stability of their own relationship, and the ease with which he understood, slipped into, and manipulated Aleksandra Petrova's own metaphor for her alienation from Sasha Peshkovskii — that Peshkovskii had become another person — is a sign of his maturing ability to attune himself to the emotional conditions and expressions of those around him, as well as to the power of metaphor in human relations under the constant conditions of change. And the firmness with which he could urge Aleksandra Petrova to abandon both metaphor and alienation is a sign of Voloshin's growing capacity for authoritativeness that would help him to draw people to him in the future. It would take some time for Voloshin to bring this talent for easing strained human relations to full fruition; yet even in the early years of his Symbolist experience, it would ease his welcome into the domestic Symbolist realm.

While in Paris in 1902 Voloshin established his first important contact with that world by making friends with the older and successfully published Symbolist Konstantin Bal'mont, about whom he had written a challenging but nevertheless apparently well-received review while still a student. Over the next few years he was to become an intimate of the Bal'mont family circle, as well as a significant fixture of the Symbolist gatherings in Bal'mont's home, for two reasons, both having to do with Bal'mont's wife, Ekaterina Alekseevna. First, Voloshin fell in love with, and eventually married, Ekaterina Bal'mont's cousin, Margarita Sabashnikova. Thus he established a significant kinship tie to the circle. Second, and probably more important, he won Ekaterina's trust and affection to such a point that, for a time, Voloshin spent a part of every day with the Bal'mont family. Many years later, after Voloshin's death in 1932, Voloshin's second wife was to include Ekaterina Bal'mont among the many friends whom she asked for personal memoirs about Voloshin. While the memoir Ekaterina wrote has overtones of the typical memorialistic adulation, it is sufficiently specific to convey a sense of why she came to like and trust him so much: with his capacity for easing the stresses of interpersonal tension, he had a great deal to offer a household that was often threatened by instability.

Konstantin Bal'mont was emotionally high-strung, drank a great deal, and spent many nights on the town. He was also attractive to women and took advantage of that quality. When the two men first began to spend time together in Paris, each was warned by his friends against the other's company. Ekaterina Bal'mont, left behind with their children in Moscow, heard of this new friendship between her husband and the presumably wild and dangerous Maximilian Voloshin in Paris with unease and concern. So she was much astonished when, upon returning from a walk with her daughter Nina one day, she met Voloshin himself at her door in Moscow. Nina had run home ahead of her, and as Ekaterina approached her home, "to my surprise, I saw Nina in the arms of some stranger. At first I took fright, fearing that something would happen to my daughter, knowing that she would never willingly go into the arms of a stranger, especially one who looked so odd: small, stout, in a long green student's coat, very shabby with black instead of gold buttons, and a soft wide felt hat. With an easy gentle movement he put my daughter on the floor, took off his hat, shook his curly head, and, straightening his pince-nez, came close to me, looked me in the eye shyly and at the same time firmly, and said: 'You are Ekaterina Alekseevna, I am from Paris and bring you greetings from Konstantin. Ninika and I are already acquainted—I am Voloshin.'"[6]

Ekaterina Alekseevna immediately felt herself drawn to this man who had stepped so deftly yet respectfully right into those spheres of concern where she felt most vulnerable: her daughter's safety and her relationship with her husband. His ability to do this bespoke a broader capacity for interpersonal relations that could be invaluable to her in managing her domestic situation, which always lay in the background of the circle gatherings that took place in her house. However simple, even humble, his talent in this regard, it was very important to Voloshin's success in gaining access to the domestic foundations of Bal'mont's popular Symbolist gatherings.

Voloshin was good with children, for example. He played with them on their level but did not forget the obligations of adult responsibility. As Ekaterina Bal'mont still remembered many years later, he once offered Nina some oranges and was then told she was forbidden to eat them. He quickly drained this situation of its potential for tears and disappointment by opening the door from the children's room to the dining room, where the other guests sat, and telling Nina that they would throw these balls out there. "Which 'uncle' do you want to hit?" he asked, and, directed by Nina, Voloshin proceeded to hit two guests with oranges, letting Nina throw one for herself.[7] Voloshin, who maintained his relationship with Nina into her adulthood, was attentive and attuned to children all his life, though he never had any of his own. Not only would this strengthen his welcome into those domestically based intellectual circles with children in the background, but it would also contribute to the building of his own circle and, eventually, cult. For it was children and adolescents who would make up the foundation of his circle, and it was children who would later as adults remember him with affection and write admiring memoirs about him many decades after his death. Children could play important roles in Russian circle and network life, as well as in shaping the social memory of that life; a number of Russian cult figures would later be admired for their connections with children.[8]

Ekaterina's apprehensions about Voloshin's relationship with her husband were also soon relieved. During that first visit she asked him carefully if the report she had heard was true, that Bal'mont in his activities had come to exchange night for day. "Max very calmly said that Bal'mont nevertheless spends half the day in the library and reads till evening. He fails to sleep only when he is in a nervous condition. 'And such nights you spend together?'—I asked, trying to make the question sound as natural as possible. 'Of course one cannot leave him alone at such a time. You probably know that.' And he said that so simply and sincerely that I already could not doubt that the rumors which had reached me were false." Ekaterina's further association with Voloshin never undermined this first conclusion. "When much later I saw how Max, always sober, accompanied Bal'mont in his night wanderings, sometimes till morning, carefully preserving him from conflicts and brawls in the street or in restaurants, escorting him either home or to Voloshin's—I understood that their friendship had been like that from the very beginning."[9]

Ekaterina liked many other things about Voloshin. He was always having money troubles, and borrowed money repeatedly, but his creditors trusted him because he paid them back with unusual precision and punctuality, "for a Russian." (Clearly those early rigorous lessons from his mother in this area of human relations had had an impact on his financial habits.) When others needed money, he was quick to lend or give it himself. He was polite and respectful; sometimes, Ekaterina seems to have felt, too respectful of the literary lions who attended the Bal'monts' domestic literary gatherings. He was soft-spoken but nevertheless definite in his opinions. He disliked and discouraged sly gossip. He kept his troubles to himself and always kept his associations with others on an even keel; as had been noted long ago by Valentina Viazemskaia, it was virtually impossible to quarrel with him. Altogether he was a very attractive guest, and having once slipped through the membrane of the Bal'mont household he became a welcome intimate.[10]

Ekaterina Bal'mont was not the only one to recognize his value in the intelligentsia household. As he gained increasing access to the Symbolist networks, his personal emotional talents for inspiring trust and ease among those around him did much to ensure his success in that world during the early years of the century. Because of these talents he was able to make his way, most of the time maintaining his dignity, through the Symbolist maze of quarrels and ever-changing personal relationships. Andrei Bely, that acute social observer, took careful note of Voloshin's social skills, writing that "he entered into all the subtleties of our circles, discussing, reading, making peace, debating, quickly grasping the most delicate situations that had been created without him, finding ways to solve them, serving as adviser and confidante."[11]

Clearly these talents were not exclusively domestic in significance; they extended well beyond the domestic realm into literary and intellectual life, where Voloshin had a similar impact. Bely was especially aware of the importance to the literary scene of Voloshin's skills as a peacemaker. Writing in the later 1920s, another era of intelligentsia strife that was to have devastating consequences because of the growing interest of the young Soviet state in its outcome, Bely wrote of this earlier period: "Voloshin was essential to Moscow in those years: without him, the smoother of sharp corners, I don't know how the sharpening of opinions would have ended up between 'us' and our malevolent mockers; in Symbolist demonstrations he was precisely a placard with the inscription 'angel of peace'; Valerii Briusov, on the other hand, was more of a placard with the inscription 'devil'; M. Voloshin 'smoothed'; Briusov 'sharpened corners'; Briusov gained his ends in a dry, guttural voice like the scream of a carrion-crow; 'Max' Voloshin, on the other hand, ruddy and pink with a voice humid like pink oil, oiled our ears."[12]

It is necessary to note that Briusov and Bely became bitter enemies later in their lives, whereas Voloshin and Bely strengthened their relationship in the 1920s, when Bely came to spend his summers in Koktebel'. Quite possibly Voloshin's charm had gained by comparison in Bely's memory and memoir twenty years later. Yet the memoirs about Voloshin during this period, as well as those about his later activities as circle leader, repeatedly emphasize his ability to facilitate peaceful and successful relationships both between others and himself, and among others who happened to be around him. The large number of such descriptions leads one to believe that there was something to them, as do the signs of peacemaking activity in his youthful letters to Aleksandra Petrova. Beginning with a natural talent for intuiting the feelings and anxieties of those around him, Voloshin seems to have grown increasingly skilled in understanding and managing the struggles in his community at the fin de siècle for social and emotional equilibrium.

SYMBOLIST "LIFE-CREATION" BETWEEN COMMUNITAS AND STRUCTURE; OR, THE BAD FATHER AND THE HOUSEHOLD THAT EXPLODED

It was inevitable that as Voloshin insinuated himself ever further into Symbolist life he would become caught up in the inner workings of its complex relationships. A central contradiction of those inner workings was the potent and potentially explosive intermingling of the communitas spirit of Symbolist life with the traditional structures of power and control that underlay its organizational networks. Those drawn into the entanglement of the two could suffer greatly—as did Voloshin. For he was equally susceptible to each of these cultural forces, and seemingly helpless in the face of the two combined.

The spirit of communitas, with its emphasis on intimate, principled I-Thou relations in the interest of self-transformation, was unquestionably a powerful element of Symbolist culture. Impassioned, fervent, many in the Symbolist world were driven by a kind of personal commitment to its ideas that extended far beyond the mere writing down of words or laying out of paint on canvas. One example of this commitment was the vibrant phenomenon of Symbolist life that came to be known as *zhiznetvorchestvo,* or "life-creation": a form of self-consciously symbolic behavior in daily life reminiscent of the theatrical, ritualistic element of Turner's communitas as the mutual effort among group members at self-transformation.[13] As Khodasevich tells us in his memoir *"Konets Renaty,"* and as literary scholar and cultural historian Irina Paperno and others have demonstrated, many Symbolists deliberately shaped even the most personal aspects of their lives in obedience to artistic and philosophical ideas in a way that could have an indelible impact on their lives and their relationships with one another.[14] It was not always pursued with serious intent; members of Andrei Bely's Argonaut circle (the Symbolist circle often most closely identified with *zhiznetvorchestvo*) created a complex and idiosyncratic vocabulary to communicate to one another the symbolic meanings of daily life with great playfulness. But it could lead to intense exaltation as well as pain and sorrow, as in the case, for example, of several triangular and other nontraditional Symbolist love affairs propelled by the desire to live out Symbolist theories of love and sexuality.[15]

Irina Paperno explains the meanings and motivations of *zhiznetvorchestvo* as fundamentally religious in nature, most deeply rooted in the Christian tradition. As in the Christian narrative of the birth of the spiritual son of God into the earthly realm, the Symbolists, through life-creation, were seeking to make the Word Flesh.[16] This compelling interpretation helps to illuminate the mystical side of Symbolist ideology as well as to place *zhiznetvorchestvo* into a broad range of other spiritual or mystical Symbolist pursuits. Many Symbolists engaged not only in *zhiznetvorchestvo* but also in profound (or sometimes not so profound) explorations of Catholicism, Buddhism, Greek paganism, Rudolf Steiner's Anthroposophical movement, Swedenborgianism, and tarot and palm readings, for example. Surely one attraction of these often theatrical, ritualistic pursuits of the Symbolists was their potential for facilitating communitas-style self-transformation in a time of rapidly changing social and cultural circumstances. In the looming modernity of fin de siècle Russia, a temporary retreat from the regular order of things for the sake of fashioning new selves by such spiritual means reveals the essence as well as the value of communitas in the face of modernity.

And yet the Symbolist movement, like much of the modernist experience, was shaped at least as much by structure—by the forces of traditional power and hierarchy—as by the anti-structure of communitas. For all the purity of their intellectual and spiritual commitment, many of the Symbolists were well aware of the new and growing commercial and technological means of making their ideas known to the world, of having an impact on the national discourse, and they were very ambitious. These ambitions laid them open to the demands that traditional structure made on their intellectual community in a number of ways. They had to cope with the problem of seeking funding and support through patronage from the autocracy and the merchantry; with the effort of network formation, as they sought one another out not only for communal support and commitment but also to form strategic professional alliances so as to bring their work into the public realm of anthologies, journals, and publishing houses; with the not unusual difficulties among ambitious intellectuals, in other words, of organization and power.[17]

That, in turn, made them vulnerable to the predominant structural forces of Russian intellectual organization: that is, to the networking and patronage traditions that were, this book argues, deeply rooted in the Russian intelligentsia domestic sphere, and therefore in the power relations that reigned in that sphere. For as was the case throughout much of the Russian intellectual experience, it was in the household that so much of the Symbolist activity of circle and network formation, of planning, plotting, and preparing for public self-presentation, took place. It was in the household that circles met, amid the forces and tensions of domestic association, with the familiar patriarchal power dynamics of male and female, of older generation and younger. These dynamics had an indelible impact on the development of Symbolist professional activities. And they had further implications not only for professional life but also for the more idealistic, spiritually motivated realm of Symbolist circle life, for example, for *zhiznetvorchestvo*, which also often played itself out in the domestic sphere.

That *zhiznetvorchestvo* was susceptible to the influence of power and hierarchy is not entirely surprising. As Priscilla Roosevelt's research on gentry theatricality demonstrates, the practice of self-transformation through symbolic dramatization and masquerade that so engaged the Symbolists at the fin de siècle had deep roots in the history of hierarchical power in Russia.[18] One manifestation of this Russian practice was the theatrical Westernization of Russia as first sought by Peter the Great and later pursued by Catherine the Great, both pressing the Russian gentry ever further into new Western "cultured" identities, compelling them to live out the ideas and ideals of what they saw as "Western" through imitation of Western dress and behavior in the eighteenth century. This practice led quickly to the appearance of such artificial objects of fun as the *petimetr* and the *koketka*, as the emerging Russian tradition of attempted self-transformation through make-believe gave rise to that pervasive sense of role-playing that semiotician Iurii Lotman (who draws a specific connection between this broader tradition of Russian theatricality and the Symbolist "theater of life") has described as a significant component of Russian elite identity.[19] And, as Roosevelt has shown, the gentry were more than eager to spread this theatrical form of social transformation into the countryside in their own expressions of power. Just as Peter and Catherine first made Westernized mannequins of the gentry for their salons and other "cultured" activities, so the gentry, out on their estates, could force their serfs to stand unmoving for hours at a time as decorative living Greek statues (symbols of Western "culture" as potent as one might find) in a painful demonstration of submission to superior power.[20]

Thus, while Symbolist *zhiznetvorchestvo* could serve as a means of radical self-expression and self-transformation of the most exalted sort, it also had a historically founded potential in Russia at least to reflect, and at times to enforce, the underlying systemic structures of power, especially under conditions of social change. In this case, those structures were the patriarchal power relations of the domestic sphere as they influenced social and professional life among the Symbolists. Through his encounter with Symbolist *zhiznetvorchestvo*, as well as with other seemingly pure spiritual opportunities for self-transformation, Voloshin experienced the potential for conflict and personal damage in the potent Symbolist circle cocktail of idealistic, self-transformative anti-structure, and the raw, hard forces of structural power.

Early in 1903 Voloshin met the woman who was to become his first wife, Margarita Vasil'evna Sabashnikova. Margarita came from a very wealthy merchant family, but, like her cousin, Ekaterina Bal'mont, she had a considerable talent for drawing and painting, and was attracted to the world of the arts and the intellect. By Margarita's own description many years later, she was childlike and naive, not an easy person to understand or to get along with. Early in the relationship between Max and Margarita, Ekaterina warned him: "You must not think that she can love you. She is strange." Almost incapable of forming close relationships, Margarita had come to trust only two people, Ekaterina said, herself and Max: "Only you, I am afraid, will have to suffer a great deal."[21] When Ekaterina went on to suggest, with concern, that Max was wasting his joie de vivre in this relationship, he responded, according to his diary: "Maybe the difference lies in words: what others call suffering, pain, I call joy."[22] Max was intensely attracted to Margarita in a way that can only be understood through his diary of that period, and against the background of the intensifying concern with gender relations and sex at that time in Russian history.[23]

In the diary we see a Voloshin for whom memoirs about him, even letters he wrote, do not prepare us. This was not the confident, authoritative Voloshin who resolved quarrels and helped others to manage their problems while a guest in their homes. On the contrary, this was an uncertain and even at times a tortured Voloshin, deeply ambivalent about his sexuality and his relations with women, and seeking self-transformation through intense I-Thou openness and honesty with himself and others.

"Nature makes use of all means, pure and impure, in order to direct the masculine to the feminine and bring them together," he wrote in 1904. "My relationship with women is absolutely pure, so in my soul lives a dream of all perversions. Not a single form of satisfaction exists that would not seduce me on the boundary between dream and reality." On the other hand, he continued, "I've noticed with surprise that all my friends are women. With girls I discuss everything. With women—many things. With men—nothing. That's also sex, but sex removed to a higher order. It is possible only with absolute purity of relationship. And that's also sex. The same great power of sex, carried over to another realm. The same power that seduces my dream at night." He went on to find a kind of solution to this sense of confusion and disjointed identity in sublimation for the sake of art: "In [art] is the absolute purity of sex, because it grows out of the flame."[24]

In a sense, Voloshin's intense attachment to Margarita might be seen as another kind of sublimation, springing out of the conflict between Max, the asexual, pure friend of women, and Max, the "perverted" lover. Margarita was an artist, after all—and she was apparently not interested in sex. She wanted an intimate but asexual association with him, one that would enable her to develop artistically and spiritually. Their premarital relationship (also the later marriage, if rumor is correct) remained largely, if not entirely, chaste, as was not unheard of in the complex panoply of Symbolist sexual relations.[25] Dedicating himself to Margarita the artist and woman friend, Max could avoid, at least for a time, facing the lover in himself. Yet this did not render his feelings for her any less overwhelming. He grew to be deeply, almost abjectly, in love with her. The complexity of this fragile Silver Age love affair was greatly compounded by the intervention of two other compelling personalities of the period whose power over the two hapless young lovers was greatly enhanced by their traditional status as mother and father figures, as well as by their claims to authority in matters of spirituality and self-transformation: Anna Rudolfovna Mintslova and the Symbolist Viacheslav Ivanov.

Anna Mintslova, the daughter of a Petersburg lawyer, claimed Ekaterina Bal'mont as one of her closest friends and was mystically inclined. Together, she, Voloshin, and Sabashnikova explored several of the many byways into religion and superstition that preoccupied many of their contemporaries. All three became involved in Rudolf Steiner's anthroposophical movement; though Voloshin quickly fell away from anthroposophy, it was to become a lifelong source of comfort and direction for Margarita. Other byways of interest to them included palm reading and astrological prophecy. Voloshin's diary, which in the mid-1900s often consisted of the quotations of others, faithfully recorded several such readings and prophecies, especially those of Mintslova.

Mintslova did not hesitate to use her mystical "powers" to exert psychological control over those who let her. Reading Max's palm in the presence of Margarita Vasil'evna in June 1905, she announced, according to Max's diary: "In your hand there is an unusual division between the lines of the mind and of the heart. I've never seen anything like it. You can live only through your mind. You are incapable of love. The most terrible misfortune awaits you, should anyone fall in love with you and you discover that you have nothing with which to answer [that love]."[26] Several days later, during a time of increasing anxiety and tension in the relationship between Max and Margarita, she proclaimed, again in Margarita's presence: "I feel myself in these days in terrible ascent and feel that my words can now have power. . . . You have no sensitivity in relation to women. You don't care at all with whom you are speaking. You forget about woman. This is terribly insulting, the more so, because in the first moment of your approach, you are sensitive—and that sticks in one's memory. You will perhaps forget my words after half an hour, but I know for certain that when it is necessary you will remember them." Max, who described Anna Rudolfovna as taking his hands with "motherly tenderness" on this occasion, took her words to heart. Later in the same day, Max, alone with Margarita: "I see the childlike face and sad eyes and look into them for a painfully long time, and tears come to

Anna Rudolfovna
Mintslova, Paris,
1905.
*Courtesy of Vladimir
Kupchenko.*

my eyes. I want to say: 'You see what I am. . . . Please forgive me. Don't love me.' I say: 'I am glad that Anna Rudolfovna said all that in front of you.'"[27]

It is curious how vulnerable Max and Margarita were to Anna Mintslova, for she was in fact an object of mockery among others in their circle. The two of them had little faith in their own powers of understanding or judgment. They yearned for guidance. And in Mintslova, to them a figure of traditional "motherly" authority, on the one hand, and seemingly offering them the means of achieving true integrity and transformation, on the other, they found that guidance. We find Margarita telling Max, according to his diary: "I feel such infinite importance in my life of the appearance of Anna Rudolfovna. As if that will decide everything." Later in the same entry, the twenty-eight-year-old Max commented on his relationship with Margarita: "We always need someone older and grown up. Last year it was Ekaterina Alekseevna [Bal'mont], now it is Anna Rudolfovna."[28]

Despite Mintslova's "maternal" manipulations, and despite months and even years of agonized indecision, inarticulate feeling, guilt, misunderstanding, and hesitation, Voloshin and Sabashnikova married in April 1906 and began to build a life together. They might thus have begun to lay

Margarita Sabashnikova
and Maximilian Voloshin
on their wedding day,
1906.
*Courtesy of Vladimir
Kupchenko.*

the foundations for a joint home and household of their own. But there was
little potential for this in their relationship. As Margarita put it, "Max and I,
we went through the world like two playing children."[29] Neither of them
seemed to consider the broader domestic implications of the relationship.
Margarita later described herself as having gone into this marriage with little sense of what such a lifetime commitment might mean; it was not a secure bond. The ease with which that other compelling figure, Viacheslav
Ivanov, intervened in and destroyed the marriage supports the accuracy of
her analysis.

Viacheslav Ivanov was a figure of great moment on the literary scene in
the mid- to late 1900s, central to the Petersburg branch of Symbolism and
to his own lively literary circle. Erudite, renowned for both his scholarly
and creative activities, charismatic, married to a very attractive and attentive woman with her own intellectual credentials, and possessed of a splen-

did large household space, the famous *Bashnia* or "Tower" apartment in Petersburg,[30] Ivanov had all the ingredients for a highly successful intelligentsia circle. But to Voloshin, he was more than all these things, for Voloshin, like several other younger poets of the time, took him as his poetic and spiritual — as well as professional — mentor and teacher.

In order to understand more fully the nature of the relationship between these two men, it is necessary to give the broader outlines of the mentor-mentee relationship in turn-of-the-century literary Russia. This relationship built on the mentorship traditions of the educated elite since about the mid-nineteenth century. Mid-nineteenth-century mentors were often both community builders and institution builders in a weakly institutionalized intellectual and professional world, taking young, ambitious folk under their wings in an attempt to build up fields ranging from the sciences to the creative arts — literary, visual, and musical — to the law. Often drawn into the household circles of their mentors, the young found not only intellectual and professional guidance but also fulfillment of the deeper needs of those moving into a new and unaccustomed social realm: an education in manners, customs, and cultural ideology. It was a relationship that drew heavily on the principles of patriarchal power, as older men rested on their hierarchical status both in providing aid to, and in holding power over, the younger.[31]

A number of qualities went into the making of such a mentor among the literary elite at the turn of the century, although they did not uniformly manifest themselves in every mentor. The ability to draw and inspire potential mentees, to fill them with excitement and new self- and mutual understanding, represented the side of literary mentorship that was rooted in the literary circle as communitas. On the more practical side, the ability to aid and support one's pupil or mentee effectively in his (the gender-specific "his" is used advisedly here) efforts to attain the public realm was also important. Those with the capacity to establish and build up literary outlets for their clients, such as journals and publishing houses, those in positions of power in the literary world, such as journal editors, all were good mentor material. As in the case of mentorship in other areas of intellectual and professional endeavor, possession of a substantial household space, as well as the means for entertaining community gatherings, was another valuable attribute, as was a sound association with a female partner and supporter. It was at such gatherings that contacts among the aspiring and between the aspiring and the powerful could be made and fostered, and, of course, talents displayed, in semi-formal poetry readings and other domestically based cultural events. All these activities could contribute to professional advancement both in giving the opportunity for honing one's skills as well as for gaining access to public outlets for one's work. Such gatherings lay at the heart of professional literary circle and network life, and those who could create this kind of community, and keep it harmonious and cooperative in pursuing the broader ambitions of literary life, were vital to the intellectual scene. Literary mentorship was deeply embedded in the broader pattern of network and circle association.

A common pattern in the establishment of the mentor-mentee relationship among literati involved the approach of the hopeful mentee to the prospective mentor by letter, asking for comments on his work or perhaps for an opportunity to meet. If the mentor acquiesced, the two would meet; if they continued to suit each other, the mentee could quickly be drawn into the mentor's household, at times even moving in. The committed mentor nourished his mentee both spiritually and physically, taking an educational interest in his intellectual, moral, and spiritual condition, on the one hand, and often inviting him to meals, on the other. In many ways the mentor was also expected to serve as a living model of how best to live (*kak zhit'*), teaching by example as well as by instruction. Although its precise terms could vary, this was generally a highly self-conscious association, combining elements of spiritual leadership with the patron-client relationship and the father-son relationship in a literary context. And, as it happened, this type of association could provide one significant element for a most successful literary circle; just as it served the mentee to have a mentor capable of running a successful circle, so the energy generated by the presence of a mentee or two could inspire and draw in a number of secondary followers.

The most prominent intelligentsia mentor of the era may have been Lev Tolstoy. Tolstoy's domestic circle was huge, composed not only of friends and relatives but also of religious and philosophical followers who gathered in his home, dined at his table, and often moved in for weeks or months at a time. Not atypically, his wife, Sofia Andreevna Tolstaia, was the one who carried the burden of the economic and material management of Tolstoy's circle.[32] Among his followers (if not necessarily among regular attendees of his domestic circle) Tolstoy also counted such literary clients, or mentees, as Ivan Bunin and Maxim Gorky. Ivan Bunin made his initial approach to Tolstoy with this classic "mentor-seeking" letter: "I am one of many who have followed your every word with great interest and respect, and who dare to trouble you with my own doubts and thoughts about my own life. I know you are probably tired of listening to the same trite and monotonous questions. Thus it is doubly awkward for me to ask you if I can sometime come and visit you, and talk with you if only for a few minutes. . . . Your thoughts have affected me so very deeply." Later in their relationship Bunin wrote in another expression of literary clientelism: "Dear Lev Nikolaevich, . . . You are one of the few whose words lift up my soul and bring

Lev Tolstoy and Maxim
Gorky, Iasnaia Poliana,
1900.

me to tears. . . . Right now I feel like crying and kissing your hand passionately, as if you were my own father!"[33] The mentor-mentee relationship
could go far beyond the merely professional, into the realm of intense emotional involvement — with strong patriarchal overtones.

Another famous Realist mentor was Maxim Gorky with his *Sreda*
("Wednesday," for the evening on which members met weekly) circle of
followers (among other devotees), who, because of the strength of their loyalty to him, were humorously satirized as the *"podmaksimki,"* a type of
mushroom growing under a "maksim tree."[34] Gorky functioned as a mentor
of the most involved sort to these aspiring writers, encouraging them, giving
them professional advice, scolding them when they drank too much, and
generally providing them with a strong paternal presence. He stood in at
the weddings of two of his followers and was known to refer to his adherents
as "children," inviting one of them to move in with him for a time.[35] His status as literary editor at the Marxist journal *Zhizn'* enabled him to offer them

not only a professional outlet for their literary labors but also to work closely with them in reviewing and editing their work. He also founded and issued the *Anthologies of the Znanie Cooperative*, which featured much work by *Sreda* circle members. The appreciation engendered by these relationships often found expression in adoring "contemporaries memoirs" written by his devotees; several members of Gorky's *Sreda* circle became contributors to the hagiographic Soviet tome *Gorky in the Memoirs of Contemporaries*.[36] Indeed, whole dynasties of mentorship can sometimes be delineated in the Realist literary realm through examination of such memoirs: from Tolstoy to Ivan Bunin to Valentin Kataev, for example, each "disciple," later writing about his mentor, establishing a kind of literary genealogy.[37]

The mentorship phenomenon, as it was linked to circle leadership, manifested itself among the Symbolists as well. Dmitrii Merezhkovskii and Zinaida Gippius reigned as a couple in a domestically based circle of the 1890s, which later evolved into the Religious-Philosophical circle. In the World of Art movement, Aleksandr Benois established his sway over the group early on in the schoolboy art history circle (also domestically based, and called the "Nevsky Pickwickians") that included most of its original members, and Sergei Diaghilev, though younger and in the early years viewed as a mere provincial, later emerged as the gifted impresario of the World of Art movement. While other major figures of Symbolism such as Valerii Briusov and Andrei Bely were apparently less inclined toward the labor and responsibilities of personal mentorship (though Briusov was a phenomenal institution builder, organizing and running, above all, the Symbolist journal *Vesy*), in the later years of Symbolism it was Viacheslav Ivanov who seized upon that role with the greatest enthusiasm. Ivanov did much to enhance the energy and prestige of his household circle by including young male clients such as poets Mikhail Kuzmin and Sergei Gorodetskii, as well as Maximilian Voloshin.

Voloshin's relationship with Ivanov, whom he described as having "the face of a father," was deeply personal. Just as his diary is full of quotations of the prophecies of Mintslova during this period, so it contained a number of pages of quotations, often without comment, from his conversations with Ivanov. These conversations, beginning in Geneva in 1904, reveal the breadth of influence that Ivanov had over Voloshin both intellectually and spiritually. In one such dialogue, as recorded by Voloshin, Ivanov offered the following analysis of Voloshin's poetic skills: "[Y]ou have eyes connected to the tongue without mediation. In your poems it is as if the eye speaks." This was not necessarily praise, as Ivanov saw here a kind of pallid unwillingness to "transubstantiate, re-create nature," as was the Symbolist goal. Because of Voloshin's stated desire to leave nature untouched, to experience it only, not to re-create it, Ivanov called him a Buddhist (Voloshin was, in fact, interested in Buddhism at the time) and declared that "the virus of Buddhism is anathema to me." To Buddhism, which he described as governed by pity, Ivanov counterposed Christianity as the religion of love, "pitiless love." Voloshin thereupon endeavored to bridge this opening chasm by raising the question of sex: "I consider sex the foundation of life. It is the living, tangible nerve that binds us to the eternal source of life." And he then went into his theory of art as a pure form of sex. This appealed to Ivanov: "In that case, then, you are beginning to approach us. You are no Buddhist. There is no tragedy in Buddhism." Voloshin's reply to Ivanov echoed the reply he had made to Ekaterina Bal'mont when she warned him against becoming intimate with Margarita: "Life is happiness for me. It may be that much of what others call suffering, I call happiness. I include suffering in my concept of happiness."[38]

Much in this conversation between mentor and student, though indeed reflecting serious intellectual and spiritual discourse, also offers us a glimpse into the logic of personal ideology and power that was soon to reveal itself in the encounter between these two men. In Ivanov's sense of the malleability of nature, in his rather Nietzschean will to control and transform, we see a foreshadowing of the way in which he would feel free to transform the lives of Max and Margarita. And in Voloshin's almost child-like veneration of Ivanov, his eagerness to please him, his unwillingness to manipulate nature, and his acceptance of suffering as a natural part of life, we can trace the emotional logic of his response to Ivanov's incursions.

In October 1906 Max and Margarita moved into the Ivanov household in St. Petersburg to live with Viacheslav Ivanov and his wife, Lidiia Zinovi-eva-Annibal. This household, which was maintained in the semi-spherical corner of a building overlooking the Tauride Garden, was the scene and source of a multiplicity of overlapping circles. The Wednesday evening salons, semi-public in the sense that those who came had at least some tenuous personal connection to the Ivanovs through the intelligentsia network, were already growing famous for the prestige of those who lectured there and the high spirits of their participants. Not all those who attended were enamored of the circle. Zinaida Gippius wrote disparagingly that members of the salon were engaged only in "dancing in a ring, singing bacchanalian songs, and wearing loose chlamyses and garlands."[39] Many other memoirists, however, claimed a far more enthusiastic association with this salon, which, along with its setting, the Tower, has entered Petersburg literary legend.[40]

It was not only the salons that drew the Ivanovs' guests to the apartment: "People could spend weeks in its distant rooms, lie on the soft couches, play on musical instruments, draw, drink wine, without bothering and without seeing anyone—either strangers or inhabitants of the 'Tower.'"[41] Indeed, some close friends moved right in, making of this household a kind of modernist bohemian version of the extended elite household. An inner circle formed around the household, including Max and Margarita, who at first lived one floor down in two narrow bedrooms and later moved directly into the apartment; the disciple poets Mikhail Kuzmin, who moved in somewhat later, and Sergei Gorodetskii; the painter Konstantin Somov; and Peter Struve, to name only a few. Residents of the Tower shared at least some meals with the Ivanovs (Lidiia Zinovieva-Annibal did her own cooking, apparently out of desire rather than financial need); Ivanov's stepdaughter, Lidiia, the daughter of Zinovieva-Annibal, tells us that nine or more people regularly sat down for dinner together.[42]

A consciousness of the powerful domestic structural traditions of gender and sexuality was deeply embedded in Ivanov household associations, even though some attempted to challenge those structures. The close inner circle at the Ivanov household at this time was primarily masculine, except for Margarita Voloshina and Lidiia Zinovieva-Annibal. By all accounts Lidiia, who was warm, emotional, dramatic, forceful, and eccentric in her habits and dress, was more than enough woman to make up the balance. She was also, like the nineteenth-century poet Alexander Pushkin, a descendant of Annibal, the famous African in the court of Peter the Great in the early eighteenth century. And she was a writer of considerable talent herself along with Zinaida Gippius and Anastasiia Verbitskaia among the earliest Russian women to explore female identity and sexuality (both heterosexual and homosexual) through literature.[43] When Viacheslav Ivanov decided to form an exclusively male circle in the household, in the interest of exploring new forms of masculine spirituality, Lidiia Zinovieva-Annibal tried to form her own similarly motivated circle of women, but with indifferent results.

"At these gatherings," Margarita Voloshina wrote in her memoirs of this female circle, "we were supposed to have other names, wear other clothing, in order to create an atmosphere which would raise us out of the everyday. Lidiia was called Diotima, [and] I was named Primavera, because of my supposed similarity to the Botticelli figure. Other than the worthy, harmless wife of the writer Tshulkov and a grammar school teacher, who misunderstood the thing and behaved in a somewhat bacchanalian fashion, there were no other women who wanted to take part. The evening dragged to an end and no new spirituality was born of it; so the attempt was dropped."[44] For reasons which will soon become clear, Lidiia does not emerge as a strong protagonist in Margarita's memoir. If Margarita's description is accurate, however, the paradox is noteworthy that while a woman of Lidiia's intelligence and flair could be the life of the circle in a group composed of both sexes, her interest in organizing a group of women alone could end in such failure. Despite her efforts, the attraction and prestige of masculine power prevailed in this area of social life.

Lidiia, though initially uncertain, was much taken by Margarita's intelligence, beauty, and artistic talent. So was Viacheslav. Together they drew her further and further into the household. As time went on, Max became extremely busy with his journalistic work, and left Margarita isolated and to her own devices. Voloshin's mother, Elena Ottobal'dovna, moved into the household as well, but this apparently did not alleviate Margarita's loneliness, though she and Elena Ottobal'dovna got along well. Margarita found herself frequently going upstairs for company—where it appears that Viacheslav in some sense fell in love with her. She, too, was drawn to him—by his age (forty-one) and status, by his charm, and by his self-assurance about the matter. Differences in outlook between herself and Max became more evident to her, and soon she found that "I could no longer say 'we' of Max and myself."[45]

Although it has been argued that Lidiia "was looking for a woman" and was therefore instrumental in instigating a relationship among the three of them, her response to these developments proved ambivalent.[46] When Margarita first approached her and, given the circumstances, offered to leave the Tower household, Lidiia replied that she wanted her to stay. But in her memoirs Margarita questioned Lidiia's true feelings in this regard; she wondered if Lidiia really believed in this three-way affair or whether she saw it instead as the only way to preserve her own relationship with Ivanov. Lidiia seems to have made a genuine effort to love Margarita, but Margarita describes her as saying at one point: "When I don't see you, a protest against you rises up in me; when we are together, everything is fine, and I am again at peace."[47] To Margarita's reported disappointment, the two did not see Max as part of the relationship; just as Lidiia felt much ambivalence toward Margarita, so Ivanov felt intense hostility and jealousy toward Voloshin.

This growing relationship reflects the way that the spirit of communitas could be mingled with the power of patriarchy in domestic and professional relationships among the Symbolists, especially in the later years of the movement. It was, on the one hand, an expression of *zhiznetvorchestvo*, that profound commitment to "making flesh" of Symbolist ideals and ideology.[48] Lidiia and Viacheslav were attempting to live out an ideal of Eros and of Russian communalism through the establishment of a sacred triple union. This is how the two Ivanovs seem most consciously to have seen it themselves, drawn to the idea of such a union as a means of transcending individualism and possessive love: "We cannot be two," Lidiia wrote in her diary, "we should not close the circle. . . . Our rings of love are for the ocean of love!"[49] In this, their effort reveals an expression of the ritualistic, theatri-

Viacheslav Ivanov,
Lidiia Zinovieva-
Annibal, and
V. K. Shvarsalon,
Zagore, 1907.
*Courtesy of Vladimir
Kupchenko.*

cal side of communitas, as Lidiia and Viacheslav sought to transform their lives by acting out an idealized vision of human relations.

But this relationship also reflected the raw encroachment of domestically based gender and generational power into the colorful practice of *zhiznetvorchestvo.* Given the subordinate status of the Voloshin couple as members of a younger generation, and especially Voloshin's own dependent status as a professional and intellectual disciple of Ivanov, whom he also viewed as a surrogate father, this spiritual experiment reveals the manipulation of those roles in the interest of the elder over the younger and less powerful, and of the more powerful male over all of them in the context of the household. Ivanov and to a lesser, more ambivalent extent Lidiia were using their traditional power to press Margarita and also Max into a condition not entirely unlike that of the enserfed living "Greek" statues of the gentry in the countryside in the late eighteenth and early nineteenth centuries. The roles of Margarita and to a lesser degree Max were in a sense to fulfill the transformative theatrical fantasies of those more powerful than themselves.

Writing in Germany some fifty years later, Margarita described it as a situation in which feelings and ideas had completely taken over. "I was entirely swept up in this subjective world," she wrote, unable to master her emotions. "In his selflessness, Max, far from scolding me for my ignorance of the world, found my weakness touching and lovable and handled me with tender protection."[50] Margarita may have expected or hoped for his intervention, but Max did nothing to prevent (or otherwise influence) the three-way relationship that was emerging. There are no signs in his diary that he was at first angry with any of the three for leaving him out, despite Ivanov's open hostility. To some extent, he believed that he should give Margarita up to Ivanov. But for a time he could not bring himself to act upon that idea, as he was still deeply in love with her. Throughout this period we find in his diary an ever-deepening sense of pain and paralysis. (Among other things, he wished that his mother had not been around to witness this.) The pain and the situation in general seemed to peak in March 1907.

On the evening of March 2 Max came back to the Tower from a trip to Moscow: "Home. Nine o'clock in the morning. All sleep. I wander through the empty gray apartment, and it seems to me that the Tower has emptied out completely. Amoria [his nickname for Margarita] is not here—she is sleeping in Lidiia's room. Like a child, I am offended and hurt that no one met me, no one waited for me. I would like to see only her, to speak with only her."[51] In the next few days he slowly began to pull himself together and to make some decisions. On the 10th he went to an exhibition of paintings by the famous Crimean landscape artist Konstantin Bogaevskii: "I had not expected to see so much nature. I was amazed and stunned. It seemed to me that centuries had passed since I had seen anyone. I was distracted. I recognized no one and spoke irrelevantly. Then I came to myself a little bit. Returning, I made some important life decisions. I decided that I cannot tie my own life plans to Amoria's plans." He would leave for Koktebel' for the summer and then go to Paris in the fall, and Margarita either could come along or not; "right now I need several years to focus myself and to work alone."[52]

That his decision was the correct one seemed to be confirmed the following night, when the misery and confusion in this by now entirely dysfunctional household came to a head. "Restlessness and anguish prevented me from sleeping for a long time," Max wrote. "I looked out into the corridor. In Amoria's room—darkness. I lay down. I lit the lamp again and read, then put it out. Suddenly Amoria walked in [saying,] 'I couldn't sleep out of worry and I wanted to see you.' She went out to Lidiia. I went to sleep." Several hours later Margarita came in to Voloshin again and said that she and Lidiia had talked, but Voloshin was too sleepy to have much of a response. As Max was washing the next morning, Margarita came in: "'Yesterday I wanted to come spend the night with you. But that sickened Viacheslav. I didn't come.' Indignation rises up in me," Max wrote, "it's hard for me to fight it down, even to concentrate."

This led to a confrontation with Viacheslav, in which Viacheslav told him, according to Voloshin: "'If this will set you at peace: my passion toward Margarita is not blind. She will become mine only if it is unavoidable. Even the attraction of passion is not sufficient.'" Viacheslav's words did not seem calculated to set Voloshin's mind at rest in the long run, but the four of them spent that day together in a friendly way. Late in the day, after tea, "we [are] all on Amoria's bed in Viacheslav's room. General peace and goodwill. 'I worry about every single new day,' says Lidiia. Everyone feels the same. Everyone rushes to separate, to rest, to calm down after the inhumanly tense atmosphere of the past days."[53]

This household circle had exploded; ceasing to function as a community, it had collapsed under the strain of powerful and complex personal emotions. The close entanglement of transformative communitas relations with the power structures of Symbolist circle life had proven too dangerous to the survival of the community; principled self-transformation, on the one hand, and patriarchal power, on the other, had caught the domestic circle as between gears and torn it apart, causing a great deal of personal damage along the way. And it was Ivanov, the most powerful person in the community both as traditional patriarchal figure and spiritual leader, who had the greatest responsibility for this development. This course of events helps us to understand why memoirist-commentators of the period focused so narrowly on leadership figures as being responsible for community harmony and why they valued so highly those who fulfilled their responsibilities in maintaining harmony.[54] It also provides insight into why they so lauded, in circle leaders, the quality of humaneness, of sensitivity and appreciation for the feelings of others. Ivanov had failed to demonstrate that quality of humaneness in his treatment of those around him, and thus the circle was forced into a state of crisis with far broader implications than the merely personal, given its social and professional function.

The saga of the love affair among Lidiia, Ivanov, and Margarita continued to unfold over the next months. Viacheslav and Lidiia visited Margarita a few times that spring and summer in Tsarskoe Selo, where she was staying with her family. But although Margarita was ready to commit herself to Ivanov, after the winter of 1906–1907 she never again aroused his interest in the same way. She discovered this, to her sorrow, toward the end of the summer of 1907, when she returned to the Tower for a visit: Lidiia was quite hostile toward her, and Ivanov was chilly. Voloshin learned of their treatment of Margarita when she came to visit him in Koktebel' in September. They went for a walk together in the hills: "All was fading. The sunset was pure and cold, just like sunrise. The uninhabited valleys were golden-black and wild. She looked up at me and pressed her head against my knee and said: 'If only I could see him once.'" Neither Viacheslav nor Lidiia had come to meet her at the train station; instead, they had sent Lidiia's daughter, Vera, to meet her. Upon her arrival at the Tower, "[h]e embraced me and led me into the room. 'We must decide whether or not we are necessary to one another.' Lidiia kissed me with a cold, unwelcoming face. . . . And he behaved entirely differently toward me—like a father. He said: 'If you want, we will send for your mother or for Max.' We talked for a very long time. Then Lidiia called him, and it was clear from her voice that she was crying. She said: 'I can't live this way anymore.' . . . He tried to calm her."

Voloshin held Margarita's head and looked at the sky. "And I felt that all that *I* had felt for Viacheslav was at an end."[55] His anger grew over the next few months, perhaps in part because it became increasingly evident that, although Ivanov was no longer interested in Margarita, the marriage between Max and Margarita was over. Toward the end of September Anna Rudolfovna Mintslova came to Koktebel' for a visit. Voloshin quotes her in his diary as railing against Ivanov: "He destroys, breaks people. . . . No one has the right to break and destroy, to do *experiments* on people." She also says: "What kind of teacher of life is he?" and adds, "He has no disciples."[56]

Voloshin's long quotations of others are no doubt filtered; but in this case it does not matter whether the vocabulary of Mintslova's condemnation is more her own or Voloshin's. More important is that Ivanov is described as having failed as a mentor: as a "teacher of life [*uchitel' zhizni*]" profoundly responsible for his mentee's welfare and education, both spiritually and professionally. Voloshin's continued musings on the topic further develop the concept of the mentor and his responsibilities: "Viacheslav is not a teacher. A teacher experiences for the disciple. [Ivanov] experiences for himself and breaks people." And in another conversation with Mintslova, he concludes: "The path of the disciple is not for me."[57] If Ivanov had been an irresponsible patriarch in the sense of damaging community harmony, then, according to Voloshin, so, too, had he been an irresponsible mentor, taking advantage of Voloshin's weakness as client, spiritual charge, and "son" rather than protecting his interests. Ivanov's pursuit of personal ideals and principles with, and sometimes at the expense of, those dependent upon him reflected a broader pattern in Ivanov's mentorship activities:

just prior to his relationship with Margarita, he had also instigated a similar relationship with another of his mentees, Sergei Gorodetskii.[58]

Never again would Voloshin look up to another male in the same way that he briefly had admired Ivanov; his desire for mentorship had been satiated. Yet through this deeply abrasive experience he had caught a glimpse of the positive potential of both the transformative powers of *zhiznetvorchestvo* and the structural powers of mentorship. The yearning for self-transformation compelled those engaged in this romantic experiment to penetrate deeply into radically new social identities and relations, even if the ultimate effect in this particular case was destructive. If pursued with a greater degree of sensitivity, of humaneness, this phenomenon presented tremendous possibilities for social and individual motivation. Voloshin had also seen the positive potential in the structural powers of patriarchal mentorship in the domestic sphere; used well, access to such power could give an individual in this fluid society tremendous potential to catalyze a broader community around him. As Voloshin had experienced, the overwhelming combination of spiritual leadership and patriarchal mentorship had its dangers. But the positive potential remained. And, finally, he could also see the structural value of a secure emotional and economic partnership, such as that which originally existed between Viacheslav and Lidiia, for the maintenance of a domestic base. Yet perhaps he had also learned that the person one adores as a partner may not always be the individual with whom one can make a happy life of mutual interdependence or build a stable household.

The question of settling down was just beginning to take hold of Voloshin. Surely it is no accident that the theme of nature, and especially of the natural beauty of the Crimea, was beginning to appear more frequently in his diary at this time. Nature offered an escape, a counterpoint and alternative to the overwhelming tangles of urban life. The Crimean landscapes of Bogaevskii gave him the strength to reach certain decisions in Petersburg; the still loveliness of the Koktebel' hills at dusk provided the natural and narrative setting in which he heard Margarita's story and turned for the first time definitively against Ivanov. This was the first summer in which he began to invite guests to stay with him in his dacha in Koktebel'. Not only Margarita and Anna Rudolfovna came to accept his hospitality and take part in his household but several others did as well. One day early in the summer he met two new guests and spent the day with them among the Tatar markets and bazaars of the region. "Then, already in the twilight, we arrive in Koktebel'. The house comes to life for the first time and glows from every window. I go out into the garden and joyfully look at it, lit up and full with domestic life, decorated with vines, living at last."[59]

THREE

Voloshin and the Modernist Problem of the Ugly Poetess

A MENTOR OF WOMEN

Voloshin would never again take a master to his heart the way he had taken Viacheslav Ivanov but, having seen the power of this role, it was not long before he would test his own potential to play it. Voloshin, however, turned out to be a mentor with a difference. Building on his early sensitivity to the weaker female element in the intelligentsia household, he became a mentor of women in a world where mentorship was primarily masculine, and where access to the public arena was difficult for women to attain. This was a lengthy and not uncomplicated process. Along the way he found that he had to consider again — and yet again — the place of love and sexuality in mentorship and professional life. And he also engaged in a renewed exploration of modernist *zhiznetvorchestvo*, this time through masquerade and illusion.

In all these efforts a new theme emerges in Voloshin's relations with the Symbolist world, that of resistance, indeed of outright challenge, to its traditional power structures as he continued to experience them and as he saw them affecting the women he supported. Through his new mentorship activities, he was in a sense rising up against that system, although it was an awkward and partial revolution, and perhaps not fully intentional. Even so, it was a significant expression of agency, since for the first time he truly began to intervene in his culture to effect its transformation. In so doing he laid the foundations for his own future circle in Koktebel', which was to take form as a revitalized and purified expression of communitas in the modernist world.

In order to understand the difficulties of women in the Symbolist world, and what Voloshin had to offer them, it is necessary to consider further their structural place in the culture of the literary *kruzhok* at this time.

A paradox of that place was that while women as wives and mothers were often vital to the maintenance of both the emotional and material foundations of *kruzhok* society, it was not at all easy for them to break into it as independent thinkers and writers. The few who did, such as Zinaida Gippius and Lidiia Zinovieva-Annibal, were usually supported by a man with whom they were married or had some other romantic and domestic relationship.[1] This was the case because, although the *kruzhok* networking world offered men a direct conduit from the private domestic realm to the sphere of public self-expression, this transition was far more difficult for women to negotiate. Given the relatively precise delimitations of their activities in *kruzhok* society, it was awkward and culturally inappropriate for women to break out of their traditional domestic roles for the sake of public aspiration. Distaste for female literary ambition even extended into textual criticism and analysis; the very notion of a female poet could be seen as an offense against good taste in Russian modernism. The "poetess" was inherently undignified, an "unconscious parody" of the poet, as Svetlana Boym tells us in her work on Marina Tsvetaeva.[2]

At a more practical level, women seem to have had particular difficulties in gaining access to that core of literary network relations, the mentorship system. This may in part have been because it was difficult for them to maintain dignity when leaving their own domestic sphere and entering that of a potential mentor. One piece of anecdotal gossip floating about in Moscow and Petersburg around 1911 concerned an untalented but endlessly persistent female poet, Maria Papper, and her attempts to find a poetic mentor. In an inappropriate, undignified manner, she would enter the homes of famous male poets through the kitchen, and be given food and drink until the cook or housekeeper found a moment to approach the master of the house. The master invariably hated her poetry and sought to get rid of her as quickly as possible; but even having boots flung after her failed to diminish her humiliating persistence.[3] While the superficial point of this story is that she was a poor poet, it would surely lack resonance without the subtext of her impropriety in thus exposing herself as a woman. Maria Papper's attempt to network for mentorship created a disturbing conflict between traditional and new, more challenging female identities.

It was precisely in this matter of creating new professional identities that Voloshin was to prove most useful to ambitious literary women. First of all, lacking at this time a stable household of his own, he was more than willing to spend time in the households of the women he wanted to support. There, amid familiar domestic surroundings, protected from the hurly-burly of the public realm, he offered them time and attention to their work and helped to acclimate them to the unaccustomed identity of ambitious literary female. Memoirist Evgeniia Gertsyk, who analyzes Voloshin's

Adelaida Gertsyk
with her son,
Nikita, 1915.
*Courtesy of
Vladimir
Kupchenko.*

relationships with women in some detail, writes of his particular sensitivity
to the intellectual and personal challenges that lay before her ambitious sister, Adelaida, in becoming a female poet. "He went into every line of Adelaida's poetry, engaged himself with interest in her childhood memoirs,
deepening and broadening what she had barely thrown together. In those
years, when her tender spirit suffered from almost any contact, Max was
easy for her; around him it wasn't necessary to dress oneself up for show in
complicated feelings, you could be anyone at all around him."[4] Attempting
to enter the public realm as creators in their own right could put a strain on
women; the pressure of attempting to build and "dress up" a public persona
could drive some right back into themselves. Voloshin was peculiarly attuned to this problem and possessed a singular skill in helping women to
transform themselves into creators with public ambitions. In this he was ac-
tively reinterpreting that mentorship role he had seen Ivanov playing, the
role of the "teacher of life" aiding a mentee in the difficult process of self-
transformation, in the interest of professional development and upward
mobility for literary women.

The four women with whom Voloshin became most closely involved as
a mentor were Margarita Sabashnikova, Adelaida Gertsyk, Elizaveta Dmitrieva (Cherubina de Gabriak), and Marina Tsvetaeva, in more or less that
order. We have already seen that he was drawn to Margarita Sabashnikova
partly because of the attraction of supporting her artistic endeavors. Both of

Margarita Sabashnikova [detail]. Date unknown. *Courtesy of Vladimir Kupchenko.*

them uncertain about their sexuality, and Margarita searching explicitly for an intellectual and artistic supporter as opposed to a lover, she and Voloshin appear at first to have believed that the mentor-mentee relationship was ideally suited to their needs and could easily be integrated with marriage. Yet the agonizing depth of Voloshin's love for Margarita complicated the matter. This first major act of mentorship was greatly hampered by Voloshin's desire for romantic possession, and by his attempt to establish a secure romantic and domestic association with Sabashnikova. Their experience was an indication of the difficulties faced by men and women alike when they attempted to cross traditional gender boundaries for the sake of new professional and intellectual relationships.

Throughout the period of his attachment to Sabashnikova, Voloshin addressed his poetry to her as to a kind of lovely romantic idol. He did this much as Symbolist Alexander Blok had made an idolized object of his beloved Liubov' Mendeleeva, as the famous "Beautiful Lady," somewhat earlier, creating with his poetry an image of lustrous femininity that had left a deep imprint on Symbolist culture.[5] There was a point at which this began to wear on Margarita (as earlier it had in fact irritated Liubov' Mendeleeva).[6] Evgeniia Gertsyk, who had come to know Max in the Ivanov household, was present on that final evening just before it broke up. Max read aloud to the group a poem in which he described a meeting between himself and Margarita in the woods; they walked together until they encountered a forest-mirror which reflected back at them the burning torch of the "Sun Beast" (presumably Viacheslav Ivanov): "'Let's get away!' But she gave a birdlike cry . . . And suddenly cast herself into the mirror of the darkening abyss. . . . At this loss I felt deathly pain."[7]

Margarita expressed strong exasperation. "And it's all not true, Max! I'm not jumping into a well, I'm going to Bogdanovshchina."[8]—"And you didn't call me away. . . . And why a birdlike cry? You're a liar, Max!"[9] If part of Max's original attraction to her had been founded on her need for an asexual friend and supporter, his attempt at mixing mentorship with romantic love and marriage had failed altogether. (As had Margarita's search for a mentor; she would later find one better suited to her needs in Rudolf Steiner, the founder of anthroposophy.) Max's attempt to press her into the role of beautiful, passive female object seems to have served neither of them well in the end.

Voloshin's fourth and final mentorship, namely, that of Marina Tsvetaeva, on the other hand, was phenomenally successful, as Tsvetaeva's later lavish tribute to him indicates. In her classic "contemporaries" memoir about him, she uses the language of the "mentee" to describe her relationship with him: "Everything that I learned from Max, I learned for good."[10] Voloshin was not her "teacher" solely in the intellectual sense. Though he often helped her in her writing, she was actually a better poet than he and did not particularly need him as a literary model. Rather, he was her "teacher of life," the teacher Ivanov had failed to be for Voloshin. Above all, he "taught" or helped her to accept and take hold of her own identity as a woman poet. He was able to do this first of all because he sought and could find the selves (in certain people) with whom they were happiest and most comfortable: "By his insatiability for what was genuine, he forced an individual to be his own self," wrote Tsvetaeva.[11]

But in his understanding of self Max was not so simple as to believe that there was only one to each individual; he recognized that a multitude of selves and self-images could be stored in a single person.[12] Women aspiring to literary expression sought most intensely to bring forth their creative selves. And Voloshin was especially skilled at calling up those creative selves, Tsvetaeva wrote: "Max's sharp eye was a collecting lens, collect-

Anastasiia Tsvetaeva
and Marina Tsvetaeva,
Moscow, 1911.
*Courtesy of Konstantin
Polivanov.*

ing—and so fire-igniting. Everything that was personal, that is, creative in a person, fired up and grew into the largest possible bonfire and garden." For women searching for identity in this new sphere, such support was dearly appreciated: "Max in women's and poets' lives was *providentiel,* and when they merged, as in the case of Cherubina, Adelaida Gertsyk, and my own case, when the woman proved to be a poet or, more accurately, the poet a woman, there was no end to his friendship, care, patience, attention, admiration, and co-creation."[13]

The term "identity" can be vague and insubstantial, but there are concrete ways of getting at it: in the association between one's sense of self and one's outward appearance, for example. Appearance was a matter of great concern to many in the Russian Modernist movement. A culture of costume was introduced into the Symbolist movement in its earliest stages because of its association with Russian Decadence, whose proponents dressed up in outlandish and flashy clothing that left a deep impression on those who saw them. Symbolist men wore such colorful clothing as yellow waist-coats; women took on the role of "Beautiful Lady," or bohemian, like Lidiia Zinovieva-Annibal, who was known, on occasion, to dress up for the Ivanov Wednesday evening salons in flowing white and orange gowns in the Greek style. And a few very daring women, such as Zinaida Gippius, dressed up now and then as men. Both Voloshin and Tsvetaeva were intensely aware of the literary and cultural power of image and masquerade in their world.

In her poetry, Tsvetaeva drew heavily on the contemporary themes of clothing, costume, and self, in no small part as a means of getting at the problem of female, and female poetic, identity.[14] Her fascination with appearance and self was grounded in concrete experience. During her early years as a poet (late adolescence), Marina Tsvetaeva was deeply unhappy with her appearance: it did not seem to her to fit her true poetic self. Her figure was too square and stout, her face too round, her coloring too ruddy. Her sister, Anastasiia, wrote in her memoirs: "The obvious incongruity between her soul and her appearance was the tragedy of those years for Marina. With ever more suffering eyes she looked at herself in the mirror, not for long—and turned away."[15] She tried to change her appearance, by dying her hair, for example. Unfortunately the dye changed color, from a kind of yellow-orange to a greenish shade. Finally, she had to shave her hair off entirely; and, following someone's advice that this would make it grow back curly, she decided to shave it off ten times over.

Thus, when Voloshin came to visit her at her home, she was wearing over her bald head what Anastasiia described as a very unbecoming black silk cap with a little frill.[16] Voloshin's direct response set her at ease in a way that almost none other could. "In the interval of silence," wrote Marina,

> he looks so intently that you might say it was shameless if it weren't for the wide, always widening smile of an openly favorable disposition—that makes you openly disposed to favor him.
>
> "And you always wear that . . . ?"
>
> "Cap? Always; I'm shaved bald."
>
> "Always shaved?"
>
> "Always."
>
> "And wouldn't it be possible . . . that . . . to take it off, so I could see the shape of your head? Nothing is so indicative of a person as the shape of his head."
>
> "By all means."

Not giving her time to take it off herself, he lifted it off her head for her, then asked if she would take off

"My glasses?"

He, joyfully:

"Yes, yes, your glasses, because you know, nothing hides a person like glasses."

Voloshin stepped back, looking at her, Marina wrote, with the gaze of a sculptor, and said:

"You're amazingly like a Roman seminarist. Most likely you're often told that?"[17]

She had never been told that, since no one else had ever seen her bald, as she told him. As with Ekaterina Bal'mont concerned about husband and daughter, once again Voloshin had moved right into that sphere of the greatest personal anxiety with a firm and sure step. Eliminating embarrass-ment, he had given her an alternative metaphorical view of herself, one both dignified and interesting (not coincidentally, perhaps, masculine)—a mask more conducive to the comfortable expression of her "soul" than the modernist stereotype of poetic female beauty which had left her feeling so inadequate. As Tsvetaeva was to write later, after Voloshin's death, "I owe Maximilian Voloshin my first self-conception as a poet."[18] On the basis of this first encounter, still vivid in Tsvetaeva's memory two decades later, their friendship quickly flourished.

Soon Voloshin demonstrated his skill in helping those around him to form bonds among themselves. He did this by introducing Tsvetaeva to Adelaida Gertsyk, another woman (described by Anastasiia as unattractive and somewhat deaf) whose poetic spirit and earthly appearance were equally mismatched, and who had also experienced discomfort in shaping a public image for herself. Max told Tsvetaeva that she and Adelaida needed each other, and indeed the two women soon became close friends. He also performed another, more traditional act of mentorship (indeed, he had done so even before he met her, bringing the results to their first meet-ing): he advertised her work to the public in a lively and supportive critical review of her work, as well as that of Sabashnikova, Gertsyk, de Gabriak, and Liubova Stolitsa, entitled "Women's Poetry."[19]

Voloshin's mentorship of Marina Tsvetaeva, like that of Adelaida Gert-syk, was strictly platonic; he attended closely to her literary concerns, and reassured her about her poetic and physical selves, but stopped short of the romantic love on which his mentorship of Margarita Sabashnikova had foundered. Sabashnikova and Tsvetaeva represented two extremes, one of failure, the other of success, in Voloshin's experiment in the mentorship of women: whereas his relationship with Margarita would disintegrate entirely, that with Tsvetaeva would soon lay the foundations for his future success as a builder of intelligentsia community. But there was also an intermediate stage, one in which Voloshin was still experimenting with romantic love between mentor and mentee, as well as with the relations between appearances and self-transformation as a means of providing a frustrated female poet with access to publication. The story of this mentorship is embodied in the legendary entrance onto the St. Petersburg literary scene of "Cherubina de Gabriak," a figure who lived up to almost everyone's fantasies of the ideal modernist female poet.

INTELLIGENTSIA IMPRESARIO

The legend of Cherubina de Gabriak plays out at a number of different levels. It demonstrates the significance of traditional power relations in the modernist publishing networks as well as the difficulties women had in breaking into those networks as creators in their own right. It is a tale of theatrical status reversal entirely in the spirit of communitas, as Voloshin, together with a female co-conspirator, undertook to challenge those power relations.[20] It also reveals the great vitality of an oral tradition of network gossip and *anekdoty* which helped to spread the story of Cherubina far and wide. It was through this oral tradition that Voloshin would first advertise both his challenge to some of the rigid hierarchies of Symbolist life, and his willingness to mentor women poets in order to further that challenge. In order to tell Cherubina's story we first need to look at the stage on which it was set: the late Symbolist literary journal *Apollon*. And to learn about the origins of *Apollon*, we need to return to that vital node in the Petersburg modernist literary network, the Ivanov household.

After Lidiia Zinovieva-Annibal died in the fall of 1907, it was expected that the Ivanov household would cease to be a lively center for literary gatherings. But, on the contrary, guests continued to arrive in such a stream, and with such determination to stay, that a third apartment had to be added to the household by knocking down some walls.[21] By the fall of 1907 the poet Kuzmin was a permanent member of the household; his rooms soon became the central point for a new round of literary and artistic gatherings, as many enthusiasts of a slightly younger generation began to collect there. In the spring of 1909 a new project evolved: led by the up-and-coming poet Nikolai Gumilev, some of this younger generation asked Viacheslav Ivanov, Maximilian Voloshin, and a third member of the "older" generation, Innokentii Annenskii, to give a regular series of lectures on poetics.[22] These lectures (ultimately delivered primarily by Ivanov) at first took place in the Ivanov apartment, like those given at his Wednesday salons. The presence of a stenographer enhanced listeners' sense that they were taking part in events of historical significance. The lectures attracted a growing number of participants, including one young man of great significance in our story of Cherubina, the art critic and historian Sergei Makovskii.

Sergei Makovskii was an ambitious young man with intellectual roots in the World of Art movement who modeled himself closely on its most phenomenal network and community builder, Sergei Diaghilev.[23] Infighting and difficulty with patronage and financing had led to the demise of Diaghilev's journal, *World of Art,* early in 1905; by the end of the decade the other Symbolist journals—*The Golden Fleece* (where Makovskii began his Symbolist career as a staff member) and *The Scales*—were also petering out, so that younger poets such as Makovskii and Gumilev had few outlets for their talents. Tapping the energy of the new gathering point of Ivanov's lectures (indeed, Makovskii later claimed that he and Gumilev had become involved in the lecture series for precisely this purpose), Makovskii organized a new journal, *Apollon,* modeled directly on the now dead, glossy, elegant *World of Art.*[24] Like most other journals of the Modernist movement, *Apollon* was not economically self-supporting; Makovskii possessed that essential skill (like Valerii Briusov, and to some extent Sergei Diaghilev before him) of gaining and maintaining the trust of a wealthy patron, the tea merchant Mikhail Ushakov.

Apollon soon acquired its own "household" of editorial offices. Here its staff, the so-called *Apollontsy,* could gather just as the staff of the *World of Art* journal had famously gathered in Diaghilev's home, where Diaghilev's female partner in circle hospitality, his childhood nurse, had presided over the samovar.[25] The offices became a central meeting place for writers and artists of the modernist persuasion in Petersburg, a locality in which they could exchange criticism and gossip, form acquaintances, and network. Johannes von Guenther, a young Baltic German friend of Gumilev's, later described it as a "genuine collective."[26] These offices, which were dominated by men and, as will become evident, possessed of a strong masculine flavor, formed the essential backdrop for the Cherubina drama. Among those who were closely involved in the publication of the journal, and therefore frequently on the premises, were Kuzmin, Gumilev, von Guenther (who also moved into the Ivanov household for a time), and Alexei Tolstoi.[27]

Another of the three main figures in the Cherubina story was Voloshin himself. After it became clear that Margarita continued to yearn for (a now unresponsive) Viacheslav Ivanov, Max went into a deep depression that lasted a year or more. Late in the fall of 1907 he returned to Petersburg. In January he wrote Aleksandra Petrova: "Forgive me for the silence. I was sick and hidden in my room for a month and a half. . . . [W]hy write in moments of grief and despondency?"[28] His next letter arrived in September of

1908 from Paris, where he had fled in May in an effort to get away from Ivanov, about whom he was obsessed: "This whole winter I lived only to leave as soon as possible, but that wasn't possible. The whole time a long and very difficult struggle went on inside me over Viacheslav. I didn't want to, [but] I couldn't free myself of a feeling of dislike to the point of hostility toward him, which seemed to me shameful and unworthy. So my spirit was involuntarily bound to him and to his life. And only after I left Petersburg did I begin to feel that I was *tired* of thinking about him." In the same letter he announced that in January of 1909 he would come back to Russia permanently: "I will probably not return to Paris for many years."[29]

It was not only his loss of Margarita that was causing Voloshin to rethink the patterns of his life and to make new plans. Always having before him the goal of becoming a poet, the necessity of supporting himself through journalism was becoming increasingly distasteful. Writing to Petrova again from Paris in November 1908, he asked her: "How did you guess, Aleksandra Mikhailovna, that I want to shake off journalism and find other sources of economic support?"[30] Voloshin's journalism was by no means a mere day job; he had written many well-received essays on literature and art, especially in his capacity as a reporter on the modernist scene unfolding in Paris at that time.[31] Yet he had been writing poetry for many years, yearned for publication and recognition as a poet, and sought professional opportunity in that direction. His intellectual, professional, and economic contacts came together primarily in Petersburg, especially around the Ivanov household. Thus it was that by the winter of 1909 he was back in Petersburg taking part in the lectures on poetics and in the establishment of *Apollon*. He spent the summer in Koktebel' and in the fall of 1909 returned to continue his association with *Apollon*. But now he was a happy man again: in Koktebel' he had fallen in love with another woman, Elizaveta Dmitrieva.

Dmitrieva is the third central figure in the Cherubina story: indeed she *was* Cherubina, or at least was the reason for Cherubina's existence. She was another of those female poets whose physical appearance did not answer to the powerful contemporary stereotype of the female poetic soul. Descriptions of her vary, according to the intentions of those describing her: those who wanted to magnify the distinction between her and the ethereal Cherubina (the two Tsvetaeva sisters and Voloshin himself, for example) described her as a plain, simple schoolteacher with a limp which had made her vulnerable to teasing since birth. Others saw her with a somewhat different eye; Johannes von Guenther, for example, though conceding that her physical appearance was unprepossessing, found her wit and carriage attractive to the point of "sexiness."[32] In any case, she attracted not only Voloshin but also one other soon-to-be-famous Russian poet during that summer in Koktebel'.

Elizaveta Dmitrieva,
or Cherubina de
Gabriak [detail].
Date Unknown.
*Courtesy of Vladimir
Kupchenko.*

As a young and ambitious modernist poet based in Petersburg, Dmitrieva aspired to publication in *Apollon*. But when she submitted her poetry to the journal as Elizaveta Dmitrieva, whom the editors knew because of her habit of lingering around the editorial offices, her work was rejected. So, together, she and Voloshin plotted another way to get her poetry published.

Voloshin believed that she had been rejected because of her physical appearance and Makovskii's snobbery. "Makovskii, or 'Papa Mako,' as we called him," wrote Voloshin many years later, "was exceptionally aristocratic and elegant. I remember how he consulted with me on how to establish the rule that all co-workers must appear in the *Apollon* offices in smoking jackets. Of course only ladies [*damy*] were to be in the offices, and Papa Mako intended [to have] ballerinas from the Petersburg *corps de ballet*."[33] Under these circumstances Dmitrieva suffered from an obvious handicap:

"[She was] an inconspicuous, unattractive girl—and the aestheticizing editor S. Makovskii looked upon her and upon what she read with offensive scorn," Voloshin explained in a letter to the Gertsyk sisters only a few months after the event.[34] Perhaps a little weary of modernist posturing, and certainly wanting to come to the defense of Dmitrieva, whom he described as very much alone and unprotected in the masculine atmosphere of the *Apollon* editorial offices, Voloshin instigated a masquerade in the Symbolist spirit of life-creation, and a far-reaching deception of Makovskii, by creating with and for Dmitrieva the role of the wealthy, reclusive, religiously exotic (Catholic), and presumably gorgeous Cherubina de Gabriak.

Cherubina de Gabriak never showed her face in the offices; she sent letters and her poetry to Makovskii, had passionate conversations with him over the telephone, but remained always out of reach. Her poetry moved delicately along the border between religiosity and eroticism:

> "*Sang de Jésus-Christ, enivrez moi.*"(Ignace de Loyola)

> In my dreams I am close to arrogance,
> Within me—are the temptations of sin,
> I do not know chaste blessedness . . .
>   Flesh of Christ, sanctify me!

> Like the maiden who extinguished the icon lamp,
> Rejecting the Bridegroom's Summoning,
> I stand at the heavenly fence . . .
>   Pain of Christ, heal me!

> And the mute door will arouse
> A daring thought in the fallen ones:
> What if beyond is insanity? . . .
>   Passion of Christ, strengthen me!

> Overcome with an anxious tremor—
> I now do not wish to accept
> That I considered wisdom a lie . . .
>   Blood of Christ, intoxicate me![35]

The extent to which this poetry was of Dmitrieva's own creation was to become a subject of debate; some believed that Voloshin had a large role in writing it, but Voloshin asserted that he merely proposed topics and Dmitrieva wrote the poetry. Apparently some of the poems had been written before Cherubina came into being; Alexei Tolstoi, who had also been visiting Voloshin in Koktebel' in the summer of 1909 and was now frequently present at the *Apollon* offices, immediately recognized Dmitrieva's

Koktebel' poems when they first began to arrive under Cherubina's name (he remained absolutely silent about this, however). Cherubina, in any case, consistent with the myth of her wealth and with the image of the woman poet as dilettante, refused all payment for her work.

Makovskii's own memoir reveals how entirely he fell victim to Voloshin's and Dmitrieva's imaginations, and to his own, in this affair. In Cherubina, he saw the perfect female partner for himself as "patriarch" of the *Apollon* household. He records how anxiously he awaited Cherubina's letters (written by Voloshin), telephone calls, and poems, and how agonizing were the missed encounters, when Cherubina told him that she would be in such and such a place at such and such a time, and yet was not to be found. Voloshin and Dmitrieva drew the joke out further and further, elaborating on Cherubina's personality (often with Makovskii's unwitting aid), creating a family background (Spanish; she had a despotic father and her mother had died), an educational background (she had been educated in a Catholic seminary), as well as a travel itinerary for her. Her physical appearance was also determined. Revealing the strong visual impact this imaginary figure had had on him, Makovskii wrote almost half a century later: "she had reddish, bronze curls, [and] the color of her face was quite pale, deathly pale, but [she had] sharply defined lips with slightly drooping corners, and a gait almost limping, as befitted a sorceress."[36]

Both the poetry and the person of Cherubina were an instant and smashing success. The *Apollon* offices became the background for a scene of intensive debate about her poetry and her identity. She had both supporters and detractors; curiously (or perhaps not so curiously) Elizaveta Dmitrieva became one of her more energetic critics, compounding the deception by writing lively parodies of Cherubina's poetry. But this may have been taken as personal jealousy; the *Apollontsy* were convinced that Cherubina was a breathtaking beauty. Only one man, according to Makovskii, proposed that if she was not showing herself, perhaps she had something to hide. Most convinced of her beauty was World of Art painter Konstantin Somov, a member of Ivanov's inner circle: "'Tell her,' insisted Somov, 'that I am prepared to travel [to her home] in a carriage with my eyes bound, in order to paint her portrait, giving her my word of honor not to abuse her trust, not to discover who she is and where she lives.'"[37] Makovskii writes in his memoirs that this collective masculine fantasy of female beauty was surely nourished by the powerful image of the "Beautiful Lady" of Blok's poems written a few years earlier.[38] Its fires were additionally stoked by the information that Cherubina suffered from acute loneliness and yearned for someone to trust and love. Many of the men who frequented the offices were reported to have fallen in love with Cherubina—but none more than Makovskii himself.

Impassioned and obsessed, Makovskii lingered at the *Apollon* offices waiting for communications, doggedly pursuing the illusion of Cherubina every step of the way that Voloshin and Dmitrieva led him. More important to Dmitrieva, of course, was that he published her poetry. The plain, lame schoolteacher had had no chance with him, but the calculated artificial Cherubina held complete sway over his heart and his editorial judgment. Through this masquerade, Dmitrieva's status had been reversed from an ugly and therefore lowly aspirant to a goddess-like figure.

The story spread ripples of gossip throughout Petersburg literary society, and the emotional impact of its imagery and the pertinence of the concerns it touched on were such that it found its way into a large number of memoirs about the period. Each memoirist tells the story slightly differently, partly because each experienced it differently and partly because, as the anecdote traveled, the details were changed. Marina Tsvetaeva's version, for example, contains several historical inaccuracies, as does Anastasiia Tsvetaeva's; not personally involved themselves, they were the recipients of somewhat distorted versions, like the later players in the child's game of telephone.[39] What most tend to agree on is that the story ended badly, with hurt feelings all around. Yet opinions differ on why this was the case, and on who the heroes of the tale were, and who the villains.

A principal complication was an overlapping of Cherubina's story with the story of another romance that found its way into the memoirs: that of Dmitrieva and Nikolai Gumilev, the other Russian poet who had flirted with her in Koktebel' in the summer of 1909. This story is long and complex, and cannot be related in its entirety here. Suffice it to say that, although again versions of this story vary considerably, and are even mutually contradictory at times, a disastrous attempt was made to bring the now estranged Dmitrieva and Gumilev face to face with each other by Gumilev's young Baltic German friend, Johannes von Guenther, at the height of the Cherubina sensation. So deeply did Gumilev insult Dmitrieva on this occasion that Voloshin fought a duel with him. Voloshin's challenge to Gumilev, a slap in the face, was made at a moment that had its own symbolic significance: at the time the group was posing for a collective portrait of the *Apollon* staff. Makovskii described the challenge and duel (in which no one was hurt) as a "family drama."[40]

Voloshin's memoir about Cherubina ends with the duel, leaving the impression that this was the end of the Cherubina story, and that perhaps Gumilev, or at least his friend, von Guenther (who did in fact learn the secret from Dmitrieva herself), was responsible for the ultimate unmasking of Cherubina.[41] But as other memoirs—as well as Voloshin's letters from the period—indicate, the Cherubina affair actually went on for some time thereafter.[42] Yet rumors of Cherubina's true identity began to spread, and eventually, according to von Guenther, the poet Kuzmin came to him and demanded to know whether Dmitrieva and Cherubina were identical. With von Guenther's confirmation, Kuzmin told Makovskii, who in turn made an appointment to see Elizaveta Dmitrieva.[43] According to Makovskii's account, their meeting was heartrending, as Elizaveta displayed herself in her true ugliness (as both she and Makovskii seemed to agree), and Makovskii faced the loss of his dear fantasy.

What none of the memoirists recorded, and what few indeed seemed to know, was the extent of Voloshin's love for the flesh-and-blood Elizaveta. Only his diary during the summer of 1909 in Koktebel', and his letters to Aleksandra Petrova the following winter, preserve this central fact of Voloshin's theatrical mentorship of Dmitrieva.[44] On November 26, 1908, he wrote to tell Petrova about the duel, which had taken place four days earlier, and then went on to describe the circumstances of his personal life. All was delightful, he wrote. Lilia (his name for Dmitrieva) and Margarita had become good friends, which had much improved his own relationship with Margarita. "But there is another side, very bitter and difficult," he went on. The problem was that Dmitrieva was actually already married, to a young man in the military. Dmitrieva loved him, Voloshin wrote, but felt a strong sense of duty toward her husband. Ironically Voloshin now found himself in a relationship with this young man similar to the one Viacheslav Ivanov had been in with him, Voloshin, two years before: that of the socially powerful lover openly preferred over the husband.[45] "He knows everything. He loves me. . . . You can imagine with what care and with what horror I listened at times to my own old words and guessed at the movement of the soul and the struggle."[46]

Some memoirists leave the impression that Dmitrieva vanished from Petersburg "into the provinces" immediately afterward because of the shame of her unveiling as Cherubina de Gabriak. Voloshin's letters to Aleksandra Petrova indicate that increasing tensions over Dmitrieva's painful choice between "love" and "duty" came to a head at around the same time, resulting in Dmitrieva's decision to stick by her husband.[47] Dmitrieva's own memoir about the period, written in 1926 and actually dedicated to the memory of Nikolai Gumilev (who was shot as a White spy by the Bolsheviks in 1921), reveals the agony she went through during this time but attributes it to the unpleasant conclusion of her relationship with Gumilev. "After the duel I was sick, almost to the edge of insanity. I stopped writing poetry, for five years I hardly even read poems, every rhythmic line caused me pain."[48]

Whatever the cause of Dmitrieva's abrupt abandonment of poetry and disappearance from the Petersburg literary scene—all three blows must have had their impact on her—Voloshin's second attempt at mentorship had come to a dead standstill. The form of his mentorship had been inspired in that it made for a vivid and mocking public exposure of the narrow masculine spirit that dominated modernist publishing circles. And at a time when it was very difficult for an ambitious female poet to find the reserves within herself and the acceptance from without to push her way into the modernist publishing network, Voloshin had provided a mask, an alternative identity, that made it possible for such a woman to accomplish her goal.

But the charade had carried with it the seeds of personal confusion and distress. The mask had not fit in a way that it could be maintained; further, it had forced a consciousness of cultural truths surely more painful to Dmitrieva than to Makovskii or his male associates (or to Voloshin, for that matter) about what it might take for a woman to break with some semblance of dignity into the public realm. In order to make her way into the network of intensely personal relationships that made up the Russian modernist publishing community, a woman had to be beautiful and lovable. Her most appropriate status was that of amateur, entirely uninterested in either professional or financial advancement through her literary activities; best of all was the status of romantic partner. But the strain of maintaining the several romantic relationships that provided her entrée into the literary community proved, in the end, too much for Dmitrieva. The poetic impulse in her—so dependent on audience and recognition—was crushed for many years.

For Voloshin there was depression at his loss of a second potential love partner and also, perhaps, a more precise realization of the difficulties ambitious women faced in finding a place in the modernist network. His first abortive mentorship, that of Margarita Sabashnikova, had foundered against the romantic impulse; this second theatrical mentorship had been inspired by one romance, Voloshin's with Dmitrieva, had been conceived in the framework of another, Dmitrieva's with Makovskii, and had become complicated to the point of disaster by a third, Dmitrieva's with Gumilev. If an element of what Voloshin as a mentor had to offer women was a mask, a creative identity, the romantic mask was not very effective. Never again would he as a mentor attempt to manipulate the romantic feelings of those around him through his skill in playing with the masks and metaphors that comprise human identity.

Yet the charade had succeeded in publicizing Voloshin's will to challenge the Symbolist hierarchies by supporting women who had poetic ambitions. Word of his exploit spread quickly, passing through the gossip mills of the Russian intelligentsia; it was to become a touchstone of his anti-structural identity among them. And it had its impact: the tale delighted Marina Tsvetaeva and helped to convince her of his will to support her as a female poet. With such a mentee as Tsvetaeva by his side, he could lay the foundations of his real challenge to the northern literary scene, his Koktebel' circle in the Crimea, where he would revive and purify the circle formation as communitas and, in the process, give impetus in a small but distinct way to the historical transition from Symbolism to post-Symbolism.

FOUR

The Koktebel' Dacha Circle

LAYING THE FOUNDATIONS

Many of Max's summer guests recall the day of their arrival at the Voloshin dacha in some detail.[1] "I remember the hot—silver and deep blue—morning" when she first saw Koktebel', writes Anastasiia Tsvetaeva in a pastoral rhapsody. Riding in a horse-drawn cab from the Theodosia train station, brooding still over personal difficulties back in Moscow, the younger sister of Marina Tsvetaeva watched the landscape unfold beneath the early morning Crimean sky: "And already, Max's Cimmerian steppe stretched out under the melting lilac, hilly, mysterious, scorched."

As the morning light grew stronger, she came into sight of the hills overlooking the village: "the horses gallop along the chaussée, the landscape grows brighter, awakening first in the distance and then nearer, blazing up in shadows and layers of light, casting off shadow and becoming a part of the day, of me, of my true life here. . . . And approaching us the deep blue of the sea, overpowering the low infrequent gardens where the windows of the houses, thrown wide open, glitter in the sun. The village road shudders and leaps beneath the wheels, brief glimpses of wattle fences, and to the left, far away, the left edge of the bay, a ridge of ash-yellow hills. . . . Some kind hand, unnoticed, soundless, relieves my soul of all its weight."

And then suddenly the cab driver announced: "The Voloshin dacha? We're here!" Dazed and fumbling with her baggage, Anastasiia stepped out into the entrance to the dacha, to be heartily embraced by two welcoming figures. One was Marina, who had arrived some weeks before Anastasiia, and the other was a man who made a strong impression on her: "He stood and smiled so DEEPLY, the way—people can't smile. He was silent, his head on one side [as he] looked and rejoiced. He understood everything . . . and I saw why it was that, even just approaching his house, the weight had dropped from my shoulders: a Good Spirit lived in this house."[2]

This "Good Spirit" that Tsvetaeva so effusively described was no ethereal creature. Rather, it was the painstaking and hard-working Voloshin, who was beginning, that summer of 1911, to concentrate seriously on establishing his circle. He had a number of resources and talents to draw upon for this purpose, and would need to make the fullest use of them all. Above all there was the powerful sense of anti-structural communitas, of unity in resistance to the traditional hierarchies of modernism and perhaps indeed of certain aspects of intelligentsia culture itself, that he brought to the effort as he built up the circle beginning with a small group of somewhat rebellious, difficult adolescents. It was as a leader of communitas, inspired and inspiring, that he gave his circle a sense of its reason for being. It was to this powerful and in a way mysterious sense of purpose that Marina Tsvetaeva would later refer when she wrote: "When we fell into his orbit we invariably fell under his set of laws. Max himself was the planet. And when we revolved around him we were revolving in some other large circle together with him around a luminary that we did not know."[3] There was a quality of awe, of excitement; and Voloshin constantly enhanced that quality through his continued sensitivity to and use of metaphor, masquerade, and theatricality. Through playful exploration of mask and identity, he continued to build upon his reputation as a rebel of sorts, now establishing himself as a builder of anti-traditional, anti-hierarchical community.

But he had other resources and talents to draw on as well. One of these resources was Koktebel' itself: to the Russian urban educated elite, a distant and exotic place, fortunately (from their point of view) under the secure control of Russian Imperial power. Situated on the Black Sea in the Crimea, the realm of myriad ancient civilizations and myths, Koktebel' was to its northern visitors visually extraordinary, with its yellow hills and fragrant chaparral, its glittering dead Black Sea waters and imposing cliffs. Not a mile from Voloshin's home, in the sea beside the coastal cliffs, was the gateway where, according to Greek mythology, Orpheus had sought to lead Eurydice from Hades: a rocky loop of sea sculpture rearing up from the waters. More recently the area around Koktebel' had been populated by the Bulgars and the Crimean Tatars, both Inner Eurasian tribal civilizations whose existence went back to the days of the early Rus'. With their flowing gowns and trousers, not to mention the unfortunate Bulgar habit of stealing horses, they greatly enhanced the magically evocative spirit of the place for those drawn to a Russian variety of orientalism. Koktebel' was itself a former Bulgar village, which had over the previous decades gradually been taken over by Russians in search of new vacation territory.

In this sense the village, and indeed the Voloshin household, reflected phenomena of nineteenth-century Russian social history. The development of Koktebel' as a Russian summer colony was part of a longer tale of the gradual emergence of a middle social group in Russia looking for vacation homes, often in settlements, and an exurban way of life.[4] The Crimea, with its long and seemingly romantic history not only of Scythians, Greeks, and Khazars (to name but a few of the many tribes and empires who made use of the Black Sea as a source of commercial and political power over the millennia) but also of Imperial conquest and famous literary journeys, was immensely attractive to those among the educated elite who either had or were beginning to accumulate the finances and leisure time for summer vacations. With the building of a railroad from Moscow to the Crimea in the decades following the Crimean War, more and more Russians began to stream into the area. Voloshin's mother, Elena Ottobal'dovna, had been one of the earliest of the settlers of Koktebel', making their home a veritable fixture in the growing dacha colony.

The other major resource upon which Voloshin drew was closely associated with his mother. Even such a vibrant, idealistic expression of communitas as Voloshin's Koktebel' circle required a sound material base: a house and a smoothly running household that would provide its guests and circle members with shelter, food, entertainment, and all the other amenities that were required for successful circle life. And it was through Elena Ottobal'dovna that Voloshin gained access to these basic needs. She was to become the essential female partner in his circle, not only providing emotional sustenance for those complex, ambitious young females, for example, but also offering economic support, keeping the house in order physically, and taking general responsibility for the financial arrangements for maintaining the home. These arrangements were more complicated than one might think, for the Voloshin home functioned in part as a summer boarding house for circle members as well as for other visitors. Voloshin himself was deeply uncomfortable about taking money from his guests, and thus was happy to leave that part of the affair to his mother—keeping his hands clean, so to speak, for a purer kind of relationship with his guests.[5] The relationship between Voloshin and his mother was not an easy or automatic one; their association fluctuated over the years leading up to 1911.

Elena Ottobal'dovna represented Voloshin's primary link to Koktebel'. In earlier years he had even suggested moving to the Caucasus mountains along the Black Sea rather than to dusty Koktebel'; but she made the decision to go there, and, along with several other early settlers, established the first Voloshin household in the 1890s. Voloshin began to build his own house in Koktebel' in 1903. But its construction was supervised largely by Elena Ottobal'dovna; and she continued to manage his property and affairs in Koktebel' during his years in Europe and the urban centers of Russia. Only at a moment of serious marital trouble did he turn his thoughts to the Crimean landscapes of his adolescence.[6] And only as his first marriage collapsed around him did he begin to think of establishing himself as a regular summer inhabitant in Koktebel', and of inviting guests to stay with him. But in order to shift the center of his life to the Crimea, Voloshin had to come to terms with the woman, his mother, who up until now had reigned freely there.

There were many tensions in this relationship between a mother with an extraordinarily strong personality who had raised her son single-handedly and an equally strong-willed son who had struck out as far as Paris on his own. He now wanted, in 1910, to return in some sense to the fold, but without giving up the sense of freedom and individuality he had gained through age and distance. Had his marriage not collapsed, the relationship between them might have taken a very different course. The presence of another woman to act as his main confidante and partner in emotional and economic matters, especially in household matters, could easily have shifted the balance of power away from Elena Ottobal'dovna, or at least cushioned the buffeting that occurred when these equally strong-willed individuals with disparate styles came up against each other. But lacking that other weight in their stressful negotiation of balance, Max and his mother were often bound together in matters that each might have preferred to manage independently of the other.

Money continued to be a source of particular irritability and contention between them; where emotional and economic ties crossed, sparks could fly. Yet they frequently found themselves closely bound together by their comparatively weak financial circumstances; the centrality of this aspect of their bond with each other may well have contributed to the strength of their later partnership in circle hospitality. Though fierce about her independence, Elena Ottobal'dovna found that at one point she was trapped by her economic situation; despite her vocal opposition to the practice of borrowing money, she was obliged to take this route herself. To accomplish this, she had to turn to Voloshin and his network ties for help. In 1908, protesting and uncomfortable, she allowed Max to help her borrow between one thousand and two thousand rubles from one of Margarita Sabashnikova's relatives. The Sabashnikovs were, after all, a wealthy merchant family; and although they had originally disapproved of Max and his marriage to Margarita, and although the two were separated by now, Max had won friends among the clan who were pleased to help out when they could. (Such help later included publishing a book of Voloshin's translations of the French author de Saen Victor, and loaning him travel money.)

The arrangements for security—the Koktebel' house, as this was essentially a private mortgage—and interest were complicated.[7] Thus Elena Ottobal'-dovna found herself at this time dependent in a small way on her son's aid for economic survival.

The loan was not for her alone, however; Max was also having a great deal of trouble making ends meet. Though journalistic work was not always easy to find, he generally, through networking and persistence, did manage to obtain it: a large part of the difficulty was that the publications he worked for were often slow or remiss in their payments. That he often lived abroad, usually in Paris, multiplied his difficulties in wringing his rightful honoraria out of Russian publishers. *Apollon* kept him dangling for many months at a time; as did *Golden Fleece*, while it still existed, *Rus'*, *Pantheon*, the *Moscow Gazette*, and the "Sphinx" Publishing House. At one point, exasperated and broke, he had to ask his mother to intervene personally for him: late in 1911 he sent her three consecutive letters from Paris, asking her to go directly to the offices of the *Moscow Gazette* and "Sphinx" to ask them for his money. Finally, more than a month after his first letter to her, he wrote again to say that, undoubtedly in response to her visit, the *Moscow Gazette* had sent him a telegram informing him that his money was on the way—as a postal order. "But a postal order from Moscow to Paris takes up to three weeks. . . . Just like a publishing house, I telegraph them: send me the money by telegraph, and they deliberately choose the slowest possible route," he fumed.[8] In addition to this example of how Voloshin relied on his mother to manage his financial affairs, at times he even turned to her for help in selling his work when he was too far away to do it himself.

Max also borrowed money from his mother, especially to subsidize his travels abroad, which could be the cause of emotional flare-ups. After unpleasantness over a loan she had given him in 1914, in 1915 he wrote her a postcard conveying his decision not to borrow money from her for his travel expenses this time, along with the perhaps provocative request that she not be insulted by this. She replied: "Insulted or not, I don't like the final explanation in [your postcard]: that it's better to have no accounting between us at all." Evidently responding to Max's impatient tone, she made an awkward attempt to defend herself: "Yes, Max, I often settled accounts with you, was often dissatisfied with the way that you simply didn't want to think about money, about accounting, to know where it was going to come from; simply didn't know and didn't want to think about where I got it and am getting it now[;] and again [you are] behaving like a little child about life and about me." She *would* lend him the money, she continued somewhat roughly. Despite her brusqueness, however, there were signs of a move toward reconciliation on the always irritating subject of finance. This reflected a broader process of reconciliation between the two of them which had actually begun several years earlier.

While Max and Elena Ottobal'dovna had certainly been close throughout Max's early adulthood, it was not a relationship between equals. Elena Ottobal'dovna's sometimes abrasive maternal attitude toward her son was certainly a factor in this; there was also the constraint of formality. Throughout his childhood and early adulthood, Voloshin had addressed his mother by the formal *"vy."* But soon after Elena Ottobal'dovna had witnessed the humiliating theft (from Voloshin's point of view) of Voloshin's wife by Ivanov in early 1907, Voloshin began to address her by the more intimate *"ty."*[9] It is uncertain who initiated this—the only definite sign of this transformation accessible to a historian are his letters to her—but it seems in some way to have acted as a trigger for a new stage in their association with each other.

The next hint of change is also to be found in his letters to her during this period. Elena Ottobal'dovna had been subject all along to deep depressions that caused her to require much attention and support from her son. One of those depressions had set in while she was living in the Ivanov household with Max and Margarita as their marriage was undergoing the challenge of Ivanov's incursions, so that Max's distress about his wife had been mingled with his concern about his mother. His diary indicates that he found it somewhat exhausting to come to her aid.

But just as he soon thereafter began to address her with the intimate *"ty,"* so he began as well to probe more attentively into the causes of her depressions and generally into the patterns and motivating forces of her life. Sometime between 1907 and 1909 he wrote to her: "Dear Mama, only now, reading your letter, do I realize that we have both at last come to the question without which all remains dead between us. So many times I wanted but feared to ask you about your life. But earlier it was impossible to ask. Of all people, I know you the least (both least and most)." Voloshin went on to try to explain his previous hesitation at asking her questions about her personal life and feelings: he had been unobservant in his childhood, and had taken her power for granted. "You were for me the unquestioned authority." This sense of her authority had long blinded him to the reality of her vulnerability and dependency: "Very late I noticed the suffering and unhappiness of your life. Perhaps I got my first inkling when you came to visit me in Paris the first time, and were so lonely and lost in those other surroundings. I was more clearly conscious of this on that evening when I told you that I would marry Margarita Vasil'evna. But only very recently did I realize the extent to which I am your life."

Having brought into the open this imbalance and lack of understanding in their relationship, Voloshin went on: "If you can, if you want, tell me about yourself and your life. Because I always wanted to ask you and feared to. I think it would be easiest of all in a letter and in segments. I also always wanted you to tell me in detail and everything about my father and about how I came to be and it was terrifying for me to ask you about this. Every word of your letter today is so painful and important to me. And with every word the barriers that stand between us fall."[10]

His letters to her over the next few years reveal a continued effort to increase openness and to strengthen the bond between them. In one, writing from Koktebel' in the winter, and moved almost to tears by the loneliness of this place where she had often lived during the off-season without him, Voloshin accused himself of having neglected his mother and withholding intimacy from her. He begged for her forgiveness. "And I want to write to you, because I can't say it or show it, believe that I love you deeply and strongly. Dear mama, when you come home, help me to be true and loyal with you."[11]

Max early linked the tightening of this bond with his mother explicitly with his bond to Koktebel', and with his desire to establish a new life there. At the beginning of 1909, upon hearing of the death of Elena Ottobal'dovna's mother, he wrote: "I now feel that we two have become closer, Mama, and that my life is growing more closely attached to Koktebel'. Now it is necessary to create new, more whole and harmonious forms of life and you must make me your assistant [in this]." Consciously or not, he associated the growing importance of his relationship with his mother and with Koktebel' with the failure of his marriage and his plans for the future. In the same paragraph of this letter, he continued: "When I understood that Amoria had left me for good, I felt intensely alone. But everything that happened was for the best. Everything that is, *must* be for the best. Now it is necessary to build a whole, full, and real life in Koktebel'."[12]

Lacking a wife as his partner in this domestic endeavor, Voloshin soon came to rely on his mother as the person with whom he would share the responsibilities of maintaining the Koktebel' household whose "new, whole, and more harmonious forms of life" he was so consciously plotting out. Thus he was now turning his already proven skills in successful personal association to the establishment of a more deeply rooted and more harmonious emotional relationship with his mother, the fruit of which would be the establishment of a successful intellectual circle. Essentially he was networking with his mother in a process that involved a complex material as well as emotional negotiation, so as to gain both her material and emotional partnership and support. The arduous but necessary establishment of terms between them reflected the importance of the traditional male-female leadership partnership in the social context of Russian *kruzhok* life, as well as the inner workings of such a partnership.

COMMUNITAS AT THE
HEART OF THE CIRCLE:
THE PLAYFUL *"OBORMOTY"*
IN THE SUMMER OF 1911

There is more to the story of Anastasiia Tsvetaeva's first day in Koktebel' than related above, but to that we will return later, considering, first, those whom she would find in this house other than her hosts: a small group of adolescent summer visitors who were to name themselves the *"Obormoty,"* or the "Idiots." Anastasiia was the last of the *Obormoty* to arrive in that summer of 1911, and the last to be drawn into the group. There were seven of them, members of three sibling groups: the three Efron children—Elizaveta (Lilia), Vera, and Sergei (Serezha); Bella and Leonid (Lenya) Fainberg; and the two Tsvetaeva sisters. This was a varied crowd and by no means easy to handle. Voloshin succeeded not only in handling them but also in binding them together into the legendary heart of his circle, largely through deft manipulation of their dreams, fantasies, and games, leavened by a constant intuitive sensitivity to the ebb and flow of social harmony both among his guests as well as between himself and his partner in hospitality, Elena Ottobal'dovna. The Voloshin circle that emerged in 1911 was a lively—if, as always, fleeting—expression of communitas, whose manifestation gave impetus and meaning to the circle's later success.

The Efron siblings were the offspring of a Jewish revolutionary father and an aristocratic mother, who had renounced her social class and become a revolutionary herself, and who committed suicide in 1910. They were the largest faction, and a lively, talented, and demanding set of siblings they were. Marina Tsvetaeva, whose association with Voloshin was that of treasured poetic "pupil" or "disciple" coming to live with her "master," arrived at around the same time the Efrons did; the second contingent to arrive was the Fainberg siblings, along with their friend Maria Gekhtman.

Many years later Leonid Fainberg would write his own memoir of Koktebel', a long piece entitled "Three Summers as a Guest at Maximilian Voloshin's." But his arrival with sister and friend was nothing like the joyous occasion that Anastasiia experienced: indeed, it was rather disconcerting, at least at first. This was because, back in St. Petersburg, the Efrons had invited the Fainbergs to come to Koktebel' but had failed to mention this in Koktebel', so that no one expected them. After the long journey south by train, Leonid Fainberg, Bella Fainberg, and Maria Gekhtman arrived at the Voloshin dacha exhausted but expectant. Entering the garden they stepped onto a terrace where they found Elizaveta Efron, along with three others sitting at one end of a long table.

At the sight of us she expressed no delight whatsoever. Just a simple welcome.

"Well. You came after all? But, you know, there aren't any free rooms."

Bella held her peace, but Mania [Maria] Gekhtman, maybe, objected:

"Why didn't you announce us ahead of time?"

Lilia [Elizaveta] remained entirely indifferent.

"—No problem! Somehow you'll find a place. Seryozha [Sergei]! Take Lenya [Leonid] to the Manaseinii place. Maybe they have a free room."

So the two young men walked over to a neighboring cottage but to no avail. Back on the Voloshin terrace, Sergei Efron announced that the Manaseinii household had no room either. One can well imagine the sense among the three new arrivals of being out of place and unwanted. "Just then a woman walked onto the terrace," Fainberg continues in his account, "not tall, with a remarkable brow. If this really was a woman. Her masculine face reminded one of the countenance of the chief of an ancient nation. Just so I could imagine the chief of some Gallic tribe. She was beautifully dressed. Her Cossack-style jacket was sewn, as I later found out, of Crimean Tatar towels. Her *sharovari* [wide trousers like those worn by the local Tatars], dark blue, were stuffed at the bottom into brick-orange Hessian boots with folded tops. Of her face I will say more later. For now I will add only that in her sternly drawn brow and her firmly compressed lips there was a look of one accustomed to power."

This was, of course, Elena Ottobal'dovna. While Max Voloshin's mother heard the whole story from Elizaveta Efron and learned how to pronounce Maria Gekhtman's name, Max himself walked out onto the terrace. Leonid writes: "If in his mother's appearance there shone a kind of hard inflexibility, then in Max could be seen a kind of soft inflexibility, if I may put it that way. He wasn't tall, but I sensed that something colossal had come onto the terrace. His unusually large head, broad face, with highly regular features, was essentially made even broader, greater, by an abundant mass of hair, just barely touched by early gray." This adoring description goes on for some paragraphs, providing the details of Voloshin's curly beard and sideburns, of his piercing hazel-gray eyes ("There was something of the peacefully resting lion in his eyes"), of his massive figure, and of his clothing: Max wore a long, loose brown and purple gown that reached to his ankles, and, on his feet, *chuviaki*, the light slippers of the region. Leonid had indeed been expecting something extraordinary, something bohemian —and between Elena Ottobal'dovna and Max, he was enchanted. "If his mother (though it's true, the height was wrong) resembled the chief of a Gallic tribe, then Max himself reminded one of a pagan priest among the Druids."[13]

The visual impact of Elena Ottobal'dovna and her son is almost always noted in the memoirs of their guests, who describe the sense of having stepped away from the world of ordinary conventions into a kind of charmed space where the charmingly outlandish held sway. Costume, particularly this playful manipulation of "native" trappings, was quickly to become one of the identifying marks of the Voloshin circle, and to serve as a means of drawing its members together and distinguishing them from the other "normal *dachniki* [summer residents]" of the Koktebel' colony. But to return to the terrace, as Max took stock of the tension brewing there, Leonid was about to witness another way that his host and hostess worked together to integrate this household community:

> Max looked at my sister attentively and gently.
>
> "You are Bella Fainberg?"
>
> "Yes, Maximilian Aleksandrovich."
>
> "That name suits you. Call me what everyone here calls me: simply Max!"
>
> Bella smiled, for the first time, it seems to me, since we had arrived in Koktebel'.
>
> "And you are Lenya? You are an artist?"
>
> "Oh, no, Maximilian Aleksandrovich! I've only just begun to study drawing . . ."
>
> Max approached his mother—and said something to her quietly. What exactly he said, I do not know.
>
> She turned to Lilia [Efron], and if not sternly, then firmly [said]:
>
> "Lilia! Your guests have arrived. You invited them to come visit us here. Why the Manaseiniis? How could you send Seryozha off without even consulting with me? You may sleep together with Vera. There: one room for Bella and Lenya. And I'll take care of Manya myself. Everything is set."[14]

Thus Elena Ottobal'dovna and Max divided the role of host between them at that moment. He attended to the emotional comfort of their new guests, easing the tension created by their arrival, making them feel like interesting and attractive people with whom he wanted to share his home, and setting a tone and an example of courtesy and hospitality, while she, with her sharper edge and her control of the physical arrangements, gave teeth to the requirement of this household that its members treat one another fairly and well.

Max's part in this was vital; he brought a degree of emotional control to the household that was essential to its success. Fainberg attributed Max's ability to accomplish this to an internal stability of Voloshin's personality: "One of the most valuable parts of his character was his unbreakable mastery over himself. He was never beside himself. Not rage, nor vexation, nor irritation, nor laughter or even happiness got the upper hand of his internal self-mastery, of the internal evenness[15] of his existence. . . . His fundamental external quality was smoothness, smoothness of gesture and movement, soft, good-willed smoothness, unalterably vigilant smoothness (forgive the contradiction of those linked terms). . . . Unshakable smoothness of strong-willed decisions. Unaltered smoothness of a whole life-, even daily life-system. Smoothness of daily life."[16]

That sense of self-control that Max imparted to his guests (which could indeed lead some to believe that he was passionless) served as a touchstone in determining their behavior, and contributed greatly to his success as a circle leader just as it had done to his earlier success when he insinuated himself into the Symbolist circles. His figure was catalytic in maintaining the standards necessary for the coexistence of a large group of varied personalities. Not only did he demand a certain degree of courtesy among his guests, but he also repressed sly or complaining gossip, telling one fussy young visitor that he did not care to know bad things about his guests. In all, he provided that sense of "smoothness of daily life" that made it possible for a household to function successfully—especially a household such as this, whose members could depart at any time if they were not happy. Only in such an atmosphere could intimacy and familiarity be gained, and domestically based circle alliances formed. Against the early-twentieth-century background of seemingly chronic dissension among the Russian educated elite, his capacity for calm self-mastery in the face of general emotional ferment was much remarked upon and admired. It was invaluable to circle and network life.

The styles of mother and son in handling those around them differed greatly, and this manifested itself in the way they divided up the role of playing host to Max's guests, as their behavior on the terrace illustrated. To some extent, this role-playing was simply a kind of collusion as each of them brought what she or he could to the business of running their joint household. But at times it may also have reflected the struggle between them to accommodate their differences in personality and style, to which they both gave expression through playful exaggeration. For example, at dinner that afternoon (meals representing one of the central moments of material exchange in circle life), Elena Ottobal'dovna strictly and precisely doled out the portions to all those sitting around the table. Meanwhile, Max gave vent to what the others may well have been feeling, the natural impatience and anxiety of people waiting for their food:

"Maaama! If possible—serve me first, out of order! I can't wait! I want my food!"

Elena Ottobal'dovna—in her turn—played stern fairness:
"Everyone gets their food in order!"
"But Mama, I can't wait! I don't have the strength."
"Then you'll come last!"
But the apportionment of the food ended well. We, too, got our food—
each according to his share.[17]

This sort of humorous role-playing, which manifests itself more than once in the memoirs and reflects issues of domestic power, is one indication of how Max helped to keep the tensions between them under control. But by no means did it entirely define Elena Ottobal'dovna and Max as hosts or as individuals. Many of their guests recognized the rather shy and vulnerable, sometimes unhappy woman behind the forbidding masculine exterior of Elena Ottobal'dovna; a few, such as the Tsvetaeva sisters, grew close to her, discovering her warmth and generosity. Max, on the other hand, could have his moments of disciplinary firmness, such as when the Efron siblings left a book from his extensive library lying on the beach, and he laid down the rule that no one could take his books outside his library anymore—they could read them only within its walls. No amount of complaining and moral blackmail from the obstreperous Efron children ("Now Max! You are simply nothing but an inveterate property owner. *My* book, *my* library. We didn't expect that sort of thing from you!")[18] caused him to unbend. The roles of powerful, tough-minded mother and kind, even-tempered son did reflect a reality in their relationship—which is why they were such effective roles—but the individuals were more complex.

Behind the playfully expressed polarization of their styles, there was, in fact, a strongly united front between the two on how the household was to be run. Max and Elena Ottobal'dovna may have disagreed in earnest at one point or another on household affairs, but I have seen no sign of it anywhere in the memoirs written by their guests. If there were moments of serious contention, host and hostess seem to have kept them to themselves. This united front was absolutely essential to the running of a household that often embraced such a variety of complicated and even rather difficult people. The success of their partnership, however difficult it had originally been to establish, was one of the greatest attractions of the circle.

But there were other attractions, too: for example, the lively culture of circle theatricality during that summer of 1911, which often had strong overtones of the carnivalesque out on this periphery of "cultured" Russia, and real potential for communitas-style self-transformation among its participants.[19] We left Anastasiia Tsvetaeva, on her first day in Koktebel', being embraced at the entrance to the Voloshin home by Max and her sister, Marina; as we know, there were six other young guests in the house for her to meet: the Fainbergs, Maria Gekhtman, and the Efrons. In her memoir Anastasiia mentions meeting the Fainbergs but of the presence of Elizaveta, Vera, and Sergei Efron on that first day she was given no inkling.[20] Instead, she was presented with an extraordinary masquerade by means of which household members conspired to delude her until the following morning.

As soon as they had a chance to talk, Anastasiia's sister, Marina, with what Anastasiia describes as a kind of suppressed yet artificial excitement, told her about the presence in Max's bohemian household of three suspiciously eccentric characters: first, a black-eyed, apricot-complexioned young Spanish woman by the name of Konchitta, who spoke—and understood—not a word of Russian but who had fallen deeply and jealously in love with Max. "'But what about him?'" asked Anastasiia. "'Oh, well, him . . . he can't fall in love, but he feels very sorry for her,'" Marina replied airily. The two sisters watched Konchitta through the foliage and listened to her melodious laugh. Then there was another woman, the poetess Maria Papper, whom both sisters had heard of in Moscow. Maria Papper wrote truly awful poetry and insisted on reading it out loud. "'Do you remember her poems about motherhood and pregnancy? She found a sword somewhere and uses it as a walking stick in the hills. It's a pose, but don't laugh! She's very vain.'" And Marina also told her sister about the presence of the exceedingly smug and self-indulgent poet Igor' Severianin. Anastasiia noticed him for the first time after dinner, as she sat drinking coffee with Marina: "'Look! [T]o your right . . . Igor' Severianin!'" Marina whispered. "'He sat down at the table at the end of dinner, you didn't notice him. Now he's walking through. Look at his affected way of walking. But his features are handsome.'" Anastasiia watched in fascination as, "pushing deer-like with his head through the boughs of wild grapes, a tall youth went out onto the path, very well-built, with a dark, narrow face and a thin hand with long fingers [with which he] with slow deliberation pushed a lock of hair from his forehead. He walked, averting his eyes, stepping picturesquely in his *chuviaki*, a wide belt encircling his narrow waist. Not quite having reached us, at the railing of the terrace, he stopped and slowly bent over a shrub (of roses?) Because of my near-sightedness, I couldn't see what flower it was that he chose for his gesture, but by the way his profile lengthened with delight, it was necessary to conclude that he was breathing the aroma of the '*tsaritsa* of flowers.'"[21]

Peculiar though these people were, perhaps they did not seem so terribly odd to Anastasiia in view of the unusual appearance of Elena Ottobal'-dovna, whom Anastasiia learned she was to call "Pra," short for "*Pramater*" ("Great-grandmother," with a secondary meaning: "mother of the human race") and whom she described as looking like a king, and that of Voloshin, in whom she saw both the gods Neptune and Zeus. After all, she had already met Voloshin in her own house in Moscow, and she had heard of his mother. Another rather unusual member of the household was a small, unprepossessing man named Misha, who turned out to be Max's cousin and was said to be doing experiments on a fox terrier, Tobik, who bounced all around him at the dinner table. Misha behaved in a distinctly strange and paranoid fashion; and both he and Tobik limped. Among this unconventional company, Konchitta, Maria Papper, and Igor' Severianin seemed to fit right in.

All day Anastasiia watched as the three unusual guests behaved exactly as Marina had predicted. Papper read her very bad poetry aloud, and apparently only Konchitta, who had previously gesticulated a scene of wild jealousy over her beloved Max, was able to enjoy her nonsense. Although Konchitta, of course, could not understand a word of Russian, "she ceased to be angry and, laying her hands on her knees, listened to the incomprehensible with interest." Igor' Severianin, as it turned out, had no desire to read his poetry to this audience, but while Marina and Anastasiia recited Marina's poetry in unison that evening, he walked about nearby and "sniffed all the roses in turn, bending over each one." By the time Anastasiia went to sleep that evening, Marina had extracted from her the agreement that Severianin was "handsome, but stupid."[22]

The next morning Anastasiia woke up, marveled over the calm blue ocean and the Tatars selling baskets of fruit in the silvery distance, and went down to breakfast. To her consternation, "Konchitta," with whom she had had a long and merry conversation the previous evening in sign language, was sitting there at the breakfast table speaking in perfect Russian, addressing "Maria Papper" as Vera. Furthermore, she found Marina sitting together with "Igor' Severianin" on the terrace railing and addressing him by the intimate diminutive Serezhen'ka. Though Anastasiia had been gullible, she would not admit to it. Her mind racing, she pulled herself together and pretended that nothing out of the ordinary had happened at all. Listening carefully for the real names of these deceptive individuals, she turned over in her mind what was, for her, the heart of the matter: why had Marina tricked her into calling this young man, evidently of some personal importance to Marina, stupid?

Just who had originated this *mistifikatsiia* is never made clear. It was the Efron children, of course, who were playing all three roles, expressing their creative power of improvisation. But the charade was designed to deceive Marina's own sister, with Marina herself playing the impresario of this freak show, providing the introduction and the narrative that made it stick. While the charade resonated at several different levels, it may have done so most personally in the relationship between Marina and Anastasiia. Yet the underlying creative force probably came from Voloshin himself, or at least from the fertile context of his household and presence.

All three characters were caricatures of figures familiar in Moscow and Petersburg literary circles. The Spanish "Konchitta" bore a distinct resemblance to the legendary Spanish Catholic Cherubina de Gabriac. Like Cherubina, she was ethnically, culturally, and perhaps religiously exotic as well. Her inability to speak Russian increased her quality of alien charm, while it also enhanced the drama of her scene of jealousy. That scene in itself was a kind of mockery of the melodrama of passionate love that seemed to play itself out so often in Symbolist life. And her appreciation of Papper's bad poetry, though in theory she could understand not a word, was a send-up of those who wanted so much to appear in the know that they could fall prey to art that was not only incomprehensible but of poor quality as well.

"Maria Papper" represented the woman described at the beginning of chapter 3, whose bad poetry and naive importunities on prominent male poets and potential patrons had become the source of disdainful *anekdoty* that burned their way through the intelligentsia grapevine. We find in Marina Tsvetaeva's memoir of Voloshin that he had repeated these stories to her; quite likely, therefore, they had reached the others as well.[23] To some extent the Papper figure was a caricature of the many would-be literati who aspired to success and prestige in the literary scene to the point of lacking all sensitivity to the real reaction to their capering. Perhaps there was also a comment here on the fine line between good art and the incomprehensible in a literary scene of such eccentricity and extravagance.

There may have been as well a certain poignant fear underlying this humorous caricature among ambitious individuals all too sensitive to slight and deeply apprehensive of such a negative reception as Papper had received. As a female just beginning to make her way into literary life, Marina may have found this figure striking all too close to her own fears. Sergei Efron had his own literary ambitions (never to be realized) as well, while Voloshin himself knew a fair amount about the pain and humiliation of rejection by members of the modernist scene. The Papper figure was laden with more meaning, perhaps greater anxiety, than it might seem at first glance. No one wanted to be like her.

"Igor' Severianin," played by Sergei Efron, was another real person in the literary world—a poet known for his extreme costume and his precious self-presentation. Like "Konchitta," the false Igor' represented a carnivalesque imitation of Symbolist pretensions, of the physically distant, yet potent urban modernist culture to which some of this household circle perhaps aspired, and yet simultaneously resented. The self-absorbed Decadent air, the dandyesque attire, the apparent ignorance of his true ridiculous appearance, all mocked the lack of insight or self-awareness with which some in Symbolist circles played out their "theaters of life."

But Sergei Efron's role as Severianin was significant for another reason as well. Marina was falling in love with Efron, and she would soon marry him. By playing this trick on the sister with whom she had been very close since childhood, she was playing out a ceremonial—if not especially kind-hearted—ritual of transformation and separation. Certainly Anastasiia describes her experience of this charade as a kind of separation from her sister. She fretted: "Why did Marina need me to repeat that this Severianin was stupid? (That he *seemed* stupid.) I didn't actually think that, I had agreed with her only out of "gallantry," seeing that Marina wanted me to. Now it was impossible to change that, Marina would remember. Why had she *needed* this? Something had closed here." And a few lines later, recounting the way in which Marina had talked about Sergei and herself in the first person plural, she commented: "'We.' This meant that *my* 'we' with Marina was at an end."[24] It was a sad transformation for her, but one whose significance she immediately grasped and pondered.

Strong encouragement of the theatrical manipulation of identity, mask, and self through costume and role-playing in Voloshin's home was a central attraction of this household for its adolescent guests in 1911. It was an attraction that would serve to bind the group together not only through mutual contemplation and rejection of the prevalent literary culture far to the north of them but also through mutual and self-contemplation, revelation, and transformation, on the basis of reciprocal trust and communality. These costumes and charades both required and forged consensus, fostering the growth of personal familiarity as individuals aided one another in exposing a variety of selves, through semi-formal revelation of fantasies that might hold deeper truths, fears painful to acknowledge, transformations awkward to communicate and enforce. In these activities the Voloshin circle revealed its potency as an expression of communitas and also offered a vivid illumination of how theatrical communitas can work.

At least one other such *mistifikatsiia* took place in Koktebel' that summer: Leonid Fainberg reports on it (he was not a witness, however, but learned of it through Max) as having taken place early in May 1911.[25] In order to hint away a French merchant by the name of Jules who had fallen in love with Elizaveta Efron and hoped to marry her, Max and Elena Otto-bal'dovna pretended that Elizaveta was already married, indeed to Max himself. As they devised it, Max not only was her husband but was a magus as well, organizing "mystical dances" and "magical deeds." He told Jules that Elizaveta's brother and sister, Sergei and Vera, could walk on water as easily as on land, "although for the success of such an experiment help was needed—an especially reverential mood on the part of the audience" of

Maximilian Voloshin and the *Obormoty*, Koktebel', 1911.
Courtesy of Vladimir Kupchenko.

this marvelous deed. The household also pretended that a dolphin had swum in from the sea demanding to be milked and that his milk was to be used to heal the "tubercular" Sergei Efron. According to another memoirist, it was in this charade that Elena Ottobal'dovna acquired the name "Pra": part of the joke was that she was the matriarchal head (*pramater*) of this crazy family.[26] Here again we find the humorous treatment of some of the fondest and most fatuous beliefs of such Symbolists (or hangers-on) as Anna Rudolfovna Mintslova, and of the pseudo-mysticism that generally pervaded the Symbolist world as Max had experienced it.

Yet Voloshin apparently did not allow the sharp edge of the carnivalesque to impinge upon individual comfort, or at least that was Fainberg's perception. "Maybe it will seem to someone that there was something cruel in this 'deception.' This was not the case. In the end, this was a more humane form of refusal. It would have been far crueler to say simply: 'Leave immediately, you are at the wrong address.' I now understand that all of Max's *mistifikatsii* invariably came to a good end," wrote Fainberg in his memoir. Whether the object of deception would whole-heartedly have agreed with this sanguine analysis or not, Max seems indeed to have been careful about who participated, and who was the focus, in such charades. He did not force anyone whom he hoped to keep as a member of his community into an unsuitable role or a disconcerting intimacy. Neither of the Fainbergs took part in the trick on Anastasiia Tsvetaeva, for example, though both were present. The kind of playful consciousness that made it striking and apropos for the Tsvetaeva sisters and the Efrons to forge their relationships in this fashion was not for Leonid and Bella. Fainberg writes:

"As far as we new arrivals were concerned, we were not appropriate objects for such experiments. I was still a boy, and Bella . . . Max with his exceptional intuition sensed, from her face, that such things were impermissible. . . . She not infrequently blushed out of shyness, a trusting girl, defenseless. . . . In general, Max was consistently kind-hearted toward Bella, carefully friendly."[27]

Other forms of play that summer also contributed to the transformation of its guests, at least into unified members of the community if not always into radical new identities, and these were not always so mocking, so specifically reactive to the northern literary scene. Domestic poetry was one such activity. In honor of his name day party on May 16, 1911, Max put out a box for literary and artistic contributions—and then made the most substantial contribution himself. The seven celebratory poems he had written were all about the household and its doings. Leonid Fainberg managed to preserve six of these poems over decades until he wrote his memoir. One was about the Frenchman Jules and his vain pursuit of Elizaveta Efron, and concluded with the lines,

> All in honor of Jules they heap nonsense upon nonsense,
> Max and Vera creep into the sea in their clothes,
> Jules is silent and in torment twists his mustache.
>
> But in the middle of the night Lilia awakens Vera:
> "If I'm married, then why is he, as a Frenchman,
> still around? For adultery?"[28]

Two poems were in honor of the household dogs, Tobik and Gaidan; another, entitled "Morning," was about the early morning behavior of Max, Pra, and their sleepy guests; and a fourth, "Eurythmics," concerned a family lesson in this anthroposophist dance exercise on the sand before the stares of the household servants Andrei, Gavrila, and the cook Maria:

> Sergei is sceptical. Pra is stern. Lilia,
> unable to overcome natural modesty
> asks everyone: "Do I look all right?"
>
> And, tiring of her demonstration,
> Vera loses her hairpins. General laughter.
> The Pathfinder steals Vera's pamphlet.[29]

And, finally, there was a poem about Elena Ottobal'dovna, or Pra, which, according to Leonid, was recited by all in chorus after dinner on the day of his arrival:

Pra

I am Pra from Pray. My whole life is a battle.
Tirelessly, I look after the house,
Deafened by the ceaseless uproar,
I feed the herd of hungry beasts.

Fulminating all day, and frying, and boiling,
I boil myself in the well-known cauldron.
I split Marie's [the cook's] skull with a crowbar
And clean out the cobwebs lodged in there.

To cook borshch and set up the samovars
I, who have worn *sharovari* for thirty years,
To curse cooks! No! Thank you very much!

But when all are prostrate before Pra,
Throwing back my mane, proudly I smoke,
Knocking off the ashes against my russet boots.[30]

Thus we return again to the partnership between Max and his mother, to the maintenance of that delicate balance between host and hostess through playful reference to power and suffering, expressions of respect and appreciation as well as gentle teasing, and perhaps a gentle ventilation of the strains of balancing power between them. But in all these poems, Voloshin was helping to shape a new self-consciousness among his guests, a heightened awareness of themselves as members of a group with its own distinct practices and relations.

Building on the initial sense of group apartness created by the costumes that he and his mother wore (as would many of his guests in future years, as the next chapter will demonstrate), Voloshin also used storytelling and play in order to enhance the sense of group identity that was associated with the Koktebel' locality. He began a tradition of taking his guests on long walks through the nearby hills and telling them stories about what they saw along the way, arousing enthusiasm for the region first among the *Obormoty* and then among his later guests. One story that left a deep impression on Marina Tsvetaeva, at least, described the region, Cimmeria, as the legendary home of the woman-warrior Amazons. Later, during the devastation of the civil war, Voloshin would joke that, when all else had come to an end there, matriarchy would at last come into its own in the Crimea.

He also worked to become an increasingly skilled, if minor, painter of local landscapes, experimenting in watercolor with the ever-changing light and color of the sea and mountains. Both his paintings and his stories led to a later expansion of his own legend in association with the Koktebel' region, to the point that a tradition grew up (which he himself encouraged) that the three hills overlooking Koktebel' formed the image of his own profile, embedding his very person in the landscape. Some in this highly educated dacha colony argued that the profile was that of the nineteenth-century poet Pushkin, but the great stony beard settled the question for any partisan of the Voloshin household. Possession of his paintings, at any rate, is to this day evidence of identity with the Voloshin circle tradition; they are carefully preserved in a number of contemporary Moscow households, to be brought out on occasion with melancholy pride.

Voloshin might never fulfill the promise of becoming a second Pushkin, as his Theodosian high school admirers had predicted. Yet he had a gift for transforming the everyday into something larger than life and thereby enabling his young guests to re-create, to reconstitute, themselves at least temporarily if not always more permanently. In addition to encouraging such playful activity among them as charades and dressing in costumes, he also offered them respectful attention and space for their own more formal creativity, in the form of literary and artistic endeavor. He took an interest in Fainberg's drawing and Marina's poetry, held readings by Anastasiia and Marina of Marina's work, and engaged them in his own poetic efforts by holding readings of his own work.[31] For adolescents still uncertain of their own roles in the adult world, and yearning for a sense of their own importance in that world, his household became a place where they could safely, without hurting one another or themselves too badly, give concentrated attention to self-fashioning in many different ways. Voloshin took their experiments seriously; he facilitated them; and he endowed them with an aura of significance. Thus he created for them that sense of a luminary that both hung at a distance as something to be attained and infused their daily lives within the circle with inspiring and invigorating light. In so doing Voloshin elevated his household from a mere accumulation of domestic circumstances into an artfully and spiritually self-conscious community.

The establishment of this domestic community meant much to Voloshin, though he had his moments of doubt. The *Obormoty* were not, perhaps, his ideal circle associates—they were his equals neither in age or experience—nor was his mother the domestic partner he yearned for. Of this he was aware, and it bothered him. Several years later, told that a local girl of sixteen was "one of his most passionate devotees," he answered "with an unhappy smile, 'This is evidently my fate: to be loved by old women and fourteen-year-old girls.'"[32]

Naturally the girl was crushed, not least, perhaps, because he had gotten her age wrong.[33] But despite this lapse in spirits and courtesy, Voloshin had indeed succeeded in establishing a solid middle ground of authority somewhere between old women and adolescents. All jokes about matri-

Ink drawing of Koktebel' region by Maximilian Voloshin, 1921.
Courtesy of Vladimir Kupchenko.

archy aside, he lived in a society in which older men could play a decisive role in shaping their communities, and could also easily emerge as "bad fathers." But Voloshin did not abuse the strength of his position. By using his authority cautiously and playfully, and by taking women and children seriously, he had laid the foundations for his Koktebel' dacha circle.

FIVE

Insiders and Outsiders, Gossip and Mythology: From Communitas toward Network Node

As Voloshin's dacha circle became more and more of an institution over the next few years, the original sense of freshness and raw self-transformation so closely associated with the *Obormoty* is less evident in the sources. The spirit of communitas seemed to be fading away, and Voloshin's circle was beginning to demonstrate more of the characteristics of "structure," to use Victor Turner's term, manifesting elements of the Russian intellectual circle as a traditional intellectual and professional network node, a core for interaction and professional development.

This was professional development of a less concentrated sort from that pursued in the great urban centers of Imperial Russia; after all, the Koktebel' dacha was a vacation home, intended as a relief from the pressures of the center. And yet the Voloshin circle had or quickly developed certain resemblances to the domestically based circle as professional networking node that had existed among the educated elite since the middle of the previous century. For example, it offered internal forums for professional self-display such as semiformal domestic poetry readings, and also provided professional outlets in the community, as members of Voloshin's circle began to attend local public poetry readings, often as a group; and sometimes circle members became involved in other local intellectual endeavors as well. And, of course, it provided that seminal networking opportunity for its members to meet one another, to gain familiarity and trust under the circumstances of proximity over time, and to consolidate personal and professional ties that would endure through the winter, when participants returned to the fray in the North.[1] The familial dimensions of this domestically based circle were also strengthened, by the marriage between the *Obormoty* Sergei Efron and Marina Tsvetaeva.[2]

If Voloshin had in the summer of 1911 proven adept in spurring communitas in the early stages of the circle, he was now relying a bit more heavily on his networking skill. The gradual transformation of his circle into a more stable and traditional social formation was possible thanks to his ability to operate his circle as a network node and to his talent for providing the stimulation, opportunity, and harmony needed to keep the institution from falling apart. Some of the traditional hierarchies of network life that have been illuminated in previous chapters were being consolidated, such as the primacy of Voloshin as circle leader and the secondary but prominent role of Elena Ottobal'dovna as his female partner in hospitality. His own mentees, particularly Marina Tsvetaeva, had a heightened status as well. But because of the recent origins of this circle in resistance to power and hierarchy, perhaps, and certainly also because of Voloshin's careful attention to the matter, relative courtesy, kindness, and protection of the weak remained an important theme.

Despite a gradual move in the direction of "structure," however, the themes of theatricality, costume, mythmaking, and storytelling did not vanish. As noted in the previous chapter, a number of playful activities continued. But their implications and impact were no longer so sharply intimate or so intensely focused on individual transformation. This was because a new purpose was emerging for such activities. No longer fully expressing the spirit of communitas, they now more nearly served the purpose of consolidating the community by determining both its internal relations and its boundaries and relations with the outside world. In other words, they were now helping to determine who was in and who was out. That costume, theatricality, and other forms of communitas-style play came to assume a role in determining the structural boundaries of Voloshin's circle was in part owing to the way they fed into the oral gossip tradition of the intellectual networks in late Imperial Russia, as the Cherubina episode has already revealed. Theatricality and costume made for wonderful little stories—the *anekdoty* described in the introduction to this book—to pass along; and membership in the circle could be determined by one's access to, as well as attitude toward, such gossipy tales.

Looking back over time, it is possible for the historian to see the outlines of a growing tradition of intelligentsia *anekdoty* about the circle, many of them about theatrical behavior, reflected in the memoirs that have been left behind. And at the core of this muscular oral tradition were the *Obormoty*, who reappear again and again in these tales, even as it becomes increasingly unclear just who was to be listed among them. For perpetuated in these tales was the legend of the original transformative communitas that lay at the heart of Voloshin's community, even as it became a more conventional institution.

By 1913 the circle began to grow rapidly. A few of Voloshin's older, adult friends had been coming all along, such as the writer Alexei Tolstoi and his family, visiting every summer since 1909. Another older guest was his "disciple," Adelaida Gertsyk, with her sister, Evgeniia. Soon other writers, painters, and sundry professionals also began to arrive. Voloshin, in addition, was also developing ties with some of the local intelligentsia who lived in the Crimea year-round, particularly with the well-known Crimean painters Kandaurov and Bogaevskii (the artist whose Crimean landscape paintings had so stirred Voloshin in Petersburg in 1907). These men, too, began to frequent the Voloshin household, not to live there but for chats in the evening or to meet other guests. Voloshin was expanding his local network as well as strengthening his ties with his urban guests from the North.

In 1913 the physical premises of the household were enlarged by the addition of a number of rooms to the larger house, including an expanded studio for Voloshin and a tower with a balcony on the top of the house. Many more guests, both paying lodgers (who continued to provide significant material support for the household) and friends, could be taken in. With the mingling of growing numbers of old and new friends and boarders, the question of insiders and outsiders in the Voloshin household was becoming ever more complex.

There were many different routes to becoming an insider. A personal invitation from Max to spend the summer, or part of it, in his home was, of course, the quickest. But one could also attain insider status through the lodging relationship, for example. Ordinary lodgers in the Voloshin household, those who had not been invited, were unquestionably outsiders, at least at first. The artist Iuliia Obolenskaia arrived as a lodger of this sort in May 1913: "We were met by Elena Ottobal'dovna Voloshina, in morocco leather boots, in *sharovari*, with a gray mane of hair, an aquiline profile, and a penetrating gaze: 'The rooms are bad,' she announced curtly, 'there are no conveniences. The beds are no good. There's nothing good. But you can look for yourselves. You can stay or leave as you please.' We stayed."[3]

In the first few days Obolenskaia had only one personal encounter with a member of the household: Max found a book of hers lying on the balcony and took it away, thinking that the *Obormoty*, at that time in residence, had carried it off from his beloved library. This brought about a brief conversation when she went to him to get it back, but nothing came of the encounter. Finally, it was the local artist Kandaurov who, while visiting Max, made friends with her and urged Max to take a look at her poetry and her lampoons of Koktebel' life. The ice was broken: "Then I was given an exam by Elena Ottobal'dovna. Then by all the young people. As a result I was numbered among the honorable 'Order of the *Obormoty*.'"[4] She went on

Osip Mandelshtam,
1909.
*Courtesy of Vladimir
Kupchenko.*

walks with her new friends, took part in household poetry readings, and was
generally accepted into the group. There continued to be a slight sense of
discomfort, of jockeying for a position of closeness to Max as head of the
household that is not uncommon in Koktebel' memoirs. But Obolenskaia
eventually became a close and consistent conversational partner with Max,
developing a relationship that would last for a number of summers.

Another individual to arrive as a lodger was Osip Mandelshtam, as much
a defining figure of twentieth-century Russian poetry as Tsvetaeva. Mandelshtam became an insider by virtue of his poetry, which Voloshin greatly
admired. But it was not an easy path: Mandelshtam was a person ill-formed,
in a way, for Russian communal life, one who apparently had certain difficulties in adapting to the exigencies of successful network relations.

His first recorded appearance in Voloshin's life was at an intelligentsia
home in Petersburg, where Voloshin, according to his own report, pro-

nounced: "There grows the future Briusov."[5] Mandelshtam's first attempt to make serious contact with Voloshin was late in 1909, in a letter from the German city of Heidelberg that was a classic appeal for fatherly poetic patronage: "Deeply respected Maximilian Aleksandrovich! Cut off from the element of the Russian language — more so than is usually the case — I am compelled to form a clear judgment of myself. Those who refuse to give me their attention only help me in this. I was helped in this way by Merezhkovskii, who, recently passing through Heidelberg, did not wish to listen to a single line of my poems, and also by Viacheslav Ivanov, who, despite sincere good feeling toward me, has never answered the letter he asked of me. I have only just met you. But for some reason I hope that your participation in my difficult work will be a little bit different. If you wish to make me happy with your opinion and advice, my address is [etc.]."[6] The tone of this approach did not appeal to Voloshin, and he never answered the letter. But of the five poems that Mandelshtam sent him, four were later, in mid-1910, published in *Apollon*. This was Mandelshtam's debut and, from that point on, his reputation and success as a poet began to climb.

He arrived at Voloshin's Koktebel' dacha in the summer of 1915, twenty-four years old and his literary reputation already well established. Other guests that summer included the Tsvetaeva sisters, the poet Sofia Parnok, and Sofia's sister. During the summer of 1915 Mandelshtam produced varied impressions on the other guests and on Pra (Voloshin was in France then). Mandelshtam was acknowledged to have intelligence and humor, but he also caused annoyance through his self-importance and social awkwardness. Pra became particularly irate when he left books from Voloshin's ever controversial library lying around.

Sofia Parnok and Marina Tsvetaeva formed their own subgroup in the household that summer: though Tsvetaeva was still married to Sergei Efron, she and Parnok had been lovers since the previous fall. Parnok apparently did not like Mandelshtam at all. Perhaps an element of competition was involved, for this summer the Voloshin household was to serve as a locus for yet another turn in Marina's romantic alliance building. In the spring of 1916, after the dissolution of her relationship with Parnok, she would enter into a love affair with Mandelshtam. When he returned to the Voloshin household in the summer of 1916, Mandelshtam was a solid member of the household. His poetic gift contributed greatly to his acceptance there (as well as to the later prestige of the circle). Yet he was not always welcome among other guests in the household; as will be shown further on, he became an object of complaints and jokes among some of them. Or perhaps it was affectionate teasing? It is hard to tell at times.

Vladimir Khodasevich,
1913.
*Courtesy of Vladimir
Kupchenko.*

Then there were those insiders who had not really wanted to be inside, such as the poet Vladimir Khodasevich. Khodasevich's creative work in the early years of the century did little to draw him into any of the more ideologically inclined modernist circles; he affiliated himself with a classical literary tradition in the vein of Pushkin.[7] In life, as in his work, Khodasevich was something of a loner, not inclined to attach himself to a crowd—as becomes evident in his letters to his wife in 1916, when he spent the summer in Koktebel'.

Arriving in Koktebel' at the beginning of June 1916, Khodasevich wrote to his wife to let her know that he had arrived "living and healthy"; the weather was fine, not too hot, and he had just missed some rain. He had found a room (not in the Voloshin household) and settled in. On June 7 he sent her a detailed account of how he had spent the previous day and a description of his adventures with some of his fellow vacationers. Late in the afternoon he had had a visitor: a schoolteacher with whom he had shared a train compartment on the trip south. Since he liked the man, they went out together to the beach and sat down there. "Now a misfortune occurred: from behind a little hill, four cows with terrible . . . horns came bearing down on us as we sat, but then, even worse: Mandelshtam! With him after me, I ran 100 thousand meters [*sic*] up a rock face. He did the same. I cast myself into the sea, but he caught me among the waves. I was polite but exceptionally dry. He is living at Voloshin's. That horror I haven't met up with yet. But I have no fear. I will . . . make it known that I *love solitude*. Devil take it, I'm no bohemian."[8]

Despite his distaste at the thought of Voloshin and his bohemian household, Khodasevich found it difficult to evade them. Apparently, in response to one of a series of questions from his wife, he soon wrote again to explain: "Max lives here *avec sa mère*, Mandelshtam, and the artist Shevarshidze. I see little of them. I was at Max's yesterday, I sat for an hour." Khodasevich's opinion of Osip Mandelshtam did not improve during this visit ("Mandelshtam is stormy: Sofia Iakovlevna [Parnok] is right. Simply stupid, without any distinguishing features"), but his resistance was breaking down. Soon thereafter he wrote: "Everything has turned out happily for me. On the 6th [of July] I move to the Voloshins', where for the same amount of money I will have a *quiet* room with a private terrace. I will not be harassed, as I told Max." And a quiet room he got, and apparently little harassment, at least at first; on July 7 he wrote, "I moved to the Voloshins'. Everything is very nice. I have my own terrace; it will be good to lie on it." His main problem there seemed to be that, although he did not smoke much himself, Mandelshtam cadged his cigarettes and "enveloped [him] in smoke."[9]

From this point on, Khodasevich was quickly drawn into the local intelligentsia life to which Voloshin gave his better-known guests access — and to which he gave access to his better-known guests, in the sense of urging them to perform in public and to make themselves generally available to the public. On July 16 Khodasevich wrote: "I'm famous here. They write about my arrivals and departures in the newspaper." And on the 26th: "Yesterday they again took me to Theodosia to read at a concert. I didn't feel like it, but I had to. I was a great success. I won't go again for anything. It bores me to tears." Nevertheless, though he hated the poetry readings, he made a number of artistic and literary friends in the region, no doubt partly because of the introduction Voloshin was able to give him. Whether he willed it or not, Khodasevich had become a member of the Voloshin household circle.[10]

Let us now turn to the question of outsiders who remained outsiders, that is, to relations between the Voloshin household and the rest of the dacha colony of Koktebel'. Voloshin's household is described repeatedly by his memoirist-adherents as the focal point of cultural life in Koktebel'. A kind of meeting ground between circle members and the other citizens of

Diamond Café (Kafe "Bubny"), 1912–1913.
Courtesy of Vladimir Kupchenko.

Koktebel' was to be found at a local restaurant known as the "Diamond Café," where concerts, dance performances, and readings were held in which many members of the Voloshin household participated extensively. Here, where insiders and outsiders came face to face, the boundaries became apparent. Graffiti and caricatures on the walls of the Diamond Café in 1916 provide a glimpse into Max's image in this broader community: "Drawn right at the doors [to the café] was a fat disheveled person in an orange tunic, along with two poetic inscriptions: 'Fat, slovenly, and rumpled Max Kirienko-Voloshin,' 'Awful Max—he is an enemy of the people, he is expelled, nature gasped.' On the other side of the door was another fat, very important person: 'Enter, halt! Behold Count Alexei Tolstoi!'" Next to the caricature of Voloshin was a "little person in a bowler, a black suit with a stand-up collar, a propped-up, foolish face with a mustache. The inscription: 'A normal *dachnik*, a friend of nature. Be embarrassed, naked monsters!'"[11] Who drew these caricatures and made up the inscriptions remains a mystery: whether it was the work of an insider or an outsider, tension between the circle and the community, however humorously expressed, is evident.

The tale of an excursion to the Diamond Café by the Voloshin circle for a poetry reading one evening in the summer of 1916 helps to delineate circle relations with the outside world. It began, according to Elizaveta

Krivoshapkina, with a great feast of grapes, smoked mutton, sheep's-milk cheese, and Crimean bread on the Voloshin terrace for all members of the household: "By the time we gathered to walk to the 'Diamond,' Koktebel' was already sinking into deep blue. Dusk came early; the summer was coming to an end. Khodasevich, having stumbled against a rock, is seized and supported under both arms. In the dark it can be heard how he laughs and says that if he falls, then he won't stand up and read his poetry." They walked on in a little group through the dusk. "Two shadows alongside discussed, in low voices, how to change one line in the Koktebel' 'Crocodile.'[12] Mandelshtam had taken offense at the lines 'She appeared at the "Diamond." / Intelligent people were sitting there, / But then she also ran into Mandelshtam.' Someone among those accompanying us proposed the change: 'To the sound of many trumpets . . .'"[13] Soon the group arrived at its destination. "The windows of the 'Diamond' glowed yellow. There were many people. A platform had been built on top of the tables, which had been moved together, and it was lit by two kerosene lamps."[14]

Khodasevich read first, but to no very great effect; Mandelshtam was received with greater appreciation. Then Marina and Anastasiia Tsvetaeva recited Marina's poetry in unison. After them came Voloshin: "For those who had gathered here, mostly 'normal *dachniki*,' it was necessary to read about love. And when he concluded with the lines, 'Love him precisely and truly, / Love him to the very heart,' he was applauded loud and long. From behind us, a malicious snigger and the words: 'Max dragged some applause out of them.'"[15] Some ballerinas performed as well as some singers, and the evening was finished off with the song "The Crocodile," a parody of a contemporary popular ditty about the meanderings of a hungry crocodile. The parody referred, one by one, to the more prominent citizens of the Koktebel' colony that summer. We have already noted the reference to Mandelshtam; Khodasevich was included as well ("Khodasevich appeared, / Prince of the overseas, / But she didn't Eat any part of him"), and so were Max and Pra ("Maximilian Voloshin took fright / And he, and Pra, / Didn't sleep all night"). Some of the Koktebel' citizens, we are told, took "The Crocodile" seriously as they sang it, and others not so seriously.[16]

Against the background of the Diamond Café we catch a glimpse of Max's role and the role and image of his circle in the community. In encouraging and arranging for his guests to make their talents accessible, Max was advertising his circle as a valuable contributor to Koktebel' society; in his own reading, he gave his audience, at least on this occasion, exactly what it wanted to hear—love poetry. But there was clearly a degree of irritation on both sides. The bohemian, provocative behavior and costumes of Max and his guests created a distinct group image, and set clear boundaries between the circle and the broader community. Those boundaries were strengthened by public acknowledgment (in the graffiti, for example) that Voloshin's crowd defined itself in part through its aloofness from that community.

As suggested above, the boundaries between insiders and outsiders were reinforced by a growing oral tradition of circle identity.[17] This tradition found its beginnings in group identification with the 1911 group of adolescents, the *Obormoty*. Although the original *Obormoty* were no longer the only or even the main summer guests as the century entered the teens, and some of them were no longer even coming, their name nevertheless persisted and began to refer to an ever larger group. Writing of her stay (at first only as a summer lodger) with the Voloshins in 1913, artist Iuliia Obolenskaia tells us that during her time there, "the old friends the '*Obormoty*' arrived: the Efrons, the Fel'dshteins, the Tsvetaevas, Maia Kiuvile."[18] As we know, neither the Fel'dshteins (an artist and her lawyer husband) nor Maia Kiuvile (the pen name of poet and translator Maria Kudasheva, at the time married to a Russian aristocrat but who would later marry the French author and Soviet supporter Romain Rolland) were of the original group: the membership of the *Obormoty* was evidently beginning to expand, at least as recorded by new members of the household.

In 1914 another young girl arrived at Voloshin's door: Elizaveta Krivoshapkina, whose uncle, Rudolf Redlikh, a photographer, lived in Theodosia and, as a friend of Kandaurov and Bogaevskii, was part of Voloshin's local network. One day that summer she drove with a family member to the Voloshin house and was impressed by its many rooms: "These rooms were inhabited by the merry tribe the '*Obormoty*': artists, poets, and a few people of other professions. They all wore little clothing: they were barefoot or wore *chuviaki* [the native sandals] on their bare feet; the women in *sharovari* [Turkish trousers] and with uncovered heads, shocking the 'normal *dachniki*.' They had their own hymn, which began with the words: Fall in, company, *obormoty*, / In honor of our ruler Pra . . ."[19] The military overtones of this "hymn" are something of a surprise (the influence of World War I?), but through Krivoshapkina's eyes we see, in 1914, a firm group identity with strong traditions of behavior, of theatricality and costumery, and of *Obormoty* gratitude toward Pra. We also see hints of the tension between the Voloshin household and other members of the Koktebel' dacha colony.

Another reference to the *Obormoty* may be found in the memoirs of Vikentii Veresaev, a man who was to play an important role in Maximilian Voloshin's life during the civil war, and who would become a member of Voloshin's circle when it was revived thereafter. Veresaev did not come to live in Koktebel' until the fall of 1918, when many of the Russian intelligentsia began to arrive in the Crimea as they fled the dangers and privations of the civil war in the North, yet somehow he seems in his memoir to know a great deal about the earlier history of Voloshin's house: "A whole company of talented young people and admirers from far and near grouped themselves around [Voloshin]. They called themselves the '*Obormoty*.' . . . Voloshin's mother bore the '*Obormot*' sobriquet 'Pra.' This was a lean, masculine woman. She went about with her hair cropped, in *sharovari* and boots, and smoked. The girls in this company of '*Obormoty*' went around in fantastic costumes, reminiscent of Greek [dress], and did rhythmic dances and exercises in the evenings. Sometimes ceremonial processions into the hills would be organized to worship the rising sun, in which Voloshin played the role of pagan priest, raising up his arms to God—the sun. Those visitors who took active part in this '*Obormot*' company included A. Tolstoi, the artist Mitulov, and others."[20] By now we have *Obormoty* (Tolstoi and Mitulov) entirely removed from the original adolescent circle, still identified and unified by theatrical behavior.

But the first question to be asked is how Veresaev, who was not himself present at the time, knew so much about Voloshin's prerevolutionary circle. His description echoes several different stories: those of Pra and her costume and smoking habits, the girls' costumes, the "rhythmic" exercises. Yet he could not have been an immediate witness to all that he described. And while both Obolenskaia and Krivoshapkina were actual witnesses of what they report, their reports, too, indicate knowledge beyond what they actually detail. We do not learn how they knew that these were the *Obormoty*, whether Krivoshapkina ever actually saw them line up and sing their military-sounding "hymn," or whether this was just a story she had heard, for example, any more than we know precisely how Veresaev learned so many specifics about the prerevolutionary circle.

A close reading of the memoirs about Voloshin's prerevolutionary circle reveals a number of such mirrored images and even repeated language. For example, twice we have seen Voloshin described as a "pagan priest"—once by Leonid Fainberg, who describes him as having the appearance of such a priest, and once by Veresaev, who describes an activity in which Voloshin actually played the role of a pagan priest. Another recurrent description is of Voloshin as Zeus. Pra is repeatedly described in terms of her *sharovari*, her boots, her hair, and her smoking. And, of course, the *Obormoty* come up again and again, even if their membership has changed: a happily unified community of artistically talented "admirers" of Max who engage in a variety of entertaining bohemian activities.

In these tales we find a complex mythology carried forward by means of the intelligentsia oral tradition of storytelling, and then ensconced in the memoir literature. Oral *anekdoty* about the theatrical doings of the original *Obormoty*—the charades, the poetry, the dances, and the walks in the hills—must have been passed on and around in such an appealing way that, even as the original members themselves began to vanish, newcomers were ready and eager to carry on the tradition. The legend and tradition of the *Obormoty* and their feats formed the heart of the Voloshin circle; later circle participants built upon it as a means of achieving group identity and unity. In all, the emergent insider mythology of the Voloshin circle shows the gossipy discourse of the Russian intelligentsia at its most compelling and creative, as it contributed to the forging of a communal identity and to the shaping of a community around a core legend of the original members of theatrical communitas.

What was Voloshin's role in all this? That he was a master in exploiting the mythmaking potential of the *anekdot* is evident from Tsvetaeva's memoir about him. Analyzing his talent for endowing the ordinary and the everyday with legendary proportions, she wrote: "Max would tell stories about events the way a people tells them, and he would tell about individuals the same way as about whole peoples. The exactness of his description was always beyond doubt for me, as the exactness of every epos is beyond doubt. Achilles cannot be other than what he is, otherwise he is not Achilles. . . . Mystery-making, on certain lips, is already the beginning of truth, and when it grows into mythmaking, it is—the whole truth."[21] This description points to Voloshin's significant talent for manipulating the core myths of his culture, and for building and advertising community by appealing to the needs and fantasies of his fellows. It seems more than likely that Voloshin made use of this skill to advertise himself and his circle in the name of the *Obormoty*, in order to maintain the intensity of the communal glow he had first lit in 1911 through his support and manipulation of domestic artistry and theatricality. There is certainly evidence that Max was the source of at least some of the stories that contributed to circle identity, stories about the *Obormoty* and also the story of Cherubina de Gabriak, that founding myth of Voloshin's anti-structural confrontation with modernist hierarchy.[22] But however they began, revealed in these stories as they were passed along orally and then made their way into the written memoir tradition is the spirit, if not the reality, of intimate, transformative theatrical communitas at the heart of the Koktebel' circle. Through them, those who looked back upon Voloshin's prerevolutionary circle in later years would continue to shape its identity and boundaries even long after the circle itself had ceased to exist.

SIX

Voloshin Carves Power out of Fear

SETTING A NEW SCENE

As Voloshin's circle plunged with the rest of Russia into years of war—World War I, the Revolution, and the Civil War, with the latter having the greatest impact on the Crimea—every fragment of playfulness would be ripped away from the circle like leaves from a vine, and the twining stems thus exposed would demonstrate the toughness, the bitter vitality, of intelligentsia network relations under pressure. Fear and hunger, illness and loss, would gradually eliminate every extraneous quality of Voloshin's social network; these agonies would force a return to structure and tradition, and, for the time being, would render communitas, whether myth or reality, irrelevant.

Similarly, the qualities that had made Voloshin an instigator and leader of communitas would dwindle in value both to himself and his associates, while his skills in gaining social and economic support through interpersonal relations would come to the fore. He had quietly nurtured these more traditional, pragmatic skills over a long period. They had first been called forth by his childhood and young adult experiences of domestic networking, as well as networking with the state (for example, to facilitate his journey to Tashkent), and were, of necessity, kept in modest tune during his years as a social leader responsible for the material and organizational foundations of his circle. Now, under new and rapidly changing circumstances, he had to hone these skills and press them toward new creative limits and new purposes. They became the tools of resistance not to literary lions but to the threat of physical destruction to himself and his associates. In exercising these skills Voloshin did far more than survive, however: by the early years of Soviet control he had, through his networking activities, carved out a new locus of personal power both regionally and with the expanding government in the North. This new locus would form the basis for reviving his household summer circle, though under greatly altered terms.

He was able to accomplish this because of the ways in which power was being transmuted and redistributed throughout the region and, indeed, the country as a whole. Voloshin was quicker than some to perceive this transition and its implications, as he sought to keep his footing. What he needed, first of all, was protection from immediate physical danger; next he needed food and then shelter, as will be described in this and the following chapter (which may be read as a single narrative and analytical unit). And the place to turn for these needs was a series of bureaucracies. Initially these were primarily the military organs of both the Whites and the Reds, for whom military control included power over life and death, movement, and access to many essential goods and services. Then, as the Reds achieved ever more extensive victory, they began to establish new civilian institutions for tightening their grip on national resources as well as for the sake of political, economic, and social transformation. Those new Red institutions of the greatest importance to Voloshin were the bureaucracies controlling intellectual life and activity, built with great rapidity upon the preceding Red military organs, and backed by their might.

It soon became apparent that an important way to gain access to the kinds of power held by these bureaucracies was through personal appeal to their personnel: either by revitalizing preexisting personal ties with them or forming new ties by means of the dyadic encounter. This worked because those in power, the representatives of both military and civilian might, were highly susceptible to such appeals. At first few and far between, uncertain whom to trust and whom to provide with the newly won and tenuously held fruits of power, many of the new power holders seem to have been particularly ready, even eager, to act upon such individual appeals. Personal ties offered a certain assurance, represented a certain familiarity, in a chaotic situation; they were certainly a long and familiar tradition of Russian bureaucracy.[1] This is why Voloshin's long-nurtured networking skills were now of particular value: as it turned out, he was peculiarly capable of operating at this nexus of personal and bureaucratic associations.

This nexus had historical implications well beyond Voloshin's tale. Viewing it from below, from the perspective of such individuals as Voloshin, we can glimpse a broader picture of the growing entanglement of personal associations rapidly permeating these proliferating bureaucratic institutions. It may well be that this infiltration began at the very time those institutions were forming, a possibility that offers a new perspective on a long-standing historical debate, namely, whether the origins of the "Soviet system" lie in the years of the civil war, as the Bolsheviks established control over national resources and over the population through War Communism, or whether that system is rather an expression and product of Stalinism. My research for this book supports the argument that the origin of at least one aspect of the Soviet system lies in the civil war period, for it reveals the continuity not only of bureaucratic control but also of a system of personal ties and networks underlying that control. Indeed, my focus from below exposes continuity in the experience of bureaucracy and personal ties for those who sought to survive those years not just from War Communism but also from White military control.[2]

It was, in any case, at this volatile intersection between unstable but proliferating bureaucracy, and the spreading tentacles of personal association, that Voloshin was able to carve out his locus of power over the next few years. There was a great deal of fluidity at this intersection, and much that could be accomplished if one had the will to do so. There were friends to rally, bureaucrats to influence, and institutions to establish. Given his talents, and a fundamental willingness to engage with those who had control over his destiny, Voloshin found room not only to maneuver but gradually to gain access to bureaucratically controlled advantages of various sorts for himself and for his associates, who ultimately came to depend on him for those advantages. Eventually the institution that he would establish would be a reconstitution of his circle, resting still on the domestic base of his home, but now in its final form as a state entity. He became a state-based patron of those who participated in this institution, and they became his clients—a form of association that would seem as alien to the I-Thou relationships of communitas as can be imagined.

Voloshin was by no means the only individual to build up such a locus of power and, in the literary scene, far from the most prominent or powerful. The final section of the next chapter describes some of the others from the literary world who took a similar course, from such relatively minor figures as Mikhail Gershenzon to individuals like Maxim Gorky and Anatoly Lunacharsky, who would have far greater impact on the fate of writers under Soviet power. For a broad pattern can be found in the activities of such men, and this pattern had real implications for the course of events and, above all, for the future association between the Soviet literary intelligentsia and the Soviet state. Such figures, or loci of power, would encourage the formation and integration of whole networks of economic dependents into the emerging Soviet system. Thus they would eventually bind the intelligentsia to the Soviet state through welfare and privilege during the 1920s as effectively as any threat of physical harm could do. This was by no means the purpose of many or perhaps even most of those who engaged in these activities, but it was an outcome with its own tenacious historical logic, as argued in this chapter and the next.

Voloshin's experiences during the civil war and the early Soviet period illustrate why certain people chose to act as they did. It made a great deal of cultural and practical sense, to individuals such as Voloshin, to build up these networks of patronage and to provide their members with access to resources and other kinds of support to the best of their ability. For Voloshin, it was simply a day-to-day matter of taking the kind of responsibility for his associates that had already been a part of his prerevolutionary identity as a mentor figure and social leader among the literary intelligentsia. The immediate stresses of the time were too urgent to allow any gazing into crystal balls, had that even been possible.

Taking on this leadership role actually required considerable courage on Voloshin's part, especially in the face of military threat, as well as a degree of chutzpah and a kind of detachment from the often explosive partisanship of the time. It could be that, at the heart of Voloshin's particular achievement of power under these circumstances, was his seemingly iron composure. This quality had already been noted by thoughtful observers of his life from his childhood, through his early peacemaking years among the Symbolists, and into his years as a circle leader. In the civil war period it would facilitate his networking activities with both (or even several) sides of a bitter and violent conflict, accommodating the Reds while still retaining the support of the Whites, and then ingratiating himself with Soviet power. This personal neutrality is first seen in his reaction to World War I.

The final and in many ways peak years of the prerevolutionary Voloshin circle—1914 to 1916—had a quality, exaggerated perhaps in retrospect, of hallowed remoteness from the storm. But this was an illusion, as none knew better than Voloshin himself, for he was in Western Europe from the beginning of July 1914 to the end of March 1916. There he had the opportunity to evaluate the situation from the start. If throughout the European continent there was a rush among intellectuals toward war, a fervent sense of its possibilities for purification and reaffirmation of raison d'être and community,[3] Voloshin belonged to that small minority of European intellectuals who were quickly repelled by the war fever and stood aside helplessly. "I believe in neither the liberating nor the purifying sense of the war," he wrote his mother in 1915. "It is neither a national war nor a war of liberation."[4]

Having left Russia and traveled through Germany and Austria to Switzerland in July 1914, Voloshin arrived to settle in the Swiss town of Dornach just as the European alliance system triggered declarations of war on every hand. Dornach, where he would stay until January 1915, was the center of the Anthroposophist movement; here he met up with Margarita Sabashnikova (now a dedicated anthroposophist) and participated in a variety of the movement's activities. In Dornach, too, he met a great many German followers of the movement and was heavily exposed to their sentiments in these early days of the war. This exposure left its mark on him. Arriving in Paris at the beginning of 1915, he wrote to his mother: "I have been in Paris already for a week. And even though Paris hourly is expecting zeppelin attacks these days, after Dornach I am experiencing a deep calming and tranquility of the spirit. Because that unbearable contradiction, which was born there of the close proximity of the German world, is now gone."

A rising swell of contradictory propaganda and rumor was rapidly dividing European from European that autumn, even Europeans with the closest of intellectual bonds. The question for Voloshin was whom to believe. After his intense exposure to the German perspective in Dornach, he made a concentrated effort in France to determine the Allied point of view. "As far as the German atrocities are concerned, I have at last found documents here [in France] that I can believe and with which I can repudiate the denials of the Germans themselves," he went on in his letter to his mother. "This makes it all the more tragic for me to consider that absolute trust in and solidarity with Prussia that all Germans *without exception* now feel. As far as the *origins* of the war are concerned, every German to the last man is convinced that Russia took military action before the declaration of war, and that Prussia was occupied by Russian military forces without a declaration of war. I am personally inclined to believe the version of the Allies but must confess that this is only an emotional trust, because, of course, in all yellow, white, red . . .[5] books published up to this time there has been much omitted."[6]

The problem of whom to believe continued to nag at Voloshin as the war progressed; the inflammatory half-truths of wartime left him bewildered and disgusted. Sometime during the first half of 1915, he wrote a poem entitled "Morning Newspapers," which began:

> With a greedy glance I race
> Through the letters of inflammable news,
> So that the soul moist with dreams
> Burns with creeping poison from morning.

The poem continued with a bitter condemnation of the "lie" that "clouds over the brain / With the viscous drowsiness of chloroform."[7] Max's mother took considerable exception to this poem, and so she apparently told him in a letter she wrote him in Biarritz in June 1915. To her it seemed traitorous, especially (Max believed) the final lines of the poem: "Oh, let us not cease to love our enemy / Or begin to hate our brother." In August (the mail was taking six weeks from Russia to France), he shot back: "No doubt you believe absolutely in that 'half-truth' created by the newspapers, that official tactical truth which is needed to support the spirit. Unfortunately I cannot believe in it at all. This conditional truth is the worst thing about the war." Allying himself with one of the more vocal cynics about the war, he added: "'Que messieujs les assassiuj commeucent [sic],' the defenders of the death penalty say to their opponents. Bernard Shaw cleverly reversed this phrase in the following way: 'let the murderers begin, and we will continue (to execute, that is).' It's the same with the war. The Germans began it, the rest continue, and imitate them."[8]

He was relatively immune to hatred of the "Hun": "I am against the Germans. But casting off all the conditional truths of this year, I don't see how the French are morally superior to the Germans (not taking specifics and individual victims into consideration)." His characteristic inclination to see all sides of a dispute, invaluable during his years as a "peacemaker" among the Symbolists and in his own household, here, too, rushed to the fore. "I understand your indignation," he went on, "but I don't understand why you accuse me of being a Judas when it would be natural to think: obviously everything is not so simple and clear, there are other points of view, other ideas about what is going on."[9]

Voloshin left Paris in March 1916 and returned to Russia via London, Bergen, Torneo, and Beloostrov. In Russia he passed through Petersburg and Moscow to arrive in Koktebel' at the end of April.[10] As we know, he spent the summer of 1916 in Koktebel' participating in household and local literary and artistic activities. He sought and obtained exemption from the draft on medical grounds in the fall. In December he and Elena Ottobal'dovna traveled to Moscow for the winter and thus experienced the February Revolution of 1917 in that city. This would be his last trip to the North until early in the period of the New Economic Policy (NEP). At the end of April the two returned to Koktebel', where the last peaceful summer and fall in Koktebel' witnessed the arrival of an enormous number of prominent Russian literati, from Tsvetaeva and Khodasevich to Ilya Ehrenburg and Maxim Gorky—though not all of them stayed in Voloshin's household.[11] The relative calm of the early months of the Russian Revolution in the Crimea, which had only a modest working class and a comparatively wealthy peasantry, helps to explain this mass influx.[12] In late October in Koktebel' Voloshin, like the rest of the country, learned of the Bolshevik coup; the civil war was imminent.

Some background to the story of the civil war in the Crimea is needed here in order to provide the historical context of Voloshin's survival. Rising nationalism among the Crimean Tatars, who first demanded autonomy and later restoration of the Crimea to Muslim Turkey, soon broke the relative peace in the Crimea.[13] The Tatars were overcome by the end of January 1918 by the Bolsheviks, who had the support of the Russian sailors of the Black Sea fleet that was anchored in Sevastopol. Theodosia, the nearest sizable town to Koktebel', was taken over by the Bolsheviks on January 2. But Bolshevik rule was also short-lived; the Germans arrived in April and the Crimea came under the control of General S. Sul'kevich, a Lithuanian who, as it became evident that the Germans were losing the world war, turned to White General Denikin for support but had to withdraw with the Germans by November 1918.

Denikin's reason for denying support to Sul'kevich was, in part, because a group of Russian liberals, members of the Crimean Kadet Party, was preparing to take control of the peninsula. With Denikin's support they did so in November. The Kadets attempted to rule on democratic principles, observing civil liberties and the rule of law, urging the strengthening of local self-government, and permitting the Tatars to continue their organizational and publishing activities. But their government was destined to fail largely because their liberal principles and their reputation for upholding those principles were effectively compromised by the military force on whom they were forced to depend for protection—the White Volunteers.

The Volunteers began to recruit a military force in the Crimea in November 1918. Drawing on the presence in that region of a large number of White refugees from the North, including many tsarist military officers, the Volunteers quickly swelled their ranks to four thousand to five thousand men. But independent of the Kadet government, they felt little compulsion to obey its precepts. Impressing themselves on the Crimean population with violence and atrocities, they rapidly earned such a terrifying reputation that a rumor toward the end of January 1919 that they would be quartered in Simferopol' caused a panic in that city.

As Bolshevik forces, pressing southward, approached the northern gateway into the peninsula, conditions rapidly disintegrated in the Crimea. With the end of World War I, there was some hope that the Allies would defend the liberal government, and indeed French and British ships began to arrive in the port of Sevastopol as early as November. But Allied efforts were hindered by misunderstandings, ignorance, and incompetence, and by the end of April 1919 they had conceded Sevastopol to the Bolsheviks. Yet the Volunteers were no farther away than the Crimean town of Kerch. Now began the bloody period so vividly described in Vikentii Veresaev's civil war novel, *At a Dead End*.[14] Pushed to this southern spit of the former Russian Empire, the White Army made its last grim stand. Those White civilians who still had some hope hung on in the Crimea desperately, in towns or villages like Koktebel', where many of them had dachas and were making a scrambling attempt to live off the land. As elsewhere in Russia, towns were torn back and forth between Whites and Reds as troops gave ground and returned, gave ground and returned, forcing repeated social transformation (of a sort) accompanied by bloody acts of power and revenge. Adding to the chaos were several other military groups such as the forces of the Ukrainian nationalist Petliura, the Greens, and the followers of Ukrainian Ataman Grigoriev. All these groups tore violently at the fabric of the Crimean society and economy, leaving it in devastation at the end of the civil war.[15]

Voloshin's response to the Russian Revolution of 1917 had been neither condemning nor ecstatic, as had been that of many other members of the intelligentsia. Rather, he seemed fully attuned to the historic significance of the event, comparing it at length to the French Revolution. But he was also aware of its potential to release uncontrollably destructive forces.[16] His poetry, having undergone a notable transformation since the beginning of World War I, reveals much about his feelings on this; it is significant perhaps that his poetry during this period is also the literary work that has done the most for his reputation as a poet. Many of his poems before the war had been written in the Symbolist mode, about art or about love, for example. Now, in light of the revolution and the civil war, he began to write an increasing number of poems about his native land.

These poems also reflected another change in Voloshin: an increasingly fervent Christian religiosity. Whereas the gods he had called on in the past had stemmed largely from antiquity, now we find more frequent—and more urgent—references to a Christian God who looks down at the bloody antics of his creatures in horror. In Voloshin's almost apocalyptic vision, deaf and dumb demons were sweeping the land, driven by rage and trailing blood; trichinae wormed their way into human bodies and blinded their possessors to the distinction between good and evil, driving them to bestiality and insanity. His poetry, with its new intense focus on the question of Russian character and destiny, and its vivid cosmology of spirits benevolent and malevolent, was attaining a new level of lyricism and power.[17]

But the poetry did not take political or military sides, and, as in his response to World War I, neither in many ways did he. With a tenacious will to survive these desperate times, Voloshin sought associates and supporters in every possible corner, ranging from the White, soon-to-be-exiled Russian author Ivan Bunin to French military officials to White military officials to gun-toting ruffians who were members of the Bolshevik Cheka. Accepting, in some curious way, the violence and devastation that engulfed Russia and frequently threatened his life, he refused to give in to despair—and networked his way to safety.

NETWORKING FOR SURVIVAL
IN THE RUSSIAN CIVIL WAR

Voloshin seems to have passed through the earliest stages of the civil war more or less undisturbed. There are few signs of any interaction with the Bolsheviks during the first period of their control of the Crimea, and the German regime in the summer and fall of 1918 left Koktebel' largely to itself. Voloshin wrote poetry and gave talks during that period, and even went on a short lecture tour when the Kadets, with their Volunteer support, came into power in November. In January 1919 he went to visit his friends the Tsetlins in Odessa on the Black Sea, to the northwest of the Crimean peninsula, and stayed there until May. Here, against the background of first White and then Red control of the city, we catch our first real glimpse of Voloshin in the civil war.

Among his closest friends in Odessa were the renowned Russian novelist and short story writer, Ivan Bunin, and his wife, Vera Muromtseva-Bunina. The determinants of their association were not simple. Bunin was famous (or notorious, depending on one's point of view) for his denunciations of what he considered the frivolous, amoral Modernist movement in Russia. A Realist author of the same literary generation as Maxim Gorky, and often linked with Gorky until the revolution drove them apart, Bunin was a literary mentee of Lev Tolstoy as well as of Anton Chekhov.[18] As one who had gained essential intellectual and emotional support from his mentors, Bunin was meticulously careful of his own responsibilities to a younger generation of writers, and this may help to explain the relationship between the two men.[19] For it appears that Voloshin, though now far beyond the novice stage, entered Bunin's home in very much the style of a client-disciple, asking for evaluations of his work, spending many hours in the company of his family circle, and eating at his table not merely as a guest but as one who needed the food.[20]

Yet, because he was not a novice, Voloshin no longer needed, or wanted, that spiritual or moral guidance so often integral to the mentor-mentee relationship. His moral character and ideas were already firm, and he was more accustomed by now to offering guidance than accepting it. And so he was, for the Bunins at times, a kind of riddle; indeed at first, although they allowed him to enter their circle and fed him, they did not like him very much. To some extent they admired the poetry he was writing about Russia; but being staunchly opposed to the Bolsheviks, they could make little sense of his feelings about the civil war. Soon after the Bolsheviks had taken over the city, various politically acceptable artists were asked to participate in a May 1 decoration of the city (in the end Voloshin, in fact, was deemed unacceptable), and Voloshin began to describe his ideas for the project. Bunin asked:

> "Are you really going to take part in this?"
>
> "Why not? I believe that one cannot escape from life. And since the Bolsheviks acknowledge science and art, one must take advantage of this because science and art are the most important things in life," he said with a sweet smile.
>
> "Then that means," I [Vera Muromtseva-Bunina, from whose diary this quotation is taken] remarked, "that we should not be angry with Gorky?"
>
> "Of course," Voloshin chimed in. "I have never been angry with him . . ." Then he launched into his theory. Voloshin believes that people are actually angels who take on a devil's form on earth, and that a crucified Seraph lives in each and every person, even in murderers and idiots. Thus one cannot turn his back on anyone but must accept all. The world has everything except love. Humankind brought love. Hate is the first step to love.
>
> Ian [Ivan Bunin] could not restrain himself. He asked that "all these Seraphim be left in peace." Voloshin hurriedly changed the subject.

The Bunin household continued to puzzle over him. Several days later Vera Muromtseva-Bunina wrote in her diary: "Voloshin has theories that reconcile one with everything. He is probably one of the happiest people on earth. No matter what happens, with the ease of a juggler he will throw a thing upward and it will fly to its place."[21]

As time passed the Bunins increasingly came to accept him, though still perhaps with ambivalence. By the time Voloshin was leaving Odessa to return to the Crimea in mid-May, Vera Muromtseva-Bunina wrote in her diary: "Over the past few months we have gotten accustomed to Voloshin. He is a man of good cheer. He accepts everything. He bears no malice against bolshevism, but he does not defend it. He forgives people not only for their inadequacies but also for their vices. Perhaps this bespeaks a great indifference to the world—but then this is not a virtue. But such calmness is pleasant amid universal excitement, irritation, and bitterness."[22]

It was not merely passive calm that drew people to Voloshin during this period. As the pressures and miseries of war mounted in Odessa, he began to take a more active role in the lives of his friends and acquaintances. He could not watch them struggle to survive conditions that at first were difficult but soon became dangerous without feeling compelled to become involved and to help them. And, in his efforts to support them, almost immediately he was forced to turn to those who were best positioned to help him achieve his mission: people with power in the White and Red bureaucracies. It was under White rule that Voloshin first demonstrated his growing ability to sway powerful people to work in his own and his friends' interests, as described by the comic Russian vignettist Teffi (pseudonym of Nadezhda Lokhvitskaia). According to her, Voloshin's methods for gaining the attention and support of the Whites were far from orthodox: "Everywhere one could see [Voloshin's] picturesque figure: his bushy square beard, thick curls, a round beret on them, flapping cloak, short trousers and gaiters. He went from one government office and important person to another, and read poems. He wasn't reading without purpose. Using his poetry as with a key, he opened the paths he needed to [open] and bustled about in aid of those who were close to him. At some point he walks into some chancellery and, while they are trying to think up a way of announcing him to the boss, he begins to declaim. The poems are dense, powerful, about Russia, about the Pretender, with historical breadth, with prophetic tendency. The office girls surrounded him in a delighted crowd, listened, exclaimed, and out of idiotic horror their very noses squeaked. Then the typewriters began to clatter—Max Voloshin was dictating his poems. The boss looked out from behind the door, took interest in the proceedings, and carried Max off for himself. Carried him off, and through the locked door could be heard the deep, measured drone of declamation."[23]

Teffi goes on to describe how Max came to her because of her connection to the White governor of Odessa (the governor had helped her to obtain good living quarters). He recited two poems to her and then asked for her aid in rescuing a woman poet whom the Whites had arrested in the Crimean town of Theodosia and who was now in danger of being shot. On receiving her promise to approach the governor immediately with this problem, he went off to tug another thread in the network system as a backup (this time the Orthodox metropolitan, since the endangered poet had attended a seminary). But it was Teffi's contact that took effect most quickly, and the woman was saved. "Afterward," Teffi goes on, "at many stages in our wanderings I met this round beret over thick curls, the flapping cloak, the gaiters, and heard the poems and the squeak of little noses reddening with excitement—in Novorossiia, in Ekaterinodar, in Rostov-on-Don. And everywhere he droned on in order to save someone or other."[24]

Teffi's juxtaposition of sharp images with expansive generalities, although possibly lacking in perfect historical accuracy, illuminates a whole little world: the confused, disordered chancelleries where office girls were easily distracted by the arrival of a Poet and a character: Voloshin. His willingness, even eagerness to find an audience here, to make use of a poet's prestige to obtain a bureaucratic hearing, to trudge from one office to another and then to another, all reveal a newly developing side of his personality under these new political and economic circumstances. Above all, Voloshin was prepared to bustle about (*khlopotat'*) for his own good and

Maximilian Voloshin, self-portrait, 1918.
Courtesy of Vladimir Kupchenko.

that of others. The Russian word *khlopotat'* is difficult to translate precisely in this context, but it is significant to our understanding of this new Voloshin. It means to obtain something by taking pains, by petitioning, by bustling about—often from one bureaucratic office to another. From now on Voloshin would become a champion in this activity.

Soon after the arrival of the Bolsheviks, and as they gained a foothold in the Crimea, Voloshin decided to leave Odessa and return to his home in Koktebel'. On the journey his networking talents would come to full flower, so he himself recounts. The story of this journey was to become a stock item in his household circle storytelling in later years, no doubt gradually altering itself over time as such oral histories do. At the urging of his second wife, he finally put it down on paper just before his death in 1932. His obvious pride in his own cleverness at times gives the critical reader of this memoir pause; certain imprecisions (such as the exact titles and organizational affiliations of those who helped him along the way) are revealed where it is possible to check his story against other documents. It appears that the intent of this memoir was in no small part to advertise his skills in networking and alliance building rather than to present an entirely objective narrative. Even so, his tale reveals a great deal about the seemingly endless permutations of networking and patronage-seeking activity that were required in this volatile period.[25]

According to Bunin, who provides the first part of this story, Voloshin in his effort to leave Odessa first obtained access to the resources of the Cheka "as it often happens, with the help of a pretty woman." It appears that the head of the Odessa Cheka (*Chrezvychainaia komissiia po bor'be s kontrrevolutsiia i sabotazhem*, or Extraordinary Commission in the War with Counterrevolution and Sabotage—the first Soviet incarnation of the secret police) had requisitioned this woman's house but had permitted her to continue to live there. Voloshin met her through a mutual friend, and through this woman he gained an introduction to Severny, the president of the Cheka in Odessa. He then also "secured the help of Nemitz, the 'Naval Commissar and Commander of the Black Sea Fleet,' who, according to Voloshin, is a poet as well, 'particularly good at rondeaus and triolets,'" reports Bunin with an audible sniff.[26] Voloshin convinced these two powerful men to invent an identity for him as someone going on a secret Bolshevik mission to Sevastopol. All that was lacking was a boat to get him there, and eventually the commander of the Black Sea Fleet came up with a sailboat and crew of Bolshevik sailors (also members of the Cheka) for Voloshin as well. It does not seem likely that Voloshin paid for any of these services (he had little if any money); he had acquired them by means of preexisting ties, and by his personal charm and capacity for emotional appeal, or dyadic networking. Clearly even Cheka personnel were susceptible to such an approach in these early, confused days of Red control. "Voloshin," wrote Bunin, "finally left Odessa on that sailing boat at the beginning of May (counting by the new calendar), with a traveling companion whom he called Tatida. He brought her to us the evening before he left. In spite of everything, it was sad to see him go. The whole thing was sad: we sat in semi-darkness, with a little home-made oil lamp (we were not allowed to use electricity) and treated our departing friend to a miserable fare. He was already in his traveling clothes: a sailor's jacket and a beret. His pockets were stuffed with various life-saving bits of paper for all occasions: one for the event of a Bolshevik search on leaving the port of Odessa, another in case they met the French at sea, a third for White Army authorities, and so on and so forth (before the Bolsheviks had entered Odessa, he had connections among both the French and White army officers)."[27]

Note those life-saving bits of paper, obtained for protection by (or against) all possible quarters! Clearly Voloshin had done even more networking in preparation for this trip than Bunin has recorded. "Nevertheless, that evening all of us, including him, felt far from calm, for who could tell how such a voyage to the Crimea on a sailing boat would end? We talked for many hours and, for once, quite peacefully, agreeing on almost everything."[28] It was a sad parting: as the group surely sensed, this small circle would never meet again. Soon the Bunins would travel west via Constantinople into emigration, and Voloshin would stay behind to end his days in the Soviet Union. As they made their final farewells, Voloshin leavened the heavy atmosphere by telling a funny story and pretending to be a bear, and then he and Tatida went off to prepare for their departure. At dawn they left with the three sailors and their sailboat to cross the bay. The irrepressible spirit that Voloshin had demonstrated in the final minutes before his parting from the Bunins never left him on the journey. "From the moment of our departure from Odessa begins my romantic Crimean adventure,"[29] he wrote years later in his memoir, and it is indeed as an adventure that he seems to have treated this dangerous journey.

Voloshin's personal networking talents came into play, so he records, almost before they had left port. Traveling under the protection of the Chekist sailors whom Nemitz assigned to help him, he and his companion, Tatida, were stopped by the French, who still maintained a blockade near the Odessa harbor. A French officer came onboard and demanded a translator; seizing the opportunity, Voloshin offered his services and then announced that they were White "bourgeoisie" fleeing the Reds. It quickly transpired that Voloshin and the French officer had mutual acquaintances in Paris; they chatted briefly—and the boat was allowed to pass. The ease with which Voloshin told convincing lies (or half-truths) under such circumstances was another key to his survival of the civil war.

On approaching the Crimean coast at Ak-Mechet' two days later, Voloshin continues, they were greeted by a rain of bullets from yet unknown attackers. Eventually it turned out to have been Bolshevik bullets, and the sailors, who knew the password to calm Bolshevik unease, managed to deliver them to the shore. But Voloshin still had to get to the other side of the Crimean Peninsula in order to get home to Koktebel'. First he, Tatida, and their Chekist sailor companions were escorted by the Bolsheviks from Ak-Mechet' to Eupatoria. But Eupatoria, held by the Bolsheviks, appeared to be a dead end: the port was blockaded by the French, and the railroad was not functioning, at least not for the general public. Having discovered all this on the morning after his arrival in Eupatoria, Voloshin went into one of the few restaurants still open for food. While eating, he was suddenly accosted by the young son of a family sitting next to him in the restaurant: "Tell me, aren't you Maximilian Voloshin? Papa sent me to find out."[30]

Voloshin approached the table at which the boy's family (consisting of two children, a woman [apparently the children's governess], and the boy's well-dressed parents) was sitting and asked: "Do you know me?" Indeed they did. The father explained that he had actually stayed in Voloshin's dacha one summer, having been sent there by a member of the Gertsyk family. "We sat together half the night," he reminded Voloshin, "talking in your studio. You showed me your drawings. I was still wearing a postal uniform at the time." Voloshin simply could not remember the man, but they chatted amiably, and when Voloshin ran into the governess the next day, he made cautious inquiries and learned more about the man: "Ah, [he lives in] his own train car? Why in his own train car? Don't tell me that he is now some kind of big-wig? . . . What do you mean, he's the commander of the [Red] Thirteenth Army!"[31] Armed with this new information, Voloshin, according to his memoir, dashed off to the railway station to rekindle this old friendship. Soon he had obtained the promise of a train ride to Simferopol' with the commander himself.

The Bolshevik sailors, of course, having been included in the invitation, were awed and delighted. Voloshin records (or claims) with pride that, up to this point in the journey, the sailors had allowed him to haul his own heavy baggage, but now they not only carried his baggage for him but quarreled over who would have that honor. The little group arrived at the railway station at four o'clock the next day and was given quarters on the train. On the way Voloshin and Tatida were invited into the commander's train car: "At first there was a long pause [and] then he [the commander] felt the need to speak soul to soul." At the end of much "instructive and interesting discussion," during which Voloshin provided the commander with companionship and a friendly audience in return for the ride, the commander gave him the name of a friend of his in the Simferopol' Cheka, someone who would be able to help him further on his way to Koktebel'.[32]

In Simferopol' Voloshin got a glimpse into how the new Red Crimea was taking shape. First, he heard through the grapevine that one of his critics was now in a position of power on the local executive committee of the Party, and this person was quoted as saying that "if Voloshin starts giving his aesthetic lectures, he'll pay for it."[33] This was an early portent of how some members of the Russian intelligentsia would use the power to harass and endanger one another that they could acquire by entering the proliferating organs of bureaucratic power. Nevertheless, Voloshin appears to have made some headway with the local Red bureaucracy, as we find in his archive a pair of *udostovereniia*, or identity papers, from the Simferopol' Bureau of People's Enlightenment, Art Section. One paper appoints him head of the Art Section in Theodosia. The other indicates the influence such identity documents can bring, namely, the ability to exert control over one's survival in a period of military intervention. This document is perhaps worth reproducing here in translation, as it demonstrates the kinds of services and goods that Voloshin needed on this journey, and could best obtain by bureaucratic means:

Mandate
The Art Section requests all Soviet institutions to whom this might apply to
provide, vne ocheredi,[34] *M. A. Voloshin with horses,* [word illegible] *passes,*
and tickets for use in the line of duty, and living space.
Head of the Section: [signature][35]

This paper is handwritten, and the last line "and living space" is added separately, in an ink that is unlike the ink used in the main body of the document; rather, it is the same ink that is used for the signature, indicating, perhaps, that this was a special request on Voloshin's part when he had the document signed. The value of such a document was surely considerable at a time when military barriers were crisscrossing the countryside, and access to means of travel and places to stay was becoming increasingly limited. The expression "*vne ocheredi,*" entitling Voloshin to horses, passes, tickets, and living space without waiting his turn, are a reminder of the consequences of bureaucratic intervention in freedom of movement and distribution of goods and services. One now had to wait in increasingly long lines, perhaps only to be told, when one's turn came up, that the particular good or service one was waiting for was no longer available, or that the individual disposing of that good or service had now ended his hours of availability. While it is not entirely clear whether Voloshin had to pay for these resources, it is evident that, under the Bolsheviks, access to economic benefits was no longer entirely determined by the possession of money but rather, at least in part, by bureaucratic association and identity.

Voloshin had another illuminating experience of the new Red Crimea upon going to see the member of the Cheka whose name he had been given. This man's first question was whether Voloshin might want to receive a document identifying him as a member of the Cheka. Upon learning that such a document might well in fact oblige him to carry out certain duties Voloshin politely declined the honor and accepted, instead, a stamped document giving him free passage to Theodosia. The value of this stamped document soon made itself felt as he continued on his journey. Upon arriving in Karasu-Bazaar in need of a change of horses, he and Tatida at first accepted with resignation the news that they would have to wait until the next day for the horses. Apparently even the Mandate from the Art Section did not prevent him from having to wait his turn in this town. Then, remembering the Cheka document, Voloshin showed it to the commander there, who, upon seeing the stamp, "simply shuddered"[36] and shouted into the telephone that horses be brought immediately. If access to a service such as a change of horses was under bureaucratic control, surely the most effective bureaucracy was the one harboring the most explicit threat of violence, namely, the Cheka. This is a fact of which a surprisingly large number of other literati, from the Futurist circles of Vladimir Mayakovsky to the radical RAPPists, would soon take note and advantage.

The set of horses they were given carried Voloshin and Tatida as far as Stary Krim, a village in the mountains not far from Koktebel'; here, Voloshin encountered further signs of the growing tangle of the Bolshevik art and culture bureaucracy. An artist acquaintance, Konstantin Astafiev, stopped Voloshin on the street to say that he, Astafiev, had become the local head of the new Party agency for the "protection of art" but that little had come of it so far, as the necessary authorization had not yet arrived from Theodosia. And he had a problem: on the nearby estate of Shakh-Mamai, which had originally belonged to the famous Crimean artist Aivazovskii, an executive committee was sitting on the artist's paintings. Despite all the artist's pleas and demands, the committee refused to return his paintings to the frustrated Aivazovskii. "I think," Voloshin reports himself as replying, "that this can be easily handled: I am on my way to Theodosia to take over the Department of Art there, and here is my authorization from Odessa.[37] I don't have a stamp yet, but I think that can be taken care of. Where in Stary Krim is the local executive committee?" Marching into the building that housed the executive committee, Voloshin proclaimed to its chairman: "Comrade, here's the problem. I've been sent from Odessa to head the Theodosia Art Department. I don't have a stamp, but [here in Stary Krim] I've discovered improprieties. I must write a document to the executive committee of such-and-such a village with regard to Aivazovskii's paintings. Would you authorize this with your stamp?"[38]

According to his memoir, the problem of the paintings was resolved just as Voloshin wished. Whether the "authorization" he mentioned was indeed "from Odessa" or, more likely, was actually the *udostoverenie* from the Simferopol' Art Section is unclear; more important, though, is that Voloshin had quickly discerned that the disorder which marked this transitional period was such that a mere piece of paper (here accompanied by a charismatic, authoritative tone) was a key to having one's wishes granted. For all the brutality the Bolsheviks deployed under their regime in disinheriting those with private property—and they could be brutal indeed—they were curiously susceptible to little pieces of paper with stamps on them.

A few moments after finishing his business with the executive committee, Voloshin witnessed another way in which the new Red cultural bureaucracy was having an impact on local affairs. Astafiev asked that he come to meet his wife, and, crossing the street to enter a small room, they found her amid piles of books—the contents of personal libraries that had been requisitioned throughout the area. Here, as in Odessa, private property was being eliminated, and if one wanted to have influence on its redistribution, the bureaucracy was the place to be. It is notable that these particular items were not even the kind of property that could give any material benefit to the Bolshevik war effort; the requisition of books was purely a matter of expanding Bolshevik control over intellectual activity.

Voloshin observed the situation carefully, having heard a rumor that his own library had recently been destroyed, and, indeed, on arriving in Koktebel', he discovered that his home was presently being searched (the local commander of Koktebel' carried off Voloshin's broken French mountain bicycle). Knowing that what little control he had over his own safety and property, as well as that of others, was increasingly invested in little pieces of paper, Voloshin did not hesitate to seek out a source from which to obtain them. After taking several days in Koktebel' to recover from the journey, and armed with the document from Simferopol' (or Odessa) appointing him head of the Theodosia Art Section, he left for Theodosia and the Theodosia *Otnarpros*, or Bureau of People's Enlightenment, and the Art Section within that Bureau.

The two main sources on Voloshin's experiences in Theodosia, namely, his own memoirs and the memoirs of his old friend, Vikentii Veresaev, Voloshin's neighbor in Koktebel' whom we met earlier as one of the mythologizers of Voloshin's dacha circle and the author of the civil war novel *At a Dead End*, are somewhat contradictory. To pursue Voloshin's narrative, his attempt to make his way into the Art Section of the Theodosia *Otnarpros* was a failure owing to personal infighting and competition among Russian intellectuals enthused by their new access to power. By no means were his difficulties with the leadership of *Otnarpros*; indeed, he found these men impressive and delightful. The head of the Education and Economy Sections, and by all accounts the de facto head of the Bureau, was an old friend, Nikandr Marks, a former Imperial Army general, paleographer, archaeologist, and folklorist who believed it was now his duty to work for the education of the Russian people, and ran the Bureau so that "in everything there was order, a system of hierarchy, and the normal forms and parliamentarianism."[39] And managing the Theater and Art Section was Vikentii Veresaev.

The problem, Voloshin explains, was Vladimir Kastorskii, who was already ensconced in the Theater and Art Section. Kastorskii was a bass singer who was entirely disinclined to let go of any control whatsoever. Armed with his document from Odessa (or Simferopol'), Voloshin suggested that Kastorskii divide responsibility, taking charge of the theater himself and leaving the fine arts to Voloshin. But Kastorskii strongly objected and apparently shot a telegram off to Odessa (or Simferopol') demanding to know whether he was obliged to share his power with Voloshin. A reply telegram soon arrived and, according to Voloshin, informed them that "the appointment of Voloshin [is] to be considered a misunderstanding." "I imagine," writes Voloshin, "that something had been written about me, and the result of some gossip was this brief formula."[40] This is an illustration of the balance of power between the center and the periphery, a lesson in the importance of having good local relations if a document from a more powerful but distant bureaucratic authority was to hold sway. Poor network relations nearby could easily undo good ones far away.[41]

One might reasonably ask why, under the circumstances, his two friends in power, Marks and Veresaev, did not help him? The answer is that Voloshin was, in fact, a less comfortable figure for the Bolsheviks than this narrative thus far may have intimated. By no means had they fully accepted him in Odessa: recall that, despite his eagerness to participate, he had been excluded from the group of artists called on to decorate the city for the May 1 celebration. According to Bunin, he had been castigated in the Bolshevik press in Odessa and had not been permitted to reply in his own defense. This had made his success in obtaining concessions from the Cheka president and the head of the navy in Odessa all the more remarkable.

Now, in Theodosia, he sometimes offended even his Koktebel' neighbor and friend, Veresaev, with what struck the earnest and politically committed Veresaev as disrespectful humor toward the Bolsheviks and their ideals; indeed, there seems to have been an awkward resurgence of Voloshin's tendency toward the carnivalesque mockery of power, in this case of Bolshevik power. While attending a theatrical meeting of the Art Section which included a number of members of the working class, Voloshin announced that, according to Oscar Wilde, art is always deliciously inefficacious. The principle to be observed, he went on, is that whatever emotion the spectator experiences while in the theater, he will no longer experience in life. "Therefore, for example, if we want to destroy the desire for war in the human being, we have to show plays calling him to war; if we want to inculcate chastity, then we should show pornography."[42]

Naturally, this sort of jocularity was entirely antipathetic to serious Bolshevik views on the value of art and literature as a tool to be used for the education of the people. Indeed, as Voloshin must surely have known, Bolsheviks were using plays and other dramatic presentations at that time precisely to call people if not to war then to the Bolshevik side of the war.[43] It is small wonder that Voloshin, himself a past master in transformation through theatricality, would find it difficult to restrain himself. But the "self-satisfied smile" Veresaev described as playing around Voloshin's lips as he proposed this principle irritated Veresaev: "I was simply embarrassed for him . . . it was embarrassing in front of the workers, who listened to his declaration with amazement and indignation."[44] To be sure, it was the workers whom the emerging Soviet bureaucratic intellectual elite were most eager to mold; the master could ill afford to have doubt cast on one of his foremost teaching aids—and certainly not in the presence of the pupils.

The animosity that Voloshin aroused with this joke and others about the Bolsheviks was long to weigh in the balance against the goodwill he had won by means of networking, and eventually, many years later, the balance would tip against him.

For now, however, Voloshin's difficulties with the Bolsheviks were about to become irrelevant to his immediate survival, at least temporarily. Back in Koktebel' in mid-June he witnessed the return of the Whites. They had never been far away in any case. While Voloshin had been in Theodosia, the nearby town of Kerch had been the scene of a grim battle between Bolshevik supporters and White Volunteers, the latter aided by the British fleet. This event resulted, writes Voloshin, in the hanging of three thousand people "on the boulevards and streets" of Kerch by the Whites.[45] The Whites continued their campaign to recover the Crimean Peninsula. As Voloshin prepared early one morning to carry the books belonging to his friend and neighbor, Aleksander Iunge (a relative of the Iunge who had originally founded the Koktebel' dacha colony), into his own library to protect them from requisition, Koktebel' came under White and British fire from the sea.

"Koktebel' was in no way defended," he writes, "but six people of the Cordon Guard fired on the British fleet with six rifles. This was entirely senseless and unexpected. The cruiser immediately answered with heavy missiles. They were aimed at the Sinopli cottage, from which the rifle shots had come. The Diamond Café blew up in fragments." Under these increasingly dangerous circumstances, Voloshin sat tight in his cottage with his mother, Tatida, and an elderly engineer from Petersburg who had come to wait for the Whites to retake control of the country. "In a word, whoever was here was awaiting precisely this event."[46] In the end, only one member of the household was injured in the barrage: a kitten.

Asked by the local Bolsheviks to act as a mediator, Voloshin took a small boat and a white flag out to the cruiser—which turned out to be filled with old White acquaintances and connections. Having carried out his duties as a mediator with the commander of the ship, Voloshin was told: "'The officers are waiting for you in the wardroom.' . . . I went there and saw a mass of familiar faces." The officers of the Volunteer fleet of that period were almost all young men, Voloshin explains: "Thus I saw in the space of half-an-hour a large number of my auditors from the Simferopol' University," where he had lectured occasionally before the revolution.[47] They demanded that he recite some of his newest poetry (the Whites generally seemed more interested in his poetry than the Reds), and so, before he departed, he spent some time with them in recitation and intellectual discourse.

This comparatively benign commencement of White control did not continue, however. Several days later Voloshin received an urgent message from the wife of Nikandr Marks, the ex-tsarist general who had won Volo-shin's respect for his efficient and even-handed management of the Sim-feropol' Bureau of People's Enlightenment. Marks had been arrested by the Whites, she told him; would Voloshin come and (presumably in his ca-pacity as one who had connections among the Whites) try to help him out? This was the beginning of Voloshin's second great "adventure" in the Crimean civil war. He set off for Theodosia that very day, he writes in his memoir. There he discovered that although the Volunteers had not taken a great deal of interest in Marks when they first took over the town, White "bourgeoisie," as Voloshin calls them, returning from their exile in such towns as Kerch and Batum, had demanded that he be arrested for his par-ticipation in the Bureau of People's Enlightenment. The danger of the sit-uation quickly snowballed: it was decided to transport Marks to Kerch to be tried as a traitor. Not only did the trial represent a threat to Marks's life, but it was entirely possible that, on the journey to Kerch, he would be shot out of hand by guards or other Whites too impatient to wait for a legal resolu-tion.

As Voloshin tells it, the story of his rescue of Marks from the hands of the Volunteers can, with all its fright, poignancy, and moments of sheer helplessness, be read almost as a primer in the nitty-gritty mechanics of net-working with wartime bureaucracies. Voloshin's first step was to obtain passes for himself and for Marks's wife so that they could accompany Marks on his transport to Kerch. The person dispensing such passes was the newly appointed military commander of the town; upon discovering an impossi-bly long line before the man's office, Voloshin found a soldier, an acquain-tance who, like Voloshin, had attended the local Gymnasium, and the sol-dier got them in to see the commander *vne ocheredi*. Having acquired the passes after some friendly discussion on the nature of war and on Marks's wartime "betrayal," Voloshin learned from another connection, the man-ager of the Theodosian harbor, when and on what train Marks would be transported to Kerch. Making their way onto a freight car next to the one in which Marks was being held under guard, Voloshin made friends with the guards, protected Marks from injury and theft, and learned as much as he could about what lay ahead for Marks as they made the thirty-six-hour train trip through battle-scarred countryside to Kerch (about 150 miles from Theodosia).

In Kerch he set off to find a connection Marks had: a wealthy White with close ties to the Volunteers whom Marks had helped out during the war with Germany. As a general in the tsarist army, Marks, apparently on the basis of his previous acquaintance with the man, had taken him from the ranks and appointed him to Marks's headquarters, even bringing him into his own home to live. As it turned out, however, even this personal obligation and household-based tie did not hold out. The wealthy White, who was entertaining some Volunteer officers, refused to see Voloshin and Marks's wife. As they stood before the man's house, Voloshin may well have understand why, for this particular boulevard, in this elite neighborhood, was hung with the corpses of Bolshevik prisoners-of-war. Voloshin and Marks's wife were in danger themselves, because they were out on the street after a 10:30 curfew and had no place to stay for the night.

On being arrested for breaking the curfew, Voloshin was taken before an officer whom he knew slightly from the Koktebel' dacha colony. "In the summers we had called him 'Husband of the Debauchee.' This name came from the fact that his wife, a plump and awkward blond, had once announced loudly and affectedly, 'Oh, you know, I'm such a debauchee.'" The Husband of the Debauchee immediately recognized Voloshin and set him free, and then another officer, witnessing the meeting, offered him a place to stay in his own apartment. Having obtained a place for "a lady" to stay as well, Voloshin accepted two street passes and went to pick up and escort Marks's wife to the apartment, where she promptly fell asleep. Voloshin, however, stayed up to assist his host, binding a wound he had received in battle and then helping him into bed. Finally, on asking the man's name, he learned that this was the man, so he had heard from Marks's guards on the train trip to Kerch, who had control over Marks's destiny. But on broaching the topic of Marks and his troubles, Voloshin was told: "You know, we have a quick kind of punishment for these kinds of people: a bullet in the back of the head and that's it."[48]

Struck by the coldness of this reply, Voloshin writes, he ceased to attempt to persuade him of Marks's innocence and took another tack: silent prayer. "This was my old, well-tried, and infallible method of dealing with the Bolsheviks." This reference to prayer, by no means frequent in Voloshin's autobiographical writings, reflects Voloshin's religious feeling during this period. "It was not necessary that my opponent knew that the prayer was for him . . . One usually prays for the one who is threatened by the bullet. And this is wrong: it is necessary to pray for the one . . . who will give the order to shoot. Because, of the two individuals—the murderer and the victim—the one who is in the greatest (moral) danger is the executioner and not the victim at all."[49]

This silent tactic, which also demonstrated Voloshin's diplomacy in not pushing his case too aggressively, had its effect. The officer finally said, "If you want to save him, then above all you must ascertain that he does not fall into my hands. Now he is in the hands of the commander. And this is fortunate, because if he had fallen into mine, my boys would have executed him immediately, without waiting for me. But now you hold a trump card."[50] The officer went on to explain that he had just received an order that all generals and admirals who had been taken prisoner and accused of working with the Bolsheviks were to be sent to Ekaterinodar. He offered to support Voloshin (by means of further documents and passes) in getting Marks shuttled off to Ekaterinodar for his trial, instead of being shot in Kerch, and did so the following day. Thus Voloshin, along with Marks and Marks's wife, now set off through the war-torn countryside to yet another city.

The journey proceeded much as it had begun; ever more experienced in the ways of the White military bureaucracy, Voloshin managed to obtain all necessary passes and tickets, and even a sleeping cabin on the transport train. Sometimes he made use of his reputation as a poet (a reputation that was strengthened by an opportunity to give a sonorous reading of his poetry about Russia enroute from Kerch to Novorossisk); at other times he used old network connections; and at still others he used charm and tact to get what he wanted.

Ekaterinodar proved a more difficult nut to crack. The town, Voloshin tells us, was teeming with White refugees and old friends; amazingly Voloshin found here his old flame, Elizaveta Dmitrieva, the one-time Cherubina de Gabriak. Here, too, he must again have met his Odessa acquaintance, Teffi, for it is here that she refers to Voloshin as going from office to office "droning" his poetry for the sake of his friends. This is precisely what Voloshin appears to have done for Marks: "First I began to make the rounds of all the generals . . . My typical day in Ekaterinodar passed as follows: all morning in offices, chancelleries, and going from one general to another." He also spent much time pursuing various acquaintances in the hope that that would aid him in his pursuit of mercy for Marks. Despite their desire to put Marks on trial, the Whites quickly discovered that there were few, if any, White officers of a sufficiently high rank to sit in judgment of Marks, who had been a lieutenant general in the tsarist army. This became a problem for Voloshin as well, as he sought to obtain access to anyone who had jurisdiction over the affair. He had to look high; apparently it was to General Denikin himself that his networking needed to take him. But Denikin, unfortunately, was almost inaccessible. "In order to meet and obtain an audience with Denikin, I counted on Shul'gin [a White author and political figure]. But he wasn't in Ekaterinodar—he had gone on some sea expedition. Professor Novgorodtsev, on whom I was also counting, was also not around. Thus all my ladders to the heights of power were unavailable."[51]

The matter prolonged itself as Voloshin continued to search for threads in the network that would give him influence in Marks's trial and fate. At one point, according to his memoir, he actually gave up in frustration and told Marks's wife that he was returning to Koktebel'. But as it happened, on the very day he was to depart, the trial was finally held and Voloshin was permitted to write a note to Denikin in Marks's defense. "Before you, Your Highness," he wrote, "lies a very difficult and complex duty: to punish, perhaps, a guilty general, but without at the same time touching and removing from Russian life a very talented and necessary professor and scholar."[52] Whether it was Voloshin's note or some other factor that brought about the desired result, Marks was released by Denikin on the grounds that, although guilty, he was too old to punish.

Voloshin's reputation gained tremendously through this affair, probably in part because of his own propagation of the story. It did not do him much good among the Whites, of course, who deeply resented his efforts to see that Marks went unpunished. Indeed, writes Voloshin, for a time thereafter "I could neither appear publicly nor show myself on the street; they pointed at me with their fingers and said: 'Thanks only to Voloshin, we were unable to shoot that traitor Marks.'"[53] Nevertheless he was becoming known in the region as one who would endanger himself for the sake of others. This reputation was a significant foundation for his growing locus of personalized power.

Voloshin accomplished similar feats at least three more times before the Whites were at last driven from the Crimea, and at least once after the Bolsheviks regained control. One of these events is recorded by journalist, novelist, and renowned Thaw memoirist Ilya Ehrenburg. Ehrenburg, who was living nearby at the time, tells us that in May 1920 Voloshin tried to hide an underground Bolshevik from the Whites, though to no avail as the man "gave himself away with a careless movement."[54] On another occasion Voloshin successfully protected the Bolshevik father of the grateful memoirist Raissa Ginzburg from another White search.[55] And on a third occasion, when the Bolsheviks had taken over again in November 1920, he protected friends from the threats of the Red Cheka just as he had protected them from the White Volunteers. When Anastasiia Tsvetaeva and her son were threatened by a drunken crowd of Chekists who had requisitioned their home, Voloshin quickly engaged the attention of another, more sober group of Chekists in town, and obtained their protection for Tsvetaeva.[56]

The last of his rescues to be described was that of Osip Mandelshtam, who, the reader will recall, had been an intimate member of Voloshin's domestic circle before the revolution. This story reveals the very considerable personal reputation and capacity for influence that Voloshin had by now developed in the region, and the dangers and responsibilities inherent in that type of power. This rescue must be seen in the context of an entire community of writers who had tucked themselves away all over this part of the Crimea, meeting in Theodosia at a café called the "Flak," a place where readings were held and that also served as a base for the planning of various poetry almanacs and publications. Among them were many individuals whose names are by now familiar to us: besides Voloshin, who was a dominant if not leading figure in the group, we find Ilya Ehrenburg; Maia Kudasheva, the former *Obormot* who would later marry the French supporter of Soviet power Romain Rolland; Sofia Parnok, the one-time lover of Marina Tsvetaeva; Adelaida Gertsyk, the woman who had been one of Voloshin's most important female mentees (Kudasheva, Parnok, and Gertsyk, along with Anastasiia Tsvetaeva, all lived together in the nearby village of Sudak); and, finally, Mandelshtam. It was indeed a gathering of old friends, or at least of former members of Voloshin's prerevolutionary circle. Another participant was Emilii Mindlin, whose memoir of these events clarifies a great deal that Voloshin and Ehrenburg, the two others who wrote about it, left obscure. But taken together, the three narratives give insight into the enormous significance of petty community gossip and personal conflict in an emerging system of personalized power.

According to Voloshin's somewhat cranky memoir, Mandelshtam actually needed rescuing twice. The first time Mandelshtam had attracted the attention of a White Cossack, who asked a Koktebel' inhabitant whether there were any "Yids" around and was told about the Mandelshtam brothers. Mandelshtam soon appeared at Voloshin's dacha in a panic, and took him back to his own rooms, where the Cossack was thumbing through his books.[57] Voloshin writes: "'But that's the Gospel, my favorite book—I'll never give it up,' said Mandelshtam in a worried voice, and then, suddenly remembering my presence, he hastened to introduce me to the Cossack: 'This is Voloshin—a local dacha owner. You know what? You'd do better to arrest him than me.' He said this frozen with terror. This had its effect on the Cossack esaul, and he said [to me]: 'I will arrest you, if Mandelshtam does not appear tomorrow in Theodosia at 10:00 in the morning.'"[58]

The matter was resolved when the colonel to whom Mandelshtam was to report in Theodosia turned out to be an admirer of Mandelshtam's poetry and immediately let him go. But both Mandelshtam and Ehrenburg, compelled by this manifestation of White anti-Semitism, decided to leave Koktebel' for the city of Batum. Voloshin must have had a hand in organizing this journey, as it was his friend, the manager of the Theodosia port (who had helped to get Voloshin and Marks's wife onto the train to Kerch), who "arranged" for Mandelshtam's and Ehrenburg's tickets to Batum. Unfortunately the departure was marred by a minor but nasty conflict over a book that was missing from Voloshin's library, which Voloshin believed that Mandelshtam had taken, and which Mandelshtam had apparently not. This misunderstanding led to a bitter and somewhat public exchange of letters between the two men that set the dispute firmly on the gossip agenda of the Theodosia literary community.[59]

The spat would have been of minor concern to anyone other than the gossips, however, had the Whites not arrested Mandelshtam just before he was to leave. Frantic and believing that only Voloshin could save Mandelshtam, Mandelshtam's brother turned for intercession to Voloshin's old friend, Maia Kudasheva (who had had a mildly romantic relationship with Mandelshtam in the recent past). Kudasheva turned to Mindlin, and together the two of them traveled on foot to Koktebel' to obtain Voloshin's influence. While Mindlin waited on the beach in Koktebel', Kudasheva went to get Ehrenburg; the three then discussed the question of who was to approach Voloshin first. Unfortunately Ehrenburg, too, had recently engaged in a minor but angry quarrel with Voloshin over material possessions, specifically over some missing crockery. Elena Ottobal'dovna's good name, fiercely defended by Voloshin, had been dragged into the affair as well. Thus we must picture the three of them, Kudasheva, Mindlin, and Ehrenburg, assembled on the pebble beach in front of Voloshin's house and, with anxiety and trepidation, going in one after the other for an audience with Voloshin as he lay ill upstairs in his bed. Kudasheva went first but soon returned, saying, according to Mindlin: "I can't talk with Max. I knew I wouldn't be able to. He feels sick, lies there in a bad temper, and doesn't want to hear about Mandelshtam. It's awful, just awful!"[60]

Mindlin was the next to try, but he met with equally little success. Only when Ehrenburg interceded did Voloshin agree to write a letter pronouncing Mandelshtam a great Russian poet who should be left in peace. Voloshin's letter was a masterpiece of irritable condescension to both Mandelshtam and the White addressee: "Since your position of service in no way obliges you to know contemporary Russian poetry, I consider it my duty to inform you that Os. Mandelshtam is one of the biggest names of the last generation of Russian poets and occupies a fully defined and honored place in the history of Russian literature . . . Of course it is not for me to stand up for O. E. Mandelshtam politically, especially as I do not know what he has been accused of. I can only say that, for those who know Mandelshtam, the accusation of Bolshevism, of Party work, is absurd. He is a frivolous, social person incapable of work and suffers from no political convictions whatsoever."[61] The next day Maia Kudasheva, armed with her aristocratic title (she had been married to a titled Russian who had recently died in the war) and accompanied by Vikentii Verasaev, who was respected as much by the Whites as the Reds for his prerevolutionary writings, took the note to Theodosia. With additional support from the White colonel who had let Mandelshtam go the first time he was arrested, they obtained Mandelshtam's release.[62]

This extraordinary tale has many implications. It reveals Voloshin's growing personal influence in the region. Even more significant is the extent to which such personal influence could be both used and abused. Personal power is rooted in personal relations, and the tangled webs of kinship, love, and petty quarrels over books and crockery described here were of infinite significance in this newly emerging system of personalized power; they could mean the difference between life and death.

SEVEN

Voloshin Carves Power, Cont'd, and the Broader Context and Implications of His Activities

FOOD

In the early Soviet period Voloshin continued to build on the reputation for personal influence that he had established during the civil war. If survival of physical violence had been his goal at first, his attention soon turned to other almost equally desperate needs: food and shelter. The greatest threat to survival was now famine. Voloshin's poem, "Red Easter," gives a vivid sense of the bitterness of that first Soviet winter and spring of 1920–21:

> In the winter, the corpses of people and horses
> Lay about along the road. And packs of hounds
> Ate into their bellies and tore the meat to pieces.
> The east wind was in the broken windows.
> But in the night the machine guns knocked,
> Whistling, like a whip, along the meat of the naked
> Bodies of men and women.
> Spring came
> Sinister, hungry, sick . . .[1]

During these months community life withered in Koktebel' as well as in the Voloshin household. Maria Izvergina, whose mother took her as a child to stay in Max's household for safety in 1921, wrote: "That year Koktebel' was empty, despite the fact that the surrounding dachas on the shore were inhabited by many people, dacha owners. Even though artists and the Kedrov family were living in Max's house, all were divided; all hung onto their rations, as if someone else would eat them. No one gathered in Max's room, all the less as Max was sick. Pra was sick, too."[2] This description is all the more poignant given that Maria Izvergina, along with her mother and young sister, had no access to rations for themselves. "We were very hungry," she tells us, offering us an image of a household under so much pressure that two children went hungry while the others kept to themselves for fear that the children might demand food.

Few members of the intelligentsia seem to have escaped the crisis of 1920–21 with their health intact. Both Max and Pra suffered considerable illness during this period, hardly leaving their rooms for long stretches of time, as Maria Izvergina intimates in her memoir. Max would never entirely recover, and Pra would die in January 1923, at the age of seventy-three. But Voloshin could not afford to stay in bed for long: he again needed to put his connections to work in order to obtain food and perhaps medicine. Voloshin's paper trail, to be picked up again with the return of the Bolsheviks and their proliferating bureaucracy, shows us how he accomplished this and, in the process, continued to enhance his small degree of control over circumstances, his tiny but vital locus of agency or power.

The Bolsheviks arrived in November 1920. By January 1921, at the latest, Voloshin had obtained a designation from the Theodosia Bureau of People's Enlightenment, Art Section, as head of the section for the "protection of artistic and scientific treasure" in the Theodosia *uezd*. This gave him some of the protective paperwork he needed. Along with the basic identity document that accompanied this new post, in January he received another *udostoverenie* from the Bureau of People's Enlightenment, dispatching him on a trip to Simferopol' and Yalta, and requesting that "all railroad organizations, War Revolutionary Committees, and responsible authorities offer MAV [Maximilian A. Voloshin] the broadest of support in terms of providing, *vne ocheredi*, means of movement, provisions, and so on."[3] Thus he was officially entitled to be supplied with provisions as well as train tickets and other travel assistance. With the aid of this document, Voloshin may well have been able to obtain food and supplies in Simferopol' and Yalta, if and when they were unavailable in Koktebel'.

Voloshin's archive is stuffed with a multitude of such documents dated April or May or June 1921. Unfortunately some have been rendered illegible by water or fire damage, but others can still be read, and the nature of the illegible ones can be surmised with the aid of memoirs. Included among the readable documents are those identifying and empowering Voloshin as head of one department of the Literary Section of the Crimean Bureau of People's Enlightenment;[4] organizer of children's colonies in Koktebel' and Theodosia *uezd*;[5] and archivist for Theodosia and Theodosia *uezd*.[6] Some of the illegible documents may refer to Voloshin's activities as lecturer at the Theodosia People's University, established by the Bolsheviks almost as soon as they arrived, under the leadership of Vikentii Veresaev. Veresaev made sure that his friend Voloshin got a job lecturing on the Renaissance to Red Army soldiers there. All these activities helped to preserve Voloshin's life, to extend his network among those in power, and to make him eligible for rations, which the Bolsheviks doled out carefully according to a system of ranks based on one's usefulness in achieving Bolshevik aims.[7] This was an important step toward resolving the problem of his own hunger.

But he was also concerned about others. As time went on, he began to look for ways to help others who were suffering from hunger and privation, especially other literary and artistic friends. At this time, however, the resources in the Crimea were too meager for mere local networking to alleviate the hunger and poverty of its citizens. In order to accomplish his goal, Voloshin had to extend the influence of his personal ties far beyond local boundaries—to the West, on the one hand, and to Moscow, on the other.

In the early 1920s word arrived in the West of the famine in Russia, and this spurred a movement, spearheaded by the American Relief Association (ARA), to send food to Russia. Because of Voloshin's contacts and his reputation in the West (among émigrés as well as Western Europeans who had known him in earlier days), his home became a clearing center for food aid sent to the Crimea from the West. In the summer of 1922 he received a package of supplies from the London-based Committee for the Relief of Russian Intellectuals (via the ARA), along with a postcard requesting that he either use these supplies or pass them on to those who needed them. Then in September, and again in December of that same year, a small flood of such packages arrived via the ARA, donated by such groups as the Pavlova Benefit Fund, the Comité Russe en France (Paris), and the Fund for the Relief of Men of Letters and Scientists of Russia (New York), as well as by the ARA itself. Individuals also donated; one donor was Marie Tsetlin—the same Tsetlin with whom Voloshin had stayed in Odessa and who had then gone into emigration. The ARA packages, each worth ten dollars, contained forty-nine pounds of flour, twenty-five pounds of rice, ten pounds of sugar, ten pounds of lard, eight pounds of tea, and twenty tins of milk. As the recipient of these packages, Voloshin was personally responsible for distributing them.[8]

Of course, news of the famine in the Crimea had also reached Moscow, the center of Bolshevik power. Some in Moscow were greatly concerned about the condition of intellectuals in the Crimea, among them the Commissar of Enlightenment, Anatoly Lunacharsky. The paths of Voloshin and Lunacharsky had crossed in Paris a number of years before the revolution; it was perhaps on this basis that contact between the two was taken up as early as the summer of 1921. Lunacharsky was eager for Voloshin to come to Moscow to give a personal report on conditions in the Crimea; Voloshin's archive contains a set of papers connected with his "summons" to Moscow by Lunacharsky.[9] But Voloshin was not yet ready to make this journey. A copy of his own letter (at this point Voloshin began to keep detailed handwritten or typewritten copies of his own letters to official individuals and institutions, to the great benefit of historians) indicates that Voloshin wrote back to Lunacharsky in August 1921, telling him that he had only just received the summons, as the "summons" had apparently been held up in Simferopol' for three months. He would come soon, he wrote, but at present he was prevented from making the journey by both his own poor health and that of his mother. In the meantime, Voloshin gave his impression of conditions in his letter. He included a list of writers living in Koktebel' and Sudak, and said that conditions were bad, that there was little food and much sickness, and that the prospects for surviving the winter were poor. Local "powers"—the Crimean Revolutionary Committee and Crimean Bureau of People's Enlightenment—were helping out as much as they could, but this did not amount to much: he (Voloshin), Veresaev, and one other citizen of Koktebel' were promised "academic rations," but so far that was only on paper.[10]

Voloshin would not, in fact, go to Moscow until 1924, but relations with the center had been established. In May 1922 he was made chairman of the Theodosia branch of KrymKUBU,[11] associated with the Central Commission for the Improvement of the Condition of Scholars (Tsentral'naia Komissiia po Ulucheniiu Byta Uchyonnykh pri Sovnarkome, or TsKUBU), an institution formed for the distribution of benefits and one that had a considerable impact on the lives of the Soviet intelligentsia in the 1920s. By September of that year he was fully involved in the distribution of rations from the center of Bolshevik power, as is revealed in a letter he wrote to a woman who was staying in his home and nursing his mother through her latest illness: Maria Stepanovna Zabolotskaia. He himself was undergoing medical treatment in Simferopol' for a severe case of polyarthritis and so was unable to attend to some of his obligations as a distributor. He therefore wrote to inform her that "in the course of the week, nine boxes of food and manufactured goods will be delivered to my apartment for writers who are receiving academic rations." He then lists the names of eleven recipients. "All of them have to be divided equally, and the textiles by agreement and by lottery." More was involved in setting up a source of supplies from the center for local intelligentsia than mere distribution, however. As Voloshin well knew, there was much paperwork to be done, and he pushed his friends to get their documents in order with the same energy that characterized his own pursuit of those documents: "Those same writers must quickly rewrite their curriculum vitae (especially carefully—

Maximilian Voloshin and his mother, Koktebel', 1922.
Courtesy of Vladimir Kupchenko.

[listing] their works and [describing] their material conditions) and send [them] to the Moscow TsKUBU . . . so that the vitae are there by the first of October. . . . Getting the academic ration depends on it."[12]

The letter continued with a series of reminders or instructions about the steps to be taken in order to keep the rations flowing, for him as well as for the others. He was careful to distribute responsibility for accomplishing these tasks among other friends as well, not leaving it all up to Maria Stepanovna; and he concluded the letter with the following postscript: "Dearest Musia, as I write to you, I keep remembering your disappointment upon receiving the letter from Ol'ga Vasil'evna—because of its dryness."[13] He scarcely desired to burden this woman, whom he was presently courting, with dull, businesslike communications, but he was too careful a man to allow such important issues as food for himself and his associates to go unattended because of unclear communication, insufficient organization, or matters of the heart.

Given all his contacts in the outside world, his concern for his own community, his dogged persistence, and his meticulous pursuit of bureaucratic detail, Voloshin was becoming more than simply a friend to those he was supporting in their efforts survive: he was becoming, in effect, a personal economic mentor, facilitating access to subsistence for his friends and associates. Money no longer played the most significant role in assuring survival; rather, connection with a bureaucratized network did. Voloshin had made himself a node in that network, and thus, not unlike the exile journalist Geyer all those years before in Central Asia, had become a local patron.

SHELTER

The preservation of his life and the lives of his friends throughout the civil war was Voloshin's first step in forging the locus of personal power upon which he would rebuild his circle; obtaining and distributing food and supplies during the famine following the war was the second step; and now the third step was the preservation of his property from the incursions of Bolshevik requisition. That property was his household. As we saw, the household was the essential physical foundation for the formation and maintenance of circle relationships in the prerevolutionary period. Thus possession and control of the domestic sphere under Soviet rule in the postrevolutionary period is of considerable concern to us. The widespread Soviet requisition of domestic space—as the Bolsheviks sought in the early years to turn the necessity of providing for those left destitute by war into the advantage of taking state control of the economy and of private property—was to have a substantial impact on circle life. The ways that Voloshin managed to handle the requisition of his home reveal a great deal not only about his networking and patronage skills in reestablishing the material foundations of his circle but also how his means of accomplishing this played into the growing system of Soviet control.

If Voloshin had assured his physical survival by networking with wartime and postwar bureaucracies, he took the same approach in assuring possession and control of his property: by obtaining the vital protective documents. He acquired his first such document during the first period of Bolshevik rule from January 1918 to April 1918, when the Bolsheviks were driven out by the Germans. This mandate, put out in the name of the Theodosia Uezd Land Authority (Feodosiskaia uezdnaia zemel'naia uprava), declared that "the property and land and kitchen garden and house situated in the village of Koktebel', Taraktishskii volost', and belonging to the poet Maximilian Voloshin, remains in his use."[14] The ambiguity of these words—indeed they are contradictory—draws our attention to the uncertain nature of property at this time. The property belonged to Voloshin, and, by order of this paper, he could continue to use it. In July 1922 Voloshin received a similar protective document from Krymsovnarkom.[15] Then at last, in January 1924, he received the most valuable *udostoverenie* of all, directly from the People's Commissariat of Enlightenment, or Narkompros, in Moscow: "The writer and artist Maximilian Voloshin is under the patronage [*pod pokrovitel'stvom*] of the government of the USSR. His house in Koktebel', studio, library and archive, as state treasures, are not subject to requisition without the agreement of Narkompros USSR. Should local powers turn against him on any grounds whatsoever, NARKOMPROS RSFSR [Rossiskaia Sovetskaia Federativnaia Sotsialisticheskaia Respublika, or Russian Soviet Federal Socialist Republic] must be notified immediately."[16]

The document was stamped and signed by Anatoly Lunacharsky himself, as head of Narkompros. The language of this permit deserves close examination. First, the blunt proclamation of patronage reveals how explicitly conceived was the relationship between Voloshin, on the one hand, and Lunacharsky as a representative and Narkompros as a branch of the state, on the other. Voloshin was now clearly labeled a client of the Soviet state. Second, what had been Voloshin's property before the revolution was now state property, and was to be protected not as Voloshin's property but as state property. Voloshin's association with that property was based on his position as a client of the state. Finally, note for the future that those "local powers" referred to here that might turn against Voloshin were no abstract threat to the Voloshin household but were very real indeed. Aside from those powers, however, Voloshin had by 1924 acquired sufficient influence to convince the state to use its own terms in order to give him, at least for now, effective possession of his complete prerevolutionary property. But how had he accomplished this feat?

Already in the earliest days of Bolshevik control over Odessa Voloshin had believed that a way to hold on to one's property in the face of the grasping Bolshevik requisitions was to give that property a communal institutional identity. At that time he had proposed turning the Bunin household into a "Neo-Realist Art School" and making the Tsetlin household, where he himself was living, into a hostel for men and women poets.[17] Now, even as the civil war drew to a close, he hastened to take a similar route in defining his own household. This, of course, was by no means a wide stretch from the identity he had conceived for it before the revolution: even at that time, as well as a summer boarding house run by his mother, the household had already been the focal point for a domestic communal association of the literary and artistic intelligentsia. Thus his conception for creating what would essentially be a new Soviet institution was securely rooted in prerevolutionary intelligentsia social organization.

Still, Voloshin had to proceed through several stages before arriving at an institutional definition of his household that would gain favor with the state. His first attempt was reminiscent of the "Neo-Realist Art School" that he had wanted to organize in the Bunin home. Working together with the head of the nearby Karadag Scientific Station, a center where naturalists gathered to study the region, Voloshin proposed the establishment of an "Experimental Artistic-Scientific Studio," under his leadership, at his dacha in Koktebel'. He argued in a written proposal that a major weakness of contemporary training in the visual arts was that students could pass right through the art schools without ever having to learn such basic principles of nature as anatomy, perspective, light, and color. The purpose of this "Studio" was to rejuvenate the study of nature from an artistic point of view through the collaboration of artists and naturalists. Voloshin's practical arguments for the creation of such a school were concrete and detailed: the availability of his dacha, long a center of artistic activity (which had twenty-five rooms available for use); the large number of artists in the region who could, working together with the naturalists, lecture and otherwise guide the students; the excellent library facilities consisting of five thousand books in his own library and forty thousand in the library of the Karadag Scientific Station; and the unusually interesting landscapes of the Koktebel' region.[18]

Together, he and Professor Sludskii of the Karadag Scientific Station went about gaining bureaucratic support for their initiative, approaching (or preparing to approach; it is not always clear from the archival documents) such institutions as the Moscow Artistic Sector, the Moscow Experimental Institute of Painting, and the Crimean Artistic Sector of Narodobraz (Narodnoe Obrazovanie, or People's Education).[19] In the process they discovered something that would have great bearing on the future development of Voloshin's household; they learned that an effective way to protect one's home was to define it not as a school but as a sanatorium. They received permission from TsUKK (probably Tsentral'noe Upravlenie Krymskykh Kurortov, or the Central Administration of Crimean Resorts) to work on developing their establishment but with the proviso that it be called an "Artistic Sanatorium" and that it take in sick artists and performers from the North. With this in mind they next went to Krymzdarovotdel (the Crimean Department of Health), which also gave its approval.[20]

Their needs, as they described them, were as concrete and precise as their argument for its existence: above all they needed absolute confirmation that the School/Sanatorium would be located in Voloshin's dacha (a clear indication of the primary goal of this endeavor!) and that Voloshin himself would be the director of the institution. They would also require support from a variety of other state organizations in establishing what they called the "domestic part" of the sanatorium, such as rations for their guests. They also asked for assurances that the guests would not be called away to engage in summer work (a hint as to what threatened intellectuals who did not appear to be gainfully employed, and whose physical services were needed by a state trying to rebuild after the war).[21]

In the end, however, Voloshin appears to have gained little from this undertaking other than a greater familiarity, perhaps, with the bureaucratic apparatus that he would need to appease in order to hang onto his household; and at least one *udostoverenie*, from the War Revolutionary Commissariat of Theodosia, dated May 23, 1921, asking that all railroads and all war-revolutionary committees support him in his efforts to complete his duties not only as "*okhris*" (having perhaps to do with art protection) and as an organizer of the children's colonies in Koktebel' and Theodosia but also as the organizer of an "Artistic Studio."[22] Despite these momentary advantages, however, he had not yet discovered a designation that would protect his home.

According to the research of Vladimir Kupchenko, the definition of his household that would finally take hold came to Voloshin in April 1923: he would turn his household into a "summer station" where all and sundry, but especially those from the North (Petrograd and Moscow) with literary and artistic inclinations, could spend their summer vacations.[23] This was much like its prerevolutionary identity, with the one great difference that its rooms would now be offered free of charge. Voloshin thus effectively removed this one-time source of income entirely from the money economy. This was early in the New Economic Policy era in Soviet history, when War Communism was being rolled back and the free market was given more play in order to revive the economy and build confidence in the Soviet government.[24] Voloshin, however, chose not to attempt reentering the realm of capitalist relations but rather bound himself securely into the growing Soviet bureaucracy of intellectual welfare and privilege. He had never, as we remember, much liked taking money from his guests, finding that an uncomfortable contradiction to his ambitions as host, and had indeed left that job up to his more comfortably "bourgeois" mother.[25] For Voloshin, as perhaps for other intellectuals equally uncomfortable with capitalist economic relations, economic exchange mediated by bureaucracy appeared to be a preferable alternative to market relations.

The consolidation of this new definition of his household was no doubt reinforced by its institutional success in the summer of 1923. This was the first summer after the civil war that it was possible for the Russian intelligentsia to the North in Moscow and Petrograd to think about vacations, and the seaside, and thus about Koktebel'. Visitors streamed into Voloshin's home. By 1924 Voloshin was set on retaining this approach to preserving his household. While making his visit to Lunacharsky (at last) in March 1924, he obtained a second protective document from him confirming the organization in his home of a "free house of rest for writers, artists, [and] scholars, and also a literary-painting studio."[26] In an effort to gain further support from the center, he also wrote one or more letters later that year asking explicitly for the patronage of Lev Kamenev, the head of the Moscow Party organization. In a fragmentary draft Voloshin outlined his institutional concept in some detail:

> During my mother's lifetime the house with its additions was rented out, but after she died I offered it to be used free of charge by writers, artists, [and] scholars, expanding . . . the traditions of the house. Since the beginning of Soviet power, not one room has been let for money. The doors are open to all, without any reservations: especially to writers, artists, scholars and their families, and—if there is space—to anyone who needs sun and rest, and can't afford to pay health resort prices.
>
> . . . I think that the Koktebel' Artistic Colony is turning out to be a useful and desirable organization, and for the arts—it is organically essential. You know yourself how difficult the economic situation of writers, poets, [and] artists is, how over-strained each one is from work and the tensions of city life, and how important it is in this situation for some to get reviving summer rest, and for others to seclude themselves for personal creative work.[27]

Voloshin succeeded in hanging onto his household "Artistic Colony" until the end of the 1920s, because he recognized that such an organization would be "organically essential" to the arts and to the Soviet Russian intelligentsia. The urban artistic and scholarly intelligentsia was indeed suffering greatly from sickness and exhaustion because of the stresses of the civil war and its aftermath. Thus the intelligentsia was in urgent need of the sanatorium, or *Dom Otdykha* (House of Rest), as organizations such as Voloshin's would soon come to be known. Yet they had also been left poverty-stricken in the wake of war and War Communism, and had no means to pay for this kind of privilege. Free access to such a household as Voloshin's was a great boon, and the state (or, at least, Lunacharsky and Narkompros) had provided this boon by supporting Voloshin in his endeavors.

Voloshin maintained the economic, bureaucratic foundations of his new circle through his continued and indefatigable activities as a client of the state during the 1920s. For example, he wrote to a variety of state organizations in order to publicize his facilities and to establish them as part of a regular system. Thus, for example, we find a letter from A. A., secretary of GAKhN (State Academy of Artistic Studies), thanking Voloshin for his proposal that GAKhN hold permanent rooms at the Koktebel' Artistic Colony, and taking him up on the proposal on the spot. Voloshin's first guests from this organization, wrote A. A., would be a Professor Lavrionov, and the letter-writing secretary himself. In a classic demonstration of the ways that personal ties continued to inform the structure of bureaucratic association, A. A. reminded Voloshin that he was one of Voloshin's "listeners and admirers from the long-past days of *Musaget*," a journal Voloshin had worked on in the prerevolutionary period.[28] Other organizations with which Voloshin had a more permanent relationship, or sought one, included the Society for the Improvement of the Crimea, the Historical Museum, the Military Medical Academy, the Society for the Scientific Study of the Crimea, the Union of Poets, the All-Russian Union of Writers, and the Literary Fund, RSFSR.[29]

Voloshin also struggled to gain certain privileges for his guests. In 1926 he initiated a campaign to free them from the ten-ruble "resort tax," a burden he claimed was difficult for them to bear. He also complained at length about his guests' difficulties in obtaining train tickets, and he requested that they be allowed to buy them *vne ocheredi*. He met with considerable resistance on some of these issues; this was because, although his household would seem to have been most securely tied into the central state bureaucracy, it remained, for a number of local bureaucrats, suspiciously informal and independent. Yet Voloshin did not easily concede defeat.

In his endless petitioning and networking with the bureaucracy in the interest of his Colony and its inhabitants, he was making himself a client of the state. By the same token, he was also becoming his guests' patron, retaining property and obtaining supplies and privileges for them, much as he had made himself a local patron of the Crimean intelligentsia when they were threatened by war and famine. All those with whom he was networking—whether his patrons or his clients—were becoming part of a vast and expanding system of bureaucratic control of material benefits, with his circle as the focal point of their mutual exchange. He had thus bureaucratized his circle, integrating it ever more tightly, from Victor Turner's point of view, into structure—the structure of traditional patronage relations and of the state, entwined as they were.

BUREAUCRACY, PATRONAGE, WELFARE, AND PRIVILEGE

Voloshin's role as a kind of traditional patron figure through networking with the state was in no way anomalous in the early days of Soviet power: it was part of a growing pattern of power redistribution that was rooted in the chaos and privation of wartime, and built upon the scrambling but increasingly effective Soviet efforts at social transformation in the intellectual world through a mixture of bureaucracy and personal ties. This pattern consisted of a growing number of such loci of power, or individuals with increasing sway over the lives of their fellow intellectuals owing to their association with the state. These were individuals who went beyond the effort merely to preserve themselves and their families, and sought, like Voloshin, to expand their influence for the sake of other individuals and groups of individuals to whom they felt a certain kind of responsibility. In this acceptance, or seizure, of personal responsibility they bore a resemblance to mentors of Russian intellectual life before the revolution.

As in the earlier period, this phenomenon in the literary world led to the increasing manifestation during the 1920s of chains or networks of people linked together by the organizational influence of such individuals. These chains or networks were often tied to specific institutions, for the new mentors were also institution builders, many of them eager to provide not just professional support by establishing institutions but also the kind of benefits they had once offered in their homes—places to live, food to eat, networking opportunities, and so on. What differed now was the factor of extensive state involvement; for the state was deeply interested in the development and fate of Russian letters and writers under its rule, and was willing to offer substantial material support. Such support was hard to ignore at a time of privation, even if many writers had wanted to do so.

It was through the personal intervention of such figures as Voloshin, and the other loci of power to be discussed below, that many writers sought access to state support. And as these patrons sought to fulfill the needs and demands of their followers, they began to link them to the state, drawing them into what would eventually prove, from a literary point of view, a dangerous intimacy with and dependence on it. But this was not a one-way process; just as the state was cultivating the dependence of writers and thereby control over them, so writers, through their patrons, were exerting influence over the emerging state structure. Through the particular demands that they were making, they were making clear their own expectations of support. And to no small extent, the state responded by enabling the establishment and expansion of a variety of state institutions that fulfilled their demands. This process appears to have continued apace throughout the 1920s, regardless of the changing literary politics and quarrels of the time.[30]

We can observe many elements of this process by surveying briefly the activities of some of the individuals who were such loci of power: writer and historian Mikhail Gershenzon, former Symbolist Valerii Briusov, author and playwright Maxim Gorky, and Commissar of Enlightenment Anatoly Lunacharsky. We can also learn what kinds of things writers were asking for, how they were obtaining them through their patrons, and which institutions were involved in or were products of this process.

"Those who lived in Moscow during these difficult years—1918, 1919, and 1920—will never forget what a good comrade [Mikhail] Gershenzon was," writes the poet Khodasevich of one he clearly considers to have been his guardian angel or mentor in these hard times. Mikhail Gershenzon supported such associates as Khodasevich in two ways. Like Voloshin, he appears, on the one hand, to have been willing to exert himself endlessly for their benefit, in Khodasevich's case finding him money and work, and aiding him in carrying out his business when he had to be out of town. Gershenzon was, like Voloshin, even willing to bustle about (*khlopotat'*) from one bureaucratic office to another in the interest of his clients. When Khodasevich had to leave Moscow for the Crimea, "Gershenzon, and no one else, *khlopotal* in my interests."[31] And from what Khodasevich writes, he was far from the only beneficiary of Gershenzon's personal engagement: "He was tremendously good at guessing the troubles of others—and not in words, but in deeds hurried to their aid."[32]

But Gershenzon, like Voloshin, sought to support his needy associates in more institutional terms as well: by helping to develop an organization for mutual aid in the literary community. The result was the first, non-Party, Writers' Union, upon which the later Soviet Writers' Union would be based. "[Gershenzon] was the most active of the organizers of the Union, and its first chairman," writes Khodasevich; without the Union, he continues, many writers might simply have collapsed; certainly it did a great deal to ease their lives.[33] Gershenzon soon stepped aside from his leadership position in the Union. But through his organizational activities he had already done a great deal to establish a network of writers, which, although originally relatively independent of a state identity, would eventually be drawn fully into the Soviet system of bureaucratized literary life. Gershenzon also worked for Narkompros, in the Literary Department, as well as for Glavarkhiv,[34] though it is unclear whether or not he was using those positions as well to aid his associates.

Valerii Briusov, who is familiar to us as a leader in the Symbolist community in earlier years, was another of these loci of power, though the nature of his influence and the way he was willing to use it was, as always, distinctly his own. His organizational leadership of the Symbolists in the prerevolutionary period had been vital, though he had been less fond of offering personal patronage than, say, Viacheslav Ivanov. In the early Soviet era he chose to enhance his power by joining the Party and its organs of administration. He took on several different influential bureaucratic roles, including head of the Library Department of Narkompros, head of the Literary Department of Narkompros, and head of the Department of Artistic Education of Glavprofopra, to name only a few.[35] True to form, Briusov seems to have engaged less in personal patronage than some others did, though, for example, in his role as head of the Department of Scholarly Libraries, like Voloshin he acted to save the library of one intellectual, that of

N. N. Fatov.[36] But in the course of his activities he did funnel substantial funding support to literati. In the documentation of Lito Narkompros we find that he chaired meetings evaluating and funding the applications of a number of literary circles asking for state support of a variety of sorts. The materials touching on his activities as a representative of the state reflect the positive enthusiasm with which the state supported literary organizations, including literary circles, during this early period of Soviet history, as well as the energy with which hopeful circle members were applying for funding.[37]

These funding applications to Lito Narkompros from literary circles also offer insight into what writers who had organized themselves into circles thought the state might offer them, such as meeting spaces for circle gatherings, material support for public readings and discussions, and funding for their literary labors.[38] One consequence of engaging in this kind of self-conscious organizational and financial relationship with the state was that such circles were required to register with the police, enabling the police as well as the NKVD (the new set of identifying letters for the Cheka, or secret police) to scrutinize their financial resources and expenditures. On a lighter note, it appears that the NKVD began to worry that some of these privileged intellectual organizations were serving as mere fronts for such commercial operations as beer halls. But these may not have been the organizations that presented themselves to Briusov's eagle eye.[39]

At a far more elevated level of influence was Maxim Gorky, who had access to the highest ranks of Bolshevik power. In the years before the revolution, Gorky had served as mentor and patron to many young writers, including members of his *Sreda* group. In the Soviet period Gorky continued and indeed vastly expanded his patronage obligations and activities but now on the basis of his access to state resources through personal ties with the Party leadership, Lenin in particular. He used his power, possibly more extensively and effectively than anyone else, not only to give personal aid to great numbers of those who approached him with individual needs but also to build up a series of organizations to provide financial support and privilege to writers.[40] This was not necessarily easy for him to do: he had opposed the Bolshevik coup in October 1917 and only with difficulty had reconciled himself to their activities; he would leave the country in frustration in 1921 and would not return until 1928.

Beginning in 1918 a veritable onslaught of needy intellectuals approached Gorky for all the things Voloshin and his associates were requesting, and more, and he did a great deal to meet their requests. These included not only protection from the threat of arrest and execution by the Bolsheviks, as in the case of Nikolai Gumilev and others, but also, to name only a few examples, exemptions from the draft, rations, living space, boots,

Maxim Gorky and
Vladimir Ilych Lenin,
Petrograd, 1920.

and even (later on) aid in surviving the hated communal apartment or assistance in moving out.[41] He also received many requests for help in obtaining the right to travel abroad, most famously from Alexander Blok (who
died, however, before permission finally came through).[42] Gorky was willing to approach even the most dangerous figures in order to respond to
some of these requests, as revealed in his correspondence with Genrikh
Yagoda, head of the NKVD from 1934 to 1936.[43] Like Voloshin but on a far
greater scale, Gorky, too, became an intermediate figure in the growing patronage chain, acting as client to the Bolshevik leaders in order to serve as
patron to those who came to him as clients. And, like Voloshin, he was
thereby accumulating an increasingly large group of dependents.

Gorky also founded a variety of state-based institutions to provide for the needs of literati in a broader and more regular fashion. In September 1918 in Petrograd, Gorky obtained Lenin's support for the organization of the *Vsemirnaia literatura* publishing house, which functioned as a kind of organizational center where Petrograd writers and intellectuals could find work and economic support.[44] Though *Vsemirnaia literatura* published comparatively few books during its existence (only fifty-three books over three years),[45] its role in the preservation of the morale and physical welfare of Petrograd intellectuals during and just after the civil war was significant. Gorky was also responsible for founding the Petrograd House of the Arts (*Dom Iskusstv*), established in a mansion abandoned by the fleeing merchant family the Eliseevs. The House of the Arts, intended to provide both living quarters and meeting rooms, was inhabited by a number of starving young intellectuals. It had a number of rooms, a kitchen, and a great "hall of mirrors," in which lectures, readings, concerts, and other group activities took place.[46]

One literary circle that particularly benefited from Gorky's state-based largesse was the Serapion Brothers, a literary circle moderate in its ideology but supportive of the young Soviet state, a group in whom Gorky saw a potential wellspring of Soviet literary talent. Although initially several of them came to him for his intellectual and professional support, they soon sought and received personal economic and other state-controlled support as well.[47] He also assisted them in other ways, contributing his work to their literary endeavors and advertising their literary skills both at home and abroad.[48] And they were particular beneficiaries not only of his personal patronage but also of such local institutions that Gorky had helped to organize as the Petrograd House of the Arts, where several of them lived and where many of their meetings took place in the early years of Soviet power. The Serapion Brothers' gradual integration into the Soviet system as beneficiaries of a variety of Gorky's patronage and institution-building activities reveals another way in which circles were being drawn into dependency on the state. Their conditioning to such dependency would have, as we shall see, real consequences in 1932 when the state undertook its most effective attack on Soviet literary independence by banning all literary circles and laying the foundation of the Soviet Writers' Union.

Gorky also took responsibility for aiding not only writers but intellectuals more broadly, and looked not just at home but abroad as well for aid to distribute to them. He was closely involved in instigating the humanitarian and welfare activities of the two institutions from which Voloshin and his associates in the Crimea most benefited during and just after the civil war, for example, the ARA (American Relief Association) and TsKUBU (Central Commission for the Improvement of the Condition of Scholars). Reaching out on the basis of his own ties and reputation abroad during the period of famine, Gorky addressed a public appeal to Western citizens through the newspapers on July 23, 1921: "The corn-growing steppes are smitten by crop failure . . . Think of the Russian people's exhaustion by the war and revolution . . . Gloomy days have come for the country of Tolstoy, Dostoyevsky, Mendeleev, Pavlov, Moussorgsky, Glinka, and other world-prized men . . . I ask all honest European and American people for prompt aid to the Russian people. Give bread and medicine."[49] U.S. Secretary of Commerce Herbert Hoover responded with a telegram outlining the political and mechanical conditions of ARA aid, and as much as eight hundred thousand tons of food and medicine arrived in Russia from that organization. A separate agreement established a system whereby individual donors from many countries were able to send food parcels, evidently of the sort that Voloshin received, through the ARA.[50]

Gorky was equally concerned to organize material support for Russian intellectuals within the boundaries of the former Russian Empire. He was a founding chairman of TsKUBU, whose earliest meetings took place (like the meetings of so many other such institutions during this period) in Gorky's Petrograd apartment in January of 1920, and at least one such meeting was graced by the presence of Anatoly Lunacharsky himself.[51] TsKUBU, under Gorky's leadership, became an organizational point for accumulating material support for the Russian educated elite as a whole, beginning with such basic needs as food and wood for heating, for example, as well as access to medical care and sanatoriums for the sick.

Nothing was plentiful, however, and so, as in the case of Gorky's personal patronage, choices were made about whom to support—and whom not to. Thus we find one TsKUBU protocol describing the procedure of going through a list of professors and assistants who were to receive rations, and excluding seventy-seven individuals from that list.[52] It can well be imagined how personal familiarity and loyalty must have played a role in this selection process, as well as questions of ideological suitability and calculated "value" to the community. TsKUBU had influence in other issues as well: the continued material support of a scientific laboratory, for example, and the exclusion of certain students from the military draft.[53] It was not unusual in these matters, often handled on a case-by-case basis, for Lunacharsky or even Lenin himself to intervene for the sake of one individual or another. Thus, for example, in the case of the professor who needed supplies to keep his scientific laboratory operating, we find a note from Lenin requesting support for Gorky in resolving this and similar difficulties.[54] Patronage from this highest level of power was, of course, the most valuable to obtain.

The documents touching on Gorky's activities in TsKUBU also reveal an important side of Gorky's character, namely, that he was an excellent administrator, and, like Voloshin, was well aware of the requirements of interacting with state institutions. Meticulous and energetic, Gorky enforced institutional order by example and by exhortation. He combined a concern for broad goals with a complete lack of embarrassment at focusing on details. Thus we find, for example, at the bottom of a document setting an ambitious agenda (not Gorky's own) for discussion at an early meeting of TsKUBU, a handwritten note from Gorky commenting incisively on the feasibility of the agenda and also reminding a member of the Commission not to be late for the meeting.[55] It was this kind of organizational skill that put TsKUBU on such a firm footing that it would successfully survive Gorky's absence when he left the country in 1921.

At a time of chaos, catastrophe, and hand-wringing, Gorky used all his moral authority and his administrative talents to support many who urgently needed all that he could do for them. It is clear that he viewed these efforts as a significant achievement, of Soviet power as well as his own. In a 1927 letter to an unknown recipient, which apparently made its way to Nikolai Bukharin, Gorky wrote: "TsKUBU is one of those institutions of Soviet power of which it may unarguably be proud before 'cultured' Europe."[56] And it seems quite likely that, just as Voloshin had been uncomfortable with market relations in the prerevolutionary period and found relief in turning to bureaucratic means of "renting out" the rooms in his house, so Gorky, too, who before the revolution had castigated writers who saw their work in market terms and catered to public taste, calling them "speculators in popularity, adventurers, those who look on authorship as easy seasonal labor," found this new institutionalized system for providing for the material needs of writers more culturally acceptable.[57]

Like Gorky, Anatoly Lunacharsky was at odds with Lenin and other leaders of the Bolshevik Party for a number of years before the revolution. Nonetheless Lunacharsky had established sufficient credentials as one attuned to the problems of supporting intellectual endeavor and yet also trustworthy from the Bolsheviks' point of view that when the latter took power in the fall of 1917, Lunacharsky was made Commissar of Enlightenment, a post equivalent to that of Secretary or Minister of Education. The People's Commissariat of Enlightenment, or Narkompros, was a rambling bureaucracy with many different departments and responsibilities, ranging from the university system to the teaching of literacy in distant, isolated villages to the running of the once Imperial, now Soviet, state theaters. As such, it had the potential for providing enormous support to intellectuals both through personal patronage and by institutional means.

Lunacharsky evidently viewed Narkompros as a means of providing personal patronage on the basis of access to state resources to as many starving intellectuals as possible. Party members—and others with more technical skills—generally stayed away from the Commissariat. Instead, it was populated largely by intellectuals such as journalists and political commentators, many of whom were hired on the basis of network relations. "Lunacharsky," writes historian Sheila Fitzpatrick, "who could never believe that Narkompros could be the worse for gaining a man of goodwill, or the wife of a comrade, or the destitute granddaughter of a distinguished writer, had the habit of recruiting staff on a personal basis and directing them with letters of introduction to the head of a Narkompros department."[58] Not surprisingly, this practice led to considerable inefficiency; for many years Narkompros was unable to make a complete list of its employees or even of its departments.[59]

But, from Lunacharsky's perspective, this may not have been the point, for he evidently took very seriously his patronage responsibilities to those who appealed to him, and viewed Narkompros as a means of fulfilling those responsibilities. A matter of considerable attention at Narkompros in the early years was the personal welfare of staff members, writes Fitzpatrick. "Special allowances of firewood were voted for the scholar K. A. Timiryazev, and for Lebedev-Polyansky, in view of his wife's serious illness and 'the impossibility of recovery with the temperature at 1 degree above the freezing point.' A. I. Yuzhin, head of the Maly Theater in Moscow, and Aleksandrov of the professional education section were given orders for issue of fur coats by the Moscow Consumers' society to replace 'those stolen from them in the execution of their official duties.'"[60] But beyond this sort of personal benefit, Lunacharsky, through the wide-ranging activities of Narkompros, probably did more than anyone else to institutionalize welfare and privilege for intellectuals. He accomplished this through the funding and control that Narkompros wielded over a vast number of institutions of intellectual life; in literature these ranged from such publishing houses as *Vsemirnaia literatura* and *Gosizdat* to such organizations as Voloshin's vacation home for intellectuals.

By obtaining and distributing this state-based support in the literary world, such well-intentioned men as Voloshin, Gershenzon, Briusov, Gorky, and Lunacharsky were helping to form tight bonds of dependence and mutual interest between writers and the state. The tentacles of the system these men had set in motion continued to extend themselves throughout the 1920s. TsKUBU, for example, went on growing long after Gorky had left it, taking on such responsibilities as providing books and journals from Moscow and abroad to its more far-flung clients, as well as food and manufactured goods until 1923, stipends, sanatorium access, and so on. The state attempted to cut back TsKUBU's state funding in 1924, but that support began to expand again the very next year. By 1926 TsKUBU had established a considerable material and institutional foundation, having built six of its own sanatoriums, a dormitory in Moscow, pensioners' homes in Moscow and Leningrad, and a House of Scholars in Moscow, under whose aegis were a library, cafeteria, auditoriums for lectures and readings, and "twenty scholarly societies and circles."[61]

Another, similar institution of importance for the literary intelligentsia was the Literary Fund, RSFSR (or Litfond RSFSR). This institution was founded in 1927 by the Federation of Associations of Soviet Writers and included representatives from trade unions, Narkompros, and the State Publishing House (Gosizdat, established by Narkompros).[62] Litfond was the nominal successor of a prestigious prerevolutionary organization called the Literary Fund, which had functioned as a self-supporting charity organization, providing loans, pensions, and educational stipends to impoverished writers and their relatives. The prerevolutionary Literary Fund had raised its money from donations, concerts, and other productions, and by publishing editions of the works of such famous writers as Turgenev and Pushkin.[63] Like Litfond RSFSR, TsKUBU probably received substantial state funding, although direct evidence of this does not appear in its archive. It, too, rapidly established its own material foundation, not only giving out loans and pensions but renting dachas in Sochi and Yalta for its members, establishing Houses of Rest, and eventually becoming involved in the building of cooperative apartment houses for writers. A number of the archival documents of Litfond RSFSR touch on the gritty details of its building and repairing activities.[64]

As both TsKUBU and Litfond grew, their activities became increasingly entwined with a broad range of economic activities of significance to writers and scholars. For example, as Litfond gave out loans, it became entangled in a procedure by which the petitioner for a loan would provide a guarantee from his publishing house that he would receive money to cover that sum from future publications; thus Litfond was (to its own frustration) in effect issuing publishing advances for (state-controlled) publishing houses.[65] If Voloshin was able to order books and journals through TsKUBU, the next rational step was that TsKUBU should take what he owed it for books directly from his monthly stipend.[66] The strands of intelligentsia economic association were gradually being drawn together into a kind of bureaucratic web binding the intelligentsia ever more intimately to the state.

As the web grew more dense, issues of state ideological control could not but intrude. For example, if state-supported TsKUBU supplied publications from abroad to its members, then naturally it became involved with the institutions of control and censorship of published matter. Thus, when

Voloshin ordered French periodicals on art and literature through TsKUBU, he received a reply to the effect that his order would have to be cleared with Glavlit, the central Soviet censorship board. This would probably not be a problem, the note continued, for so far Glavlit had turned down no requests.[67] By gaining control of the material basis of intelligentsia life in these increasingly intertwined ways, the state was also gaining ideological control.

Among the most significant aspects of growing state control of the material foundations of literary life was its tightening grip on the domestic sphere, that vital basis for literary energy and activity. As the state distributed living space to those who needed it by placing them with those who presumably had it to spare in the group living arrangement known as the communal apartment or *kommunal'ka*, the intelligentsia was forced into entirely unplanned and unwanted (from their own point of view) extended households. This brought on a good deal of complaining from intellectuals during the 1920s, as they struggled to obtain living quarters supportive of intellectual activity, and suitable to the intelligentsia sense of dignity.[68] Like Voloshin with his House of Rest, they soon discovered that a compromise was possible: if the state was unwilling to leave the disposition of domestic space entirely up to its citizens, it was sometimes willing to accept compromise in the form of group living organizations whose membership could be determined by profession.

During the civil war, this compromise brought about such organizations as Gorky's "House of Arts" in Petrograd/Leningrad, as well the House of Scholars and the House of Literati in that city, which operated in a similar fashion to the House of Arts. Later, toward the end of the 1920s and in the early 1930s, communal apartment buildings for writers began to go up. The first such establishment for the literarily inclined in Leningrad was built (with state agreement, of course) on the basis of advances paid by members of the Writers' Union and an engineers' union. It came to be known as the "Tears of Socialism," because of the building's tendency to leak when it rained (officially, it was called the House of the Commune). The Tears of Socialism, at 7 Rubinstein Street in Leningrad, consisted of a series of apartments without kitchens; a communal sort of cafeteria was located on the first floor, where all the occupants ate together. A cloakroom, kindergarten, hairdresser, and library were all part of the building's amenities.[69] Other similar (although some were far more luxurious) buildings for the intellectual elite appeared soon thereafter. In Leningrad, a building exclusively for the use of writers was established; in Moscow, a very prestigious building for writers was erected on Lavrushenskii Lane, directly across from the Tretiakov Art Museum. Access to the apartments in these buildings was, by 1934, entirely under the control of state bureaucracies;

these apartments, too, were being twisted into the thickening bureaucratic web of welfare and privilege that bound writers to the state.

This rapidly expanding system rendered the literary community increasingly susceptible to the demands of the state and would soon become deeply destructive of literary freedom. Yet it may be that this is not how many intellectuals experienced it. That intricate web may have been rendered relatively invisible, or at least obscured, by the intermediary role of those loci of power. It may well be that it was to those individuals that writers felt a sense of obligation, rather than to the state.[70] Certainly an obligation of some sort was felt, as revealed by our last view of Osip Mandelshtam, now beginning his precarious way toward the Gulag and death.

Mandelshtam considered himself a client of one particular Bolshevik leader who had a chain of clients extending far beyond the literary world: Nikolai Bukharin.[71] He pointed this out to his wife Nadezhda one day after she came to him indignant about a conversation she had had with the wife of the then head of the NKVD: "'[Writer Boris] Pilniak comes to see us,' this woman had told Nadezhda, then asking her, 'whom do you go to see?'" Osip, writes Nadezhda, "tried to calm me: 'Everybody goes to see someone. There's no other way. We go to see Nikolai Ivanovich [Bukharin].'"[72] But there was a price to pay for this patronage, as the Mandelshtams realized when they failed to pay that price and then sought to hide their failure from their patron. Upon Osip's arrest for his famously devastating poem about Stalin, Nadezhda immediately went to Bukharin.[73] "When he heard what had happened he changed color and bombarded me with questions . . . 'He hasn't written anything rash, has he?' I said no, just a few poems in his usual manner, nothing worse than Bukharin knew of already. It was a lie, and I still feel ashamed of it."[74]

That Bukharin expected self-censorship from Mandelshtam in return for his protective patronage is evident; also apparent is that the desire to please Bukharin—and not to get him in trouble with those more powerful than he—was a concern for the Mandelshtams, even if they did not allow their actions to be fully guided by this concern. Surely others felt a similar pressure. The sense of personal clientelistic responsibility leading to self-censorship was another important component of this system of bureaucracy and personal ties.

The sense of clientelism on the part of those who were receiving material aid through the intervention of loci of power is also revealed in a new development in the contemporaries memoir genre: the expression of praise and gratitude to such patron figures for their economic support.[75] Khodasevich's gratitude to Mikhail Gershenzon for his aid is manifest in the memoir about Gershenzon cited above; Briusov, although less a focus of effusive gratitude, was the object of genuine appreciation expressed in a memoir by the woman whose father's library he saved. More to the point, in a way, he was the object of what might be described as anti-cult rage for his failure to offer such aid to one petitioner for his bureaucratically based largesse, namely, Marina Tsvetaeva, who wrote an entire memoir castigating Briusov for his failure to fund a literary effort.[76] Briusov had failed to fulfill what she considered her justified expectation of support in that effort. Maxim Gorky was the subject of a large number of grateful memoirs, especially by the Serapion Brothers. Several Serapion memoirs about him appeared around the same time that Gorky returned from Western Europe to make his final home in the Soviet Union. Two more Serapion memoirs would appear later in the hagiographic volume *Gorky in the Memoirs of Contemporaries*. Even Anatoly Lunacharsky had his own memoir cult: in the archives now located in one of his old Moscow Narkompros offices, the State Literary Archive, lies a whole sheaf of unpublished adoring "contemporaries" memoirs about his activities in supporting individuals during the 1920s. The writers of these memoirs range from his secretaries to one-time agriculture students whom he supported economically and professionally to the children of people he had helped.[77]

Thus we see how some of the traditions of *kruzhok* culture, especially the more pragmatic tradition of networking and patronage—as opposed to the communitas tradition of anti-hierarchy and I-Thou relations—led the literary community into a condition that was contradictory to the spirit of communitas as well as severely inhibiting to the free development of literary self-expression. Its institutionalization was almost complete.

EIGHT

Inside Voloshin's Soviet Circle: Persistence of Structure, Preservation of Anti-structure

A NEW PARTNERSHIP
IN HOSPITALITY

As Voloshin's new Soviet circle took off with a flourish in the summer of 1924, much was familiar. Though there were many new visitors, they continued as in the past to be a mixture from all parts of the intelligentsia: artists, scientists, ballet dancers, engineers, archeologists, and many others, sprinkled with a highly visible contingent of writers. The landscape was as ever, and so was Voloshin's joy in hiking it, although by all accounts he now traveled shorter distances and talked less on these journeys, feeling the effects of ill health following his civil war traumas. The evening gatherings on the roof or in the spacious studio took place again, offering the opportunity for literary and artistic discourse among both the famous and less famous of Voloshin's visitors.

Poetry remained at the center of the household agenda. Not only was Voloshin able to attract poets of considerable talent, but his own reputation as a poet had gained owing in large part to the poetry he had written during the period of Russia's wartime agony. This poetry, like the domestic poetry he had written for the *Obormoty* many years before, served to create a sense of community, but now of community in a broader sense as Voloshin's domestic audience sought meaning in the terrible experiences that they as Russians and as members of the intelligentsia had recently undergone. Not that Voloshin abandoned his regional and domestic poetry; building on his increased skill, he continued to write and recite poetry about the Crimea and about his household. He began his poem "House of the Poet" (1926) with the words:

Maximilian Voloshin with some of his guests, Koktebel', 1920s.
Courtesy of Vladimir Kupchenko.

> The door is unlocked. Step across the threshold.
> My house is open to all paths.[1]

His efforts to create anew a vibrant domestic intellectual community were effective, especially for young people and children, many of whom would later write about their summer vacations there in the 1920s with reminiscent delight. Both Voloshin and his home made a deep impression on them.

Other elements of the circle's prerevolutionary culture persisted into the Soviet period as well. Yet they, too, underwent certain changes; the new circumstances of the circle—including not only its transformation into a state institution but also its new social, political, and economic environment under Soviet rule—shifted the balance and implications of certain of those cultural elements. In this chapter the particular adaptations of traditional *kruzhok* culture to be explored are the male-female partnership in hospitality at the heart of the circle, which persisted and was perhaps even strengthened under Soviet rule; and the habit of economic networking, which was indeed substantially reinforced and enhanced. And, finally, what happened to the spirit of communitas in all of this: had it vanished entirely, given the bureaucratization of Voloshin's circle? Or did that spirit somehow continue to play a role in the community?

Voloshin's new partnership in hospitality had a rather old-fashioned air about it in light of Bolshevik ambitions for improving the status of women. The new leaders of the country were attempting to transform the role of women in society at this time by loosening the restrictiveness of the marriage bond; this was the essence of the 1918 decree making marriage a matter of registration, and divorce a simple civil procedure as well.[2] But the story of how Voloshin forged a new partnership in circle hospitality reveals the continuing importance of the traditional male-female domestic partnership under the new economic circumstances of bureaucratization and impoverishment. For given his ambitions to preserve his summer circle as a state institution under difficult economic circumstances, it appears that Voloshin now needed someone to help him with its material side as much as ever, if not more. This does not mean that love played no part in the new partnership; on the contrary, like the old partnership with Elena Ottobal'-dovna, the new one involved careful emotional as well as pragmatic negotiation, this time leading to Voloshin's second marriage.

Elena Ottobal'dovna Voloshina's final illness began during the civil war and continued until her death in January 1923. This illness placed considerable burdens on Voloshin. He was not accustomed to running the material side of the household on his own, and Elena Ottobal'dovna became increasingly demanding under the stress of ill health. To alleviate these difficulties Voloshin brought in a nurse, or *fel'dsher*, to take care of her. This was Maria Stepanovna Zabolotskaia, a friend of Anastasiia Tsvetaeva who had come with her to the Crimea in 1919. Maria Stepanovna, as Voloshin's second wife, was to play a considerable role not only in Voloshin's Soviet circle but also in the formation of his cult after his death; the story of her background and the development of her relationship with Voloshin illuminate the meanings and motivations of that role.

By no means born into the educated elite, Maria Stepanovna came from an impoverished and unhappy background. Her father had been a (Catholic) Polish worker, and her mother came from a family of Orthodox Old Believers who had disowned her upon her marriage to a Catholic. Maria Stepanovna's father died early, leaving the rest of the family to struggle on in poverty; her brother wandered off and was never heard from again; and her mother died of tuberculosis while Maria Stepanovna was still very young. Apparently as the result of a suicide attempt when she was twelve, which found its way into the newspapers, Maria Stepanovna was taken in by the headmistress of a Petersburg gymnasium; thus, despite her childhood poverty, she was exposed to both education and material comfort in her adolescence.³ She was (like Elena Ottobal'dovna) a strong-willed and highly capable woman, especially in the household realm. That this particular domestic skill played a significant role in the growth and strengthening of Voloshin's romantic feelings toward her is evident in what remains of their correspondence with each other.

Toward the end of 1922, while Maria Stepanovna was taking care of his mother in Koktebel', Voloshin took the opportunity to try to mend his own health by going to a sanatorium in Sevastopol. While there, he received the news that Maria Stepanovna, though she had originally intended to stay on with his mother throughout the winter, was now unsure about this plan. Voloshin's return missive of November 18, rambling, repetitive, and self-contradictory, indicates the anxious state into which her letter cast him: "[When I heard that you and Pra had decided that you would stay in Koktebel' this winter,] I was infinitely happy. But I wrote to you myself that it will be very difficult. And it will be difficult. I have a very hard time with Pra. And those difficulties will fall on you as well. Dear Marusia, I myself would not ask you to live in Koktebel', because it is a great sacrifice. You wrote that you had decided to stay. I was deeply happy. But you are wavering. And I tell you precisely: it's not necessary, don't live in Koktebel'. You will lose your freedom."⁴

But Voloshin could not resist going on in this letter to tell her how much he needed her in Koktebel'. One very big problem was that he wanted Maria Stepanovna to stay with Pra while he made his long-planned trip to Moscow ("You yourself can see from all the telegrams I have received that it is essential . . ."). He believed that he needed first to go to Moscow and then probably to Berlin to ascertain that he gain financially from the publications of his works. "But I can't even raise the issue of leaving directly with Pra, because a year and a half ago she said, 'It would be better simply to give me poison, and then you can go where you want.' After that it was impossible even to talk [about it]."⁵ His problems with Pra were such, he went on, that he could hardly do his own work in Koktebel', despite an urgent need and desire to do so. But no, no, he wrote, it would be too difficult for Maria Stepanovna to stay in Koktebel': she simply shouldn't do it.

"And don't love me, Marusia," he continued, raising the emotional stakes, "that will be infinitely torturous. You will be torturously jealous, very much so, for a long time. I won't always be able to be as attentive to you as you need." And then he offered her a kind of deal: "But if you can love *not me* personally, but rather that which I do and *I must do*, that kind of love I ask and pray that you give. No one has ever loved me in that way before. It is the kind of love that I must have, Marusia. Help me to love Russia and help to find the words . . . help me to find peace. . . . I have to have stability to do my work. If you can come to love me that way, then I ask you, I pray of you: stay with me in Koktebel', be [there] forever, stay with Pra in my place, when I have to leave. . . . Make Koktebel' a place of peace and seclusion for me, which it has often been, but has, alas, ceased to be. You can do it with your love, Marusia, although you yourself will be uneasy and tortured and uncomfortable."[6]

This is an apparently honest, and indeed perhaps eloquent, masculine declaration of need as opposed to love. Underlying this proposal was a conviction on Voloshin's part (expressed elsewhere in the same letter) that his own literary fame was now, at last, beginning to grow on the basis of his poetry about Russia in war and upheaval.[7] In return for her commitment to him and his needs, as his offer to her seems to convey, Marusia could expect to acquire the prestige to be gained from aiding in the labors of a Russian poet. That Maria Stepanovna was in later years to become an ardent advertiser of Voloshin's perfections is an indication that at some level she was willing to consider such a deal. Perhaps fortunately for the strength of their living relationship, however, she did not acquiesce in the terms of this contract immediately, and there was time for Voloshin's feelings to grow or at least for him to tell her that they had grown. A month and a half later Voloshin found himself back in Koktebel' without Maria Stepanovna (she had left to work in Theodosia) and, longing for her return at the New Year, he wrote: "My dearest one, my beloved Marusia, what has happened to you? You arrived neither yesterday nor today which means that you've gotten sick . . . [ellipsis Voloshin's] and yesterday and today I walked a long way along the road and waited to meet you. Today I sat for a long time at the crossing and waited for you. What's with you? If it weren't completely impossible to abandon Pra, I would have come to Theodosia yesterday morning. . . . Yesterday evening I lit the stove and sat in your room all the long evening, thinking that you might still arrive."[8] This brought him to a theme he had first raised, significantly, in a letter to Pra herself many years before — the isolation and loneliness of the Koktebel' dacha — as he wrote her how much better he understood her feelings now that he, as she before him, had experienced that loneliness: "I can't believe you yourself waited for me like this for six months. Only now do I understand the anguish of your letters. I didn't understand anything earlier. Dearest Marusia, I need you to the point of pain, to the point of tears. . . . No doubt you find it strange and unexpected to hear such speeches from me, Marusia. Because the whole time I somehow simply accepted your love, and was myself passive. But now everything has suddenly changed. Separation sometimes gives unexpected lessons.

"And don't think," Voloshin hastened to add in a more moderate tone, "that this is all because I'm having a hard time with the housework — on the contrary, everything is going far better and more easily than I thought. Pra very patiently explained to me how to light the stoves, the stoves light up obediently. I heat up your borshch and I cook up my own concoction without any complications—but only once a day. Pra gets along well with me, doesn't get angry, and doesn't make ironic remarks."[9]

Then he turns to Elena Ottobal'dovna's medical condition. It is neither better nor worse than before, he tells Maria Stepanovna, his tone now becoming that of the concerned but ignorant relative petitioning for information from the nurse. The question has arisen as to whether to bring further medical aid, but Elena Ottobal'dovna, of course, will hear nothing of it. Should they get a doctor? Voloshin has been giving her aspirin to bring down her fever, although the aspirin seems to have caffeine in it. Finally, Voloshin asks Maria Stepanovna to pick up some money that has arrived for him in Theodosia and then to consult with a doctor, arranging for him to come to Koktebel' if necessary. But should they decide that the doctor need not come to Koktebel' himself, then she should buy groceries and supplies with the money, but he doesn't know what they need most—kerosene perhaps? You decide, he tells her. But he doesn't know when she will get the letter, he adds, concluding a document that is a masterpiece of mingled emotional passion and material need.

Nine days later Elena Ottobal'dovna died. That spring was in many ways a time of rebirth for Voloshin. He cast aside his mother's old "bourgeois" notions of earning money by renting out rooms and made his decision to enter into bureaucratic relations with the state. He began to set up his home as an Artistic Colony or House of Rest. And he won himself a new domestic partner more or less at the moment that he lost the old one. Maria Stepanovna (they would actually marry only in 1927, after he had finally obtained a legal divorce from Margarita Sabashnikova) was to prove an invaluable choice, from both the practical and the emotional points of view. This was only the beginning of their contractual relationship, very early on in the new Soviet world, but the contract was to last as long as Voloshin lived. While Voloshin networked with the state and polished his fame among his visitors, Maria Stepanovna made many of the material domestic arrangements necessary for the smooth operations of the new circle. Like Pra before her she kept the "servants" and the guests in order, making rooming and eating arrangements, and taking complaints.[10] It was a strenuous labor but a labor of love. She kept Voloshin in order, too, petted and bullied him and kept his spirits up. Without her, the Artistic Colony quite possibly might never have come to be, and certainly could not have lasted very long.

Some sort of partnership with an agreed-upon division of labor was essential in this situation; and the traditional one that they settled on came

Maria Stepanovna Voloshina
and Maximilian Voloshin,
Koktebel', 1925.
*Courtesy of Vladimir
Kupchenko.*

naturally, in a cultural sense. Voloshin needed Maria Stepanovna not as a
Maria Tsvetaeva, the newly liberated female intellectual, but rather in a
traditional domestic and material role. The shift to a heavily bureaucratized economy, with all its inefficiencies and its strongly personalized component, may have made such unpaid labors of love as Maria Stepanovna's
all the more necessary. Given that those who traditionally performed such
labor were women, it made cultural sense to continue to rely on them in
this time of economic stress, thereby bringing these traditional relations
into the Soviet system despite any ideological opposition to the exploitation
of female labor. This tale of the formation of an early Soviet male-female
partnership may help to provide insight into the persistence and the potency of traditional patriarchal gender relations in the Soviet period.

   This is by no means to say that Maria Stepanovna felt that she was getting the worst of the arrangement, for there was something to be said for the
particular deal that Voloshin was offering her. For the rest of her life she

would indeed bask in the light of his fame (less poetic or artistic than social, however, despite his expectations). And in accepting the arrangement and playing it out to its fullest in the future, Maria Stepanovna would carry not just Voloshin's name but intelligentsia culture itself into the future.

KRUZHOK CULTURE
AND THE ORIGINS OF THE
SOVIET "GIFT ECONOMY"

Another element of life in Voloshin's early Soviet circle evident in the historical sources is the deep concern among its members with material matters. Also apparent is the attempt to gain access to material advantages not just through demands upon the state, as seen in the previous chapter, but also through networking with one another. In this we see the persistence and enhancement of the prerevolutionary cultural tradition of personal networking for the sake of material or other advantage both inside and outside the circle formation. This pattern of economic relations was finally to be consolidated as the Soviet "gift economy," in which people helped one another out through personal barter exchange of material goods and services — often subsidized by the state — in the context of a bureaucratized and poorly organized economic system.[11]

The poet Elizaveta Polonskaya's visit to Voloshin's summer home in 1924 illustrates the focus on material concerns that was prevalent among the educated elite during the early Soviet period. Polonskaya, the only female member of the Serapion Brothers literary group, and inhabitant of the Petrograd House of the Arts, was prepared to be disappointed when she set off for Koktebel' early that summer. She was going only because her son was sick and in need of a southern climate after the long years of civil war and hunger in Petrograd, and because her friend Maria Shkapskaya had organized the trip. Polonskaya knew little that was good of Voloshin, that "bourgeois aesthete." To her he represented the worst of a snobbish prerevolutionary literary establishment. As an aspiring young poet in Paris more than a decade before, seeking entry into the Russian literary scene there, Polonskaya had known him as a founder of the glossy journal *Apollon* and a member of the tight, elitist circle that surrounded that journal. She and her social-democratic friends in Paris had abhorred the religious, aristocratic, reactionary poetry of Cherubina de Gabriac when it appeared in the journal. Polonskaya also knew Voloshin as an unkind and condescending critic, who had, she felt, entirely misunderstood one of her own early poetic efforts. So she was hardly eager to enter his household as a guest.

But Voloshin had been in Petrograd the previous winter, spreading word of the summer home that he hoped to open for writers and other members of the intelligentsia. And Shkapskaya, who knew him personally, told Polonskaya that Max had lost his pride and arrogance, now lived in destitution and wrote poems about the revolution, and, in short, at last "knew what life was." "Max has become a completely different person, Maria Mikhailovna [Shkapskaya] assured me—he saw all the loathsomeness of the White Army, he has repented."[12]

Still, Polonskaya expected the worst. She found it immediately when, on her arrival in Koktebel', she was offered a room of appalling discomfort.

> In my room [which had housed chickens the previous winter] stood a wooden deck chair and one stool. We asked Maria Stepanovna if it might be possible to find some nails, so as to hang up a dress and put up a curtain at the window, and she explained that nails could be bought at a co-operative across the square. Having been well trained by Maria Mikhailovna in Leningrad, I pulled a sack for hay out of my suitcase and handed it over to my hostess. She had apparently already agreed to fill the sack with hay for fifty kopecks.
>
> It turned out that there was no cafeteria in the village. It was impossible to obtain hot water. But how were we to wash ourselves? Maria Stepanovna shrugged: "In the sea."
>
> "But my son is sick. I'm afraid of washing him in the sea."
>
> Voloshina said nothing in reply. I walked out, having decided that I would not stay in such an uncultured place; I would leave for Theodosia.[13]

But the natural beauty of the area began to work on her almost at once. Walking to the beach, she found her son playing happily with Shkapskaya's children in the water, entirely unconcerned about the problems of "where to wash and what to eat." When she proposed leaving that evening for Theodosia, her son begged her to remain there, and "I myself unwillingly gave way to the charm of the warm late afternoon by the sea and began to want to stay." By the time they wandered back to the house, Maria Shkapskaya had organized the bedrooms, putting up the nails and curtains, and had arranged for Maria Stepanovna Voloshina to feed them all three meals a day for a small sum, until other arrangements could be made. It appeared that Maria Stepanovna was already engaged in negotiations with some women in Theodosia who would establish a kitchen and cafeteria in the Voloshins' home. Elizaveta Polonskaya and Maria Shkapskaya were only among the first of the expected summer guests that year. These concrete physical arrangements helped to convince Polonskaya that it would be possible to enjoy her stay in Koktebel' despite her initial anxieties, and so she did.

Many diaries, memoirs, and interviews about the early 1920s reveal an obsession during that period with the material matters of everyday life: the fancy china that had to be sold (if it had not already been requisitioned), the watch that stopped three days after its purchase for a sum that had taken months to raise, the remarkably cultured-looking neckties that so-and-so was wearing (*how* and *where* had he obtained them?!), the sugar, the meat . . . Just as Elizaveta Polonskaya, forty years later, remembered those nails and the sack she had brought from Leningrad to be filled with hay, so the young Konstantin Polivanov, son of a prominent Imperial and Soviet engineer, half a century later remembered (or at least cited) in meticulous detail the list of items he brought along to Koktebel' that same summer: a blanket, a small pillow in a white pillow case, a set of lilac-colored pajamas from abroad, a stearin candle, a towel, soap, toothbrush, two books, and a notebook.[14] The impoverished condition of the Russian intelligentsia compelled a constant awareness of such material matters, so much so that they became imprinted on memories for revival decades thereafter.

Although bathing continued to be a matter of plunging into the sea, by the time that Polivanov had arrived in Koktebel' that summer the problem of feeding the guests had been resolved. An old gymnasium friend of Voloshin—Olimpiada Nikitichna Serbina, Lipochka for short—had taken over the kitchen: "I soon understood," writes Polivanov, "that her role [was] very important in the House and that all love[d] her a great deal."[15] In return for money (described by another memoirist as a very low sum, but Polivanov mentions that not all could afford to pay it) from the guests, Lipochka and her associates provided tea in the morning and dinner for fifty or sixty people at noon. Dinner was eaten in two shifts; Max Voloshin and Marusia Voloshina ate during the first shift but remained through the second, apparently as a matter of hospitality. Otherwise the guests tended to shift for themselves. For breakfast, they had to bring their own cups and sugar for the tea Lipochka prepared. Food could be purchased across the square, from an old shopowner named Sinopli; this may have been the same Greek merchant who had originally run the Diamond Café. His first morning in Koktebel', Polivanov ran over to stand in line (about fifteen people with him, he notes) at Sinopli's shop; to his pleasure, he received his bread and meat wrapped in grape leaves.[16]

The Voloshins took no part in Lipochka's establishment, Polivanov writes, meaning, apparently, that they neither worked in the kitchen nor earned money from it. Yet they benefited in another sense: in return for allowing her to set up a cafeteria in their household, Max and Maria Stepanovna received their meals from Lipochka at no cost throughout the tourist season—a small mixture of NEP-style capitalist enterprise with barter.[17] Personal barter of all sorts was common in the early years of the Soviet regime, as the economy lurched from War Communism into the New Economic Policy, plagued by shortages and inflation which all the more effectively rendered money an inadequate means of exchange.[18] It represented the early stages of a move away from the importance of money toward the importance of bonding with the right people for all kinds of practical benefits.

While Voloshin's House of Rest was founded on what amounted to a patronage contract between Voloshin and the state, as described in the previous chapter, it also represented a far less formal barter contract between Voloshin and his guests. Voloshin dispensed the rooms of his house free of charge; in return, he expected and received economic support from the state, officially as a "scholarly worker." He did receive some degree of support from TsKUBU during the 1920s: a regular stipend of around sixty rubles a month,[19] free admission to a sanatorium for both Maria Stepanovna and himself when necessary,[20] and bread and potato rations, for example.[21] Official state support was not enough, however, to keep the family and household going. The remaining gap was filled by the informal gift giving of Voloshin's guests. As Vikentii Veresaev wrote, "Voloshin's summer clients helped him a great deal. Voloshin received packages of supplies from them all year long, he could even exchange the supplies for milk; by means of subscription they bought him a coat."[22] Konstantin Polivanov also observed this practice: "It is true that all who could in any way give material help were ready to do so: writers and philosophers sent Max their books, those who went abroad brought back good paper and water colors; sometimes [they would] pool their resources to bring in a carpenter, glazier, painter, or stone mason for some repair or other in the house."[23]

By letting out his rooms at no monetary expense, Voloshin created a sense of obligation among his guests. Regardless of their more abstract relationship with him through the state, they felt they had received something from him personally which they must pay back, not to the state but to him. They relieved their sense of obligation by offering concrete support in keeping up the house, as well as packages of supplies that may have been difficult to obtain out on the periphery of the centralizing Soviet economy. Thus Voloshin's guests participated in laying the early foundations of an informal barter system, based on personal association, which would grow and last at least as long as the Soviet system itself. It should be noted that although this process took place beyond the official oversight of the state it was nevertheless integrally influenced by the new state system; as in the case of the Little Deal described by James Millar in the 1960s, it was often founded upon personal access to what were technically state goods.[24]

Bureaucratization, with all its consequences of economic disjuncture and increasing elimination of market relations, was fostering an intensification of personalized economic networking among intellectuals. Through the tiny prism of Voloshin's circle we gain an impression of how the personal and economic interdependence of individuals was growing, building among the literati and other intellectuals on a now increasingly distant cultural past of personal networking in the prerevolutionary period.

STORING AWAY COMMUNITAS, AND A CULT, FOR A FUTURE GENERATION

Thus far our focus has been on the persistence of certain expressions of the traditional, structural side of *kruzhok* culture in Voloshin's Soviet circle. But what can be said about the cultural expressions of communitas? Some of those expressions noted in prerevolutionary literary circles included masquerade and theatricality, with overtones of the carnivalesque; the spirit of opposition to hierarchy; the intimacy and self-revelation of the I-Thou relationship; and self-transformation through all these phenomena. Closely associated were gossip, storytelling, and mythmaking as a means of maintaining the dream of transformative communitas even as its more immediate expressions faded. Some of these elements of communitas survived, or were preserved, in Voloshin's circle, as we shall see below; but they must be discussed in the context of their rapid institutionalization by the young Soviet state during the 1920s. For just as the material foundations of literary life were being bureaucratized, so in a sense were the spiritual dimensions.

These manifestations of communitas included theatricality, ritual, and dramatic display, which the Bolshevik state used as a means of carrying the revolution across the country; opposition to hierarchy and the desire for status reversal, evidenced most fundamentally in the expressed desire of the state to turn the prerevolutionary hierarchy upside down, with the working class at the top and the aristocracy at the bottom, in accordance with Marxist ideology; and also, perhaps, a growing fascination with confession to the collective as a form of I-Thou encounter. All these phenomena were nurtured to bring about the very essence of the socialist revolution: the transformation of the individual into a new revolutionary identity.[25] Also important was anti-capitalism as an expression of anti-structure. The initial resonance of all these expressions of the spirit of communitas, as well as the offers of material support from the state, surely contributed greatly to the willingness on the part of many literati to work with the Bolsheviks.

It may well be that the most compelling theme of common interest to both the revolutionary Bolsheviks and the literati was that of the possibility and power of personal self-transformation. This theme lay at the very heart of the Bolshevik identity in many ways; like the prerevolutionary literary intelligentsia, especially the modernists, so, too, the prerevolutionary revolutionary intelligentsia had sought self-transformation through what might be described as their own kind of *zhiznetvorchestvo* (life-creation), at least from the age of the *raznochintsy* of the 1860s on. For example, the publication of Chernyshevskii's utopian novel, *What Is to Be Done?*—which so influenced Lenin that he borrowed its title for one of his own revolutionary tracts— compelled a whole generation of revolution-minded intellectuals to attempt to transform themselves through imitation of its "liberated" characters.[26] Fascination with the possibilities of self-transformation, especially through imitation and performance, continued far into the Soviet period, as the Bolsheviks sought to encourage, and then gain control over, the processes of self-transformation, turning the state itself to the purpose of fashioning the new Soviet man.

In its desire to thus institutionalize the communitas theme of self-transformation, the young Soviet state might be described as what Turner calls "normative communitas," a potentially far more influential (and dangerous) institution than the mere literary or even revolutionary circle of the prerevolutionary period. Normative communitas, Turner writes, is "a subculture or a group which attempts to foster and maintain relationships of spontaneous communitas on a more or less permanent basis." He continues: "To do this is to denature itself, for spontaneous communitas is more a matter of 'grace' than of 'law,' to use theological language. . . . Quite often the strictest regimes devolve from what are apparently the most spontaneous experiences of communitas."[27] The Bolshevik state, in its attempt to spread controlled self-transformation uniformly across a vast community, was an expression of normative communitas. Its activities were in some ways reminiscent of those earlier Russian elite attempts at Westernization through compulsion, whether of the gentry elite by the autocracy, as Peter the Great shaved off the beards of men and Catherine the Great compelled her courtiers to attend literary salons, or of the serfs by the gentry, in the example of the living Greek statues mentioned in chapter 2 for which serfs stood unmoving for hours at a time. It could be said that in their attempts to create the new Soviet man, a creature of utopian altruism dedicated to communism, the Bolsheviks sought to make living statues of the people they ruled, props more or less of their own transformative fantasies.

This is not to say that communitas was fully institutionalized from the beginning. Richard Stites has described the outpourings of what may well be called the spontaneous spirit of communitas in the early years of Soviet power, following the destruction of the old order.[28] The performative expression of that spirit was especially striking, as the educated elite, along with many other sectors of society, participated in an orgy of parades, street theater, mass spectacles, and total works of art exploring the possibilities of self- and social transformation. Status reversal was celebrated in carnivalesque mockery of the overthrown structures of power, radical egalitarianism was theatrically affirmed in dress (such as the peasant shirts that many young folk wore with enthusiasm; the Russian blue jeans of that period), and even in personal address (the informal *ty* as opposed to the formal *vy*). All these things reveal the pent-up power, abruptly released, of a spontaneous spirit of radical transformation that perfectly fits Turner's model.

But Stites also depicts, as do other scholars, the compression of those radical acts of self-expression into increasingly controlled and routinized manifestations of the radical spirit as the Soviet state gained in strength and control. Theatrical ceremonies of social transformation became ever more "stiff," as he describes it, "instrumentalized," as the state sought to turn that spirit to its own purposes and thereby deadened it through its application of institutional power.[29] Katerina Clark details the processes by which this took place in Petrograd—at first through controlled organization and planning of mass public spectacles, for example ("You cannot have ritual without regimentation," she quotes one organizer as saying); then through greater selectivity of those who did the organizing; and, finally, to increasing centralization of the institutions of cultural production.[30]

Against this background of an initial vibrant enthusiasm about the dream of self-transformation, followed by increasing institutionalization of that dream, Voloshin's circle, at first glance, does not seem to have been a significant source of transformative energy. It does not appear to have been caught up very much in the initial revolutionary fervor, perhaps in part because it commenced functioning as an institution only as that burst of revolutionary energy was already fading. There was little if any of the spontaneous theatricality of the sort that had been practiced and made famous by the original *Obormoty* in 1911. And although it was now a branch of the state, the circle also showed no sign whatsoever of institutionalized theatricality dedicated to creating the new Soviet man. Though a few theatrical activities still took place, especially at parties as partygoers sought out Tatar and at one point even African costumes, even this seems to have been rare. Nor did costume contribute any longer in helping to shape group identity as it had in the decade prior to 1920, at least not in the substantial way that it had when circle members advertised their identity as insiders by wearing Greek or Asiatic robes and outrageous bathing costumes.

Nevertheless, some important elements of the circle spirit of communitas continued to reveal themselves, and each of these was in some way associated with Voloshin himself. The sole notable and consistent element of theatricality in the circle, for example, was the theater of Voloshin's own person. This was partially instigated by his actual eccentric clothing of tunics and sandals. But it was even more a function of his visitors' imaginations. Hardly a memoir is written about Voloshin's Soviet circle without reference to his appearance as exotic in some way. Describing him as Zeus, as Pan, as Homer, as a Greek god or demi-god, or even as a peasant *baba* (old woman), the memoirists seem to have let their imaginations run wild. Maria Stepanovna apparently attracted little such attention (unlike Elena Ottobal'dnovna, who had been famous for her dramatic masculine and ethnic costumes). Thus it was Voloshin himself who seemed to embody whatever sense of theatrical otherness remained in this circle, to embody the possibility, at least, of self-transformation through costume and appearance.

Another element of communitas manifested in the circle was the opposition to hierarchy, and this, too, came to be identified most closely with Voloshin. This facet was particularly appreciated by children. If Konstantin Polivanov noted in passing his delight in seeing the famous Andrei Bely bathing in the sea just like everyone else, so another child, Nadezhda Rykova, wrote with pleasure of sparring verbally with Bely as an equal. Much awed by "all the Moscow-Leningrad 'upper crust of the high intelligentsia'" who were at Voloshin's dacha in the summer of 1924, Rykova observed that although "both the 'upper' and the 'lower'" took walks, went swimming, and sunbathed on their own during the day, they all gathered together communally for discourse, poetry, and charades in the evenings. On one such evening she found herself engaged with Andrei Bely in a debate over the relative virtues of Russian and Western art. "The clamor became awful. It was easy to drive Andrei Bely wild. It reached the point where he made a tactical mistake and took it upon himself to orate: 'Little girl! Live to my age and then we'll talk!' My two companions, even younger than I, and also fundamental opponents of any authority, took immediate advantage of this, and also raised a cry: 'Ooo! An argument based on age! That's the end! For shame!'" Whereupon Voloshin himself intervened, strongly supporting this egalitarian mood. As Nadezhda Rykova tells it, "Maximilian Aleksandrovich acted as if the argument was being held between two absolutely equal sides. How easy it would have been for him to laugh at me (laugh without even being insulting), but he began to pour his balm with typical skill on both Bely and me, and soon we quieted down."[31] Aside from a return to the theme of Voloshin as peacemaker, and supporter of females and children, here again we find reference to one of the values of communitas as embodied in Voloshin's own storied self.

By all accounts Voloshin indeed treated most people with equal and notable respect and attention in a way that seems to have made a deep impression. Memoirists repeatedly cite his attractive demeanor, his extreme courtesy, his kindness, and his treatment of all, low and high, with identical and seemingly intimate attention. One young man tells of his excursion to Voloshin's home with a variety of peasants and other lower-class travelers, during which he and the others all experienced Voloshin's deep attention and civility, despite the shyness and absolute silence of his presumably ignorant lower-class visitors.[32] An element of the I-Thou relationship is also implied

Maximilian Voloshin and his home in Koktebel', 1931.
Courtesy of Vladimir Kupchenko.

in descriptions of Voloshin's attentions to others. For example, in 1945 Anna Ostroumova-Lebedeva, an artist and frequent visitor to Koktebel' in the 1920s, wrote: "Maximilian Aleksandrovich approached everyone with a gentle and attentive word. He could bring the best and most valuable, which sometimes hides deep in a person, to the surface. . . . Voloshin was the center to [which] all were drawn. He could accept everything and understand everything. . . . He was a subtle psychologist. Whomever he met, he always found those words, those thoughts, which enabled him to approach his interlocutor more intimately and entice him into a long conversation, at the end of which it turned out that they were, unexpectedly to both, close friends."[33] And Nadezhda Rykova writes: "Voloshin exuded calm and gentleness—two qualities lost to all who had just passed through the civil war. . . . And furthermore: he manifested to his conversational partner—whomever it might be—deep attention, identically to each one. . . . As a form of courtesy, this quality is to be found among people of good upbringing; but in Voloshin it was not a consequence of trained civility, but rather of genuine attention. Each human being meant something to him."[34]

In many ways this discourse of the courteous Voloshin who treated everyone with a kind of intimate generosity may be viewed in the context of the "contemporaries" memoirs tradition of creating models for appropriate behavior for the intelligentsia, as well as for creating intelligentsia identity. Praising these qualities of Voloshin with such enthusiasm, memoirists were offering alternative ideals for behavior to what many considered the rough, crude culture of behavior in the Soviet period. Such memoir citations provide evidence of a near obsession of some memoirists with what might be called "culturedness." Curiously Voloshin's original anti-structural mockery of the aristocratic airs of the *Apollon* journal circle through the Cherubina incident was turned on its head as some memoirists (such as Elizaveta Polonskaya) began to associate him with the prerevolutionary aristocratic intelligentsia, and his courtesy with what was assumed to be the cultured courtesy of the prerevolutionary Russian aristocracy. After describing Voloshin's "spiritual aristocratism," another memoirist continues: "If I may say so, he was aristocratic even in the superficial, social sense: his cordiality, his ability to carry on a conversation—an ability not only to "hold forth" but also to listen, his whole manner of carrying himself—revealed in him a highly bred human being." This writer then continues, clearly warming to his topic: "Especially characteristic was the absence of those vulgarly intonated tricks, those deliberate affectations of speech, with which little-cultured people, common Philistines, vainly attempt to compensate for the emptiness of their speech, the lack of skill and lack of talent of their discourse."[35] It is an amusing (but not necessarily surprising) trick of history that Voloshin's much admired spirit of courteous egalitarianism—and, in a sense, the spirit of communitas itself—thus became linked in people's minds with the objects of Voloshin's own carnivalesque fun.

Hence it was with Voloshin's own person that communitas was most closely linked in his circle: to the qualities of theatricality, of egalitarianism, and of I-Thou relations. But there is little sign that these qualities were viewed as having led to self-transformation among his guests. Instead, given that the memoirs citing them were often written many years after Voloshin's death, it could be argued that these qualities were in a sense being stored away for a new generation several decades later—the Thaw generation that would undergo a new bout of communitas-style fervor. These qualities of communitas—the theatricality of image, the focus on attentive courtesy as a means of anti-hierarchy, the hint at I-Thou intimacy—were all accumulating as part of the mythology of Voloshin's person and circle for revival in the future, largely by Maria Stepanovna, who would do more than anyone else to establish the cult of his person described at the beginning of this book. But at the time this was all irrelevant. By the end of the 1920s Voloshin was facing something quite different: the collapse of the patronage network that had kept his circle alive.

NINE

Collapse of a Patronage Network and Voloshin's Death

Another of Voloshin's guests, Kornei Chukovsky, observed in his diary in 1923 that some citizens of the Koktebel' community felt considerable animosity toward Voloshin. This antagonism reflected the persistence of another prerevolutionary cultural pattern: Voloshin's sometimes hostile relationship with some of his neighbors. "It's interesting that the neighbors and *dachniki* hate him intensely. When he walks naked along the beach, they shout angry words after him and complain indignantly and at length about 'this insolent fellow.' 'There would be some excuse if he were well-built, but that ugly mug!' — cackle the ladies."[1]

Years before, Voloshin had provoked tension among the local Bulgars because he wore long tunics without trousers beneath them; later, he had brought upon himself the wrath of such proper *dachniki* as Deicha-Sionitskaya with his informality and the informality of his guests on the beach. This kind of tension continued after the revolution, although it is not entirely clear just who these postrevolutionary "neighbors and *dachniki*" were. It was the case, however, that Voloshin and his summer crowd of visitors continued to be unpopular in the village of Koktebel'. He was disliked not only by offended ladies but also, and more significant, by those he repeatedly described as "local powers." The "local powers" appear to have taken particular exception to his summer colony. An early sign of the growing tensions is seen in a letter Voloshin wrote to Lev Kamenev in 1924: "The situation of the Koktebel' Artistic Colony became difficult only since the local (village and regional) powers began to exploit Koktebel' as a resort area themselves and saw me as a competitor. . . . For this reason, several attempts were made last summer to destroy the Artistic Colony by means of assessments and taxes. I was told in the form of an ultimatum to get a 'business license for the maintenance of a hotel and restaurant' immediately, under the threat of immediate eviction of all 'boarders' and the sealing of the house."[2]

Looking for bureaucratic protection, Voloshin continues, he approached KrymTsIK (Crimean Central Executive Committee). Unfortunately involving more powerful outsiders only made the "local powers" angrier: "But when KrymTsIK came to my defense, the 'power on the spot' saw this as an insult and created a tense situation in which I had to anticipate: which direction is the new attack to come from?" Hence, he explained, "I am turning to you, Lev Borisovich, as an individual who understands and treasures the interests of Russian art, with the plea that you stand patron of the Koktebel' Artistic Colony and give me the right to turn to you for defense at the critical moments of its existence."[3]

If Voloshin ever sent this letter to Kamenev, there is no sign that Kamenev replied; Voloshin had to remain satisfied with his *udostovereniie* from Lunacharsky, and with whatever protection he could muster within the Crimea. The same problem came up again in September 1928: he wrote an irate petition to the Crimean branch of Narkompros complaining that there were rumors claiming that on October 6 he was to be evicted from his house as a "nonworking element." He attributed this aggressiveness on the part of the "local powers" to their desire to make money by renting out his rooms themselves.[4] Another Crimean institution from which he sought patronage was the Society for the Improvement of the Crimea, to which he offered three or four places in his dacha in return for protection (on the side of the central and republic governments, he pointed out) against the "local powers."[5]

The local unpleasantness for Voloshin seems to have increased toward the end of the twenties — not coincidentally during the time that the great industrialization drive of the First Five-Year Plan was taking place, collectivization was being set in motion, the Cultural Revolution was heating up, and Stalin was consolidating his power.[6] The chaos and confusion of these interrelated processes reached all levels and areas of Soviet life; frequent arrests were made on political pretexts that could stem from personal grudges or the desire to obtain something from the individual being arrested (such as living space). Moshe Lewin has described how Soviets in all walks of life moved rapidly from one job to another during this time, out of fear of harassment or worse.[7]

The malice and disorder in Soviet life during this period had an impact on Voloshin's life as well. If he was beset, on the one hand, by those who wanted to lay their hands on his house, he faced a battle over his bread ration, on the other. Seemingly innumerable documents touching on this matter lie in his archive: he wrote to one office after another in Theodosia,

Simferopol, and even Moscow asking for help in getting the bread ration he was entitled to, as the local bread cooperative repeatedly refused to supply him. One can well imagine the scenes at the counter of this institution; at one point his ration card was physically taken away from him. He tended to obtain the support from the people he wrote to, but, as in the case of his appeal to KrymTsIK for the sake of his threatened household, this could provoke even more local ire. At one point he received a furious note from a local about his successful appeal to an outside and superior power: "I must tell you that you wrote complaints to RIK in vain, that wasn't nice on your part, it's unnecessary to put the question that way."[8] The documents recording this struggle run from early 1929 into 1931.

In this period of political turbulence Voloshin was also having troubles at the national level. The literary battles of the Cultural Revolution were growing shrill and dangerous in Moscow and Leningrad, and Voloshin, always closely identified with his modernist past, was quite likely to come out badly. Despite his 1919 poetry collection, *Demony Glukhonemye*, and a number of exhibits of his landscape art, he had rarely achieved publication during the Soviet period, and had been the object of fierce attacks by the Party-supported literary group RAPP. The situation so deteriorated that when, in 1929, he was in dire need of money, borrowing from his wealthier friends in order to reimburse his poorer friends, and allowing collections to be taken up for him, he urgently turned down the suggestion that an appeal for financial aid be made in the newspapers, as he did not want to attract the attention of his enemies: "I've already learned that any printed reminder of my name leads rapidly to my having a tub of slops poured over my head. And in this case I'm afraid not only for my reputation but for the existence of my 'refuge for writers and artists,' should news of it reach the press."[9]

It was also no accident that Voloshin's life was becoming increasingly uncomfortable at the very time that his most powerful and significant patron, Anatoly Lunacharsky, was rapidly losing power and status in Moscow. In 1928, soon after the notorious Shakhty show trials, Lunacharsky was accused of "cultural rightism," which essentially meant anti-Stalinism.[10] There were discussions about removing the higher technical schools from the control of Narkompros between April and July of that year; during that same summer, moreover, the head of the technical education administration of Narkompros was forced out and, ominously, replaced by the man who had just served as presiding judge at the Shakhty trials. Lunacharsky lost his job as People's Commissar in 1929, and his place in the sphere of power dwindled until he was appointed ambassador to Spain in 1933.

That Lunacharsky was losing influence—and thus his capacity and potential as a patron—is reflected in the growing pathos of the letters Voloshin wrote to him in early 1930. Voloshin wrote twice, the second time because he received no answer to the first letter. Thereafter he appears to have made no further written attempts. The two letters clearly reveal both the unraveling of a patronage network through which Voloshin had if not thrived at least survived, and the potential consequences for those whose networks were unraveling in this way. In the first letter, dated February 18, he began by referring to a mutual acquaintance, who, he said, had just written to him mentioning that Lunacharsky still held Voloshin in high regard. He went on to say that there were few left in governing circles or in TsKUBU who knew him anymore, and he added, in what may seem to be a slight lapse in logic but isn't really, that this undoubtedly had something to do with the lamentable and inaccurate article about him in the new *Soviet Encyclopedia*. He continued that it would now be half a year since he had received any support from TsKUBU. His TsKUBU stipend had been his sole form of financial support since visitors to the "House" stayed there free of charge; he accepted no money for his watercolors; and he had long been unable to get his works published. The problem he was attempting to address was that he recently had had a stroke (the previous December), and the doctors were advising him to go away for a cure. Could Lunacharsky possibly help?[11]

Voloshin then turned to the question of what would happen to his house when he died. The "local powers" persisted in their desire to seize it, but Voloshin hoped to see it remain intact and serving the same purpose after his death that it now served: a place of peace and refuge for writers and artists. "Forty years of Russian cultural life have passed through it, a whole generation of poets and artists studied, created, and meditated here. And each one left the creative traces of his presence." (The "forty years" was an exaggeration, since the house had been built only at the beginning of the century.) Voloshin wanted to donate his house to a "long-term," or stable, institution that would maintain his nonprofit tradition, enabling future poets and artists to use not only his rooms but his eight-thousand-volume library and his archive, "which is a valuable document of the epoch."[12]

The second letter, dated April 14, was more desperate. He had received no answer to the first, and his fears, he wrote, had been realized: a three-man commission had come by and was determined to take over a wing of his house and turn it into a paying concern. This commission was especially interested in certain documents in Voloshin's possession (for example, the original 1924 Mandate making Voloshin's house the property of the state by right of Lunacharsky and Narkompros, which Lunacharsky himself had signed). Later, after the commission had left, Voloshin discovered that the visit had probably been provoked by an article published about Lunacharsky entitled "A Smell of Class." In this article Lunacharsky had been accused of giving away some of the most attractive dachas in Koktebel' (including the Voloshin dacha) to people who lived in Moscow in the winter and did extra business renting out their rooms to tourists in the summer.[13]

Under these circumstances it might appear odd that Voloshin was appealing to Lunacharsky for help, as it was evident that Voloshin's problem was precisely that Lunacharsky was losing all capacity to assist him as a patron. Nevertheless Voloshin concluded his letter by saying that something had to be done right away: the last time he had been threatened like this, he had gone to Simferopol' and straightened the matter out there. Now he was too sick to go. Please, his final line read, set this letter on the right path.[14] In other words, if Lunacharsky could not help, then Voloshin wanted him to send the letter to someone who could.

Whether it was the result of Lunacharsky's intervention or of another tug elsewhere in the network, Voloshin managed to achieve what he wanted before he died. In 1931 the decision was made to offer the house to the Writers' Union; a little over a year later, he and Maria Stepanovna met with representatives of the Union to discuss the terms of his donation. By the time Voloshin died, he and Maria Stepanovna had moved to the second floor of the house, and the ground floor was in the possession of Litfond RSFSR, which used it as a House of Rest for its literary members. Two neighboring houses had also been put to the same use by this time: Litfond now owned both the Iunge and the Manaseinii dachas. The Moscow branch of Litfond had control over the Iunge and Voloshin dachas, and the Leningrad branch over the Manaseinii dacha. Building by building, the dacha colony of Koktebel' was being integrated into the bureaucracy of welfare and privilege that would lie at the foundations of the emerging relationship between Soviet writers and the Soviet state.

Max Voloshin died on August 11, 1932, of asthma complicated by influenza and pneumonia. Maria Stepanovna was distraught, according to her friend, Lidiia Arens, hurling herself to the floor and crying out: "'To whom have you left me, why did you abandon me?'" and then lying for hours in silence, sometimes surrounded by people and sometimes driving them all away.[15] Toward evening a death mask was taken of Voloshin's face. Lidiia Arens stood by and assisted the cast maker: "Vaseline had to be smeared on his eyebrows, beard, and the edge of his face by his hair, and it was necessary to touch his face, to touch it the whole time. Then the plaster was prepared, and we began to pour even layers over the face, from the nose to the sides. Then the cast maker said that the mask could be removed, but it was impossible to take it off because many of the hairs from the beard and mustache had gotten into the plaster and stuck to the mask . . . The face became warm under the cast, the eyes and the mouth began to open, the face

Voloshin's death mask,
Koktebel', 1932.
*Courtesy of Vladimir
Kupchenko.*

grew warm and soft. I became nervous and said to the cast maker that I would take scissors and cut the hairs that were caught in the plaster. Because of the wavering lamp, it was hard to see, the shadows danced, and somehow it was terrifying to do. Bravely I began to cut everything that was caught in the mask, and by this means we quickly dealt with it. Marusia wanted to approach several times, but I didn't let her and convinced her not to bother us but to lie quietly at a distance. I must admit that I was tired, that somehow my nerves were strained, and that I was glad when we had finished and cleared up. It was already night, and I went to my room in the attic."[16]

This was the first step in laying a cult figure to rest; the next step came the following day, when Voloshin was buried high up in the hills above the sea, as he had wished. Nikolai Chukovskii helped with the burial. Nikolai had visited with his father, Kornei, as an adolescent in the early 1920s, and now came to stay with the Voloshins as an adult. Voloshin's very heavy body was loaded onto a cart, and a small procession set off into the hills. The distance to the burial spot was only three kilometers, Chukovskii wrote, but they had to take a much longer back route in order to avoid the steeper part of the hill. Even so, the horse was unable to pull the body up the hill, so the five men in the group had to unload the corpse and carry it up the hill themselves. "The sun shone unmercifully and, having reached the top, we were half-dead with exhaustion."[17]

Voloshin was laid to rest in a place of beauty marked by the memorial described at the beginning of this book. Now, slowly, his cult would begin to grow.

Conclusion

For the literary intelligentsia, the moment of truth came in April 1932, when all the shrill and squabbling literary circles were banned,[1] and a massive reorganization and centralization of Russian literary life in the Soviet Writers' Union—officially established in 1934—began. The process was extraordinary: committees of the All-Russian Soviet Writers' Union (forerunner of the 1934 Soviet Writers' Union) met to arrange the liquidation of the assets of all Soviet institutions of literary life and literary expression, including large and small literary circles and clubs, publishing houses, and journals, and to set the material foundations of literary life on a new centralized foundation. Protocols of those committee meetings in May and June 1932 reveal a breadth of purpose and a sense of power that is breathtaking.[2] Members of the committee included several well-known Soviet authors, such as Vsevolod Ivanov, Leonid Leonov, Fyodor Panfyorov, Nikolai Tikhonov, and Lidiia Seifulina, among others; in Ivanov and Tikhonov there was a notable representation of Gorky's Serapion Brothers, who would continue to play an important role in the Writers' Union and in the Soviet literary community in the future.

They reorganized editorial staffs and eliminated or combined journals. Of great importance was the *"Material'no-bytavaia"* ("Material-daily life") subcommittee, whose tasks were to organize the building of housing in Moscow; to build dachas; to build a House of Literature that would include libraries, a consultative-informational bureau, a club, offices, meeting rooms, and a kindergarten; to build a House of Creation outside Moscow city limits; to improve provisioning; to improve medical services and sanatoriums; to improve the "social-legal" condition of writers, and, "finally, the routine, practical goal in connection with the planned liquidation of literary organizations—the verification and acquisition of the property and money of the liquidated organizations."[3]

This was the final step in the movement of the literary intelligentsia into structure—a particularly Russian kind of structure—after many years of existing on the fringe of the Russian polity in anti-structural or combined anti-structural and structural social formations. The Russian literary intelligentsia had been fully incorporated into the Soviet system through the Soviet Writers' Union, and had a bureaucratized state identity such as it never had had in the hierarchical *soslovie* (estate) system of the tsarist regime. It was to serve the state through support of its ideological and other goals, and in return it would receive welfare and privileges largely through the bureaucracy of the Soviet Writers' Union. These privileges ranged widely, from food in special cafeterias to maid service. Most important among them were the group living arrangements, such as the Houses of Rest and Houses of Creation, even a dacha colony outside Moscow, Peredel'kino (founded at the behest of Maxim Gorky as a means of bringing together and offering excellent working conditions to a select population of the literary world),[4] and, finally, the new and growing collective apartment buildings for writers. Such collective living arrangements lay at the core of literary elite culture and networks in the Soviet context.[5] Now fully resolved was the anxiety of the literary community about market relations, an aspect of its economic culture it had long shared with the revolutionary party now in power; now, rather than fighting it out in the grubby market, the economic relations of the literary community were mediated by the bureaucracy— and only marginally was money involved in this subsidized state system. This was the essence of the deal that was struck, the relationship established, between the literary community and the state.

But in many ways this deal was still a patronage deal. For a central aspect of the Cultural Revolution, and indeed of the purges and general decimation of the old Bolsheviks in the years that followed, was the struggle for patronage control of the state. Stalin's rise to power may be seen as the elimination of one alternative patron chain after another, by a man with a phenomenal and ruthless gift for the patronage game. Lunacharsky's loss of power had been only one early manifestation of Stalin's skill. By the time that Stalin was fully in control, he had taken over all the patronage chains and was now the state-based patron of all. He was the "Father" to whom all writers now owed their clientelistic loyalty—and most of them took their responsibilities more seriously than Mandelshtam had. The "gratitude" felt not just by writers but also by many others in Soviet society toward the patronage source of all well-being (Stalin) has been described elsewhere in detail.[6] In many ways the ever more rigid self-censorship of Soviet writers may be seen as an expression of that clientelistic loyalty writ large, as well as an expression of their fear of destruction.

Yet Stalin based his leadership on more than sheer structural power; he also drew heavily on the cultural sources of personal power that lay in the dream of communitas. He was a spiritual leader of communitas as well as a master of patronage and bureaucracy, leading his nation into a retreat from the regular order of the world for the sake of self-transformation, a refashioning of national self from which it was intended to emerge as a fully mature modern nation, as proud and powerful as Imperial Russia had been in the past. As such he was also master impresario of the rituals and ceremonies of national transformation. He presented himself as a mentor in this process of self-transformation, as a "teacher" of his nation; this, too, was acknowledged in many of the public slogans, poems, and songs written to him and about him.[7] And he seemed also to offer peace, in the form of the iron fist that gave many comfort, at least in the literary community; the crackdown on that community through the elimination of all circles in 1932 was greeted with relief by many in the literary community who had felt constant instability during the bitter, quarrelsome years of the Cultural Revolution.[8]

Stalin possessed that most potent combination of cultural leadership modes: he combined structural power, the patriarchal power of personal patronage as it had been anchored in the bureaucratic system of the Soviet Union, with power based on the dream of communitas, the dream of self-transformation. Not only was it a potent combination but it was also a lethal one for an educated elite that followed him a long way into destruction. For what Stalin lacked was something Russian intelligentsia memoirists had begun to recognize as an essential component of leadership and power in this complex cultural system combining structure and anti-structure, namely humanity. In their repeated emphasis on humaneness in such leadership figures in the community as Voloshin, memoirists were seeking a solution to the dangerous tendency of their culture to offer overwhelming power to certain individuals. A leader who possessed that kind of cultural power but lacked the quality of humaneness, the personal ability to recognize every individual as fully human and therefore worthy of regard and respect, was deeply threatening to the well-being of his followers, or subjects. The literary community would witness and begin to recognize this as Stalin pursued his political goals at the expense of many lives in the literary community, not to mention the millions, perhaps, beyond it.

The years following Stalin's ascent to power were very terrible for the literary community in many ways. Many of its members died and countless others experienced extreme fear, though a number of them survived and some even did well (although it cannot be said that great literature was produced). The purges, and then World War II, tore great rents in the circles and networks of the literary community, as they did in all the networks of the educated elite. With the death of Stalin in 1953, the Russian intelligentsia began the long slow process of evaluating and reevaluating their past and themselves. The rise of the youthful Thaw circles of the 1950s, the *kompanii*, played an integral role in this process. As memoirist Ludmilla Alexeyeva describes them, "*Kompanii* emerged in a flash in the mid-1950s, stayed vibrant for a decade [and] then faded away. . . . It was all remarkably simple: the *kompaniya* had sprung up as a social institution because it was needed. Our generation had a psychological, spiritual, perhaps even a physiological need to discover our country, our history, and ourselves." A central mission of these circles was to explore the past of the educated elite: "The old intelligentsia no longer existed, but we wanted to believe that we would be able to recapture its spiritual and intellectual exaltation. Our goal was to lay claim to the values left by the social stratum that had been persecuted by the tsars and destroyed by the revolution." These circles represented a new outbreak of the spirit of communitas in Russian history, one which would, like the earlier outburst, have an indelible impact on Russian history. Intimate, egalitarian relations were essential to the *kompaniya* experience, as its members drew themselves somewhat apart from society to begin a critique of the Soviet system and of Stalin in classic communitas style. And, as in the 1920s, they wore costumes expressive of egalitarianism (as well as of group distinction): "Our men grew bushy beards and wore homemade sweaters with Russian pagan symbols, avant-garde designs and primitivist, asymmetrical nature scenes. Most sweaters were knitted in *kompanii*, so we could observe them as works in progress." As Alexeyeva describes them, these *kompanii* were the beginnings of the Soviet human rights movement that was in many ways to play an incremental yet vital role in the downfall of the Soviet Union.[9]

It was at this time of the *kompanii*, the period of the Thaw, that Maria Stepanovna Voloshina was first able to revive memories of her husband. Her life had been difficult; she had had to fight for her right to remain in her old rooms in Voloshin's home after his death; for her right to ration cards; and for her right to a pension. In these struggles she often had to face many of the same bureaucratic institutions that had given Voloshin so much trouble in his last years. Through it all she kept her husband's memory and his archive safe for the future, burying the archive on the beach during World War II. And, tenaciously, through visits and letters, she kept in touch with her associates in the North. Like Voloshin, she paid a great deal of attention to children, corresponding with them, telling them stories when she visited them in Moscow, inviting them to Koktebel' for summer visits, where she would give them tours of the house and tell them stories of the past.[10] Despite her sometimes anxious, angry, and depressive temperament, she had a gift for communicating with children that reveals itself in her letters to them, which are notable for their kind tone, for treating the recipients as adults and yet not going over their heads.[11] A growing trickle of

Maria Stepanovna Voloshina at her husband's grave, Koktebel', 1934.
Courtesy of Vladimir Kupchenko.

more official attention began in 1949, when a scholar interested in Voloshin's work on the medieval religious figure Avakuum contacted her.[12] In 1962 her correspondence first mentions plans for a museum dedicated to Voloshin and his circle to be established in his former home.[13] By 1963 she was trying to find a publisher for a collection of his work, and also referred, in her correspondence, to an exhibition of his paintings in Kiev.[14]

Early in the 1960s she was joined in Koktebel' by a young man equally fascinated with Voloshin's life. Vladimir Kupchenko came from the town of Sverdlovsk; with a group of friends he had left his hometown to take a walking tour all over the Soviet Union—one manifestation of the journey of self-discovery and self-transformation of the Thaw generation. When they reached the village of Koktebel', he let his friends go on without him and settled down in the colony. Supporting himself by working as a tour guide, among other jobs, he became deeply involved in the organization of Voloshin's archive and eventually in setting up the Maximilian Voloshin House-Museum.[15] Though they were not always friends, both he and Maria Stepanovna did all they could to preserve Voloshin's memory in many concrete ways. Above all, they asked great numbers of Voloshin's friends, guests, and associates to write about their memories of him, which Kupchenko was to publish in 1990 in the volume frequently cited in this book, *Vospominaiia o Maximiliana Voloshine*. In preserving and re-creating the evidence of Voloshin's life, they, along with the memoirists who wrote for them, also preserved the memories of a Russian culture of circles and networks, of communitas and self-transformation, and of an ideal of leadership. Perpetuating that tradition of hagiographical narrative of the lives of individuals, they looked backward in search of an answer to that universal and yet singularly Russian question: "*Kak zhit'?*" or "How to live?" In the tales they told about Maximilian Voloshin, some believed they had found a kind of answer:

"And now, after many, many years, at the most difficult moments I remember Max's words, and his figure rises anew before me, helping me to surmount that which seems insurmountable, even to float through suffering into happiness. To the end of my days, Max will illuminate my path."[16]

In the words of one woman who replied to Vladimir Kupchenko in response to his request for a memoir about Voloshin: "Max lives."[17] And so he does, as a legend that reveals as much about those who have created the legend as about Voloshin himself. In shaping this legend across the years, over tea at the kitchen table, at the desk in the cramped bedroom-study, from one generation to the next, they placed some of their dearest hopes for the emergence of a truly good society, where good people flourish because they know how to live.

NOTES

ABBREVIATIONS IN ARCHIVAL CITATIONS

f. = fond (collection)
d., dd. = delo (file), dela (files)
op. = opis' (inventory)
s., ss. = stranitsa (page), stranitsy (pages)

AN INTRODUCTION
IN THREE PARTS

1. As one memoirist has put it, "His literary activities were more sparkling than influ-ential—of him it may be said, as of one of his own favorites, Viellers de L'Isle-Adam, 'He was renowned rather than famous.' It must be added that for all the value of his literary legacy (existing in any case for only a few) he was more interesting and valuable as a hu-man being—Human Being in capital letters, Human Being in the great style" (Erikh Gollerbakh, "On byl bole znamenit, chem izvesten," in V. P. Kupchenko and Z. D. Davy-dov, eds., *Vospominaniia o Maksimiliane Voloshine* [Moscow: Sovetskii pisatel', 1990], 505).

2. On the problem of intelligentsia identity as analyzed by Western scholars, see Mar-tin Malia, "What Is the Intelligentsia," in Richard Pipes, ed., *The Russian Intelligentsia* (New York: Columbia University Press, 1961), 1–18; Michael Confino, "On Intellectuals and Intellectual Traditions in Eighteenth- and Nineteenth-Century Russia," *Daedalus* 101 (1972): 117–149; Daniel Brower, "The Problem of the Russian Intelligentsia," *Slavic Re-view* 26 (1967): 638–639; Elise Kimerling Wirtschafter, *Social Identity in Imperial Russia* (Dekalb: Northern Illinois University Press, 1997), 90–91; and Jane Burbank, "Were the Russian *Intelligenty* Organic Intellectuals?" in Judith Farquhar, Leon Fink, Stephen Leonard, and Donald Reid, eds., *Intellectuals and Political Life* (Ithaca, N.Y.: Cornell Uni-versity Press, 1994), chap. 6.

3. The terminology dividing the intelligentsia into a variety of smaller groups includes, for example, the *scientific intelligentsia*, the *cultural intelligentsia* (an elite group consist-ing of those who contributed to national discourse through various types of cultural pro-duction), the *revolutionary intelligentsia*, the *high* (*vysokaia*) *intelligentsia*, and the *broad* (*shirokaia*) *intelligentsia*, not to mention the *literary intelligentsia*, a subgroup of the *cul-tural intelligentsia*. Some of these terms are discussed from a linguistic perspective in Otto Mueller, *Intelligencija: Untersuchungen zur Geschichte eines politischen Schlagwortes* (Frankfurt: Athenaem, 1971). As will become clear in this book, the literary intelligentsia, while distinguished by the form of its productive activity, could be closely entwined with other intelligentsia groups through both personal association and common experience.

4. For such a literary biography, see Vladimir Kupchenko, *Stranstvie Maksimiliana Voloshina* (Peterburg: "Logos," 1996).

5. For an extensive review of the term *agency* see Laura Ahearn, "Language and Agency," *Annual Review of Anthropology* 30 (2001): 109–137. One of the most influential anthropologists on the topic of agency and culture is Sherry Ortner. See her seminal article, "Theory in Anthropology since the Sixties," *Comparative Studies in Society and History* 26, no. 1 (1984): 126–166, and her more recent book, *Making Gender: The Politics and Erotics of Culture* (Boston: Beacon, 1996), in which she propounds a notion of "embedded agency" to explain the ways that people act within cultural contexts in order to change those contexts. It is a very useful concept and resonates strongly with the approach to individual agency taken in this book.

6. The first person to describe Voloshin's summer home as *dom otdykha* was Symbolist author Andrei Bely, writing in 1933 (Andrei Bely, "Dom-Muzei M. A. Voloshina," in Kupchenko and Davydov, *Vospominaniia o Maksimiliane Voloshine*, 509).

7. For a detailed discussion of the privileges and welfare involved, see John and Carol Garrard, *Inside the Soviet Writers' Union* (New York: Free Press, 1990).

8. Party Resolution, April 23, 1932, *O perestroike literaturno-khudozhesvennykh organizatsii.* See L. G. Fogelevich, *Osnovnye direktivy i zakonodatel'stvo o pechati: sistematicheskii sbornik* (Moscow: Sovetskoe zakonodatel'stvo, 1936), 50.

9. See, for example, Max Eastman, *Artists in Uniform: A Study of Literature and Bureaucratism* (New York: Octagon, 1972 [1934]); Christopher Read, *Culture and Power in Revolutionary Russia: The Intelligentsia and the Transition from Tsarism to Communism* (New York: St. Martin's, 1990), esp. 57–93. For the argument that intellectuals had more agency than they have been given credit for, see Sheila Fitzpatrick, "Cultural Orthodoxies under Stalin," in idem, *The Cultural Front: Power and Culture in Revolutionary Russia* (Ithaca, N.Y.: Cornell University Press, 1992), 238–256.

10. On this phenomenon in the medieval and early modern period, see, for example, Edward Keenan, "Muscovite Political Folkways," *The Russian Review* 45, no. 2 (April 1986) 115–182; Nancy Shields Kollmann, *Kinship and Politics: The Making of the Muscovite Political System, 1345–1547* (Stanford, Calif.: Stanford University Press, 1987); Valerie Kivelson, *Autocracy in the Provinces: The Muscovite Gentry and Political Culture in the Seventeenth Century* (Stanford, Calif.: Stanford University Press, 1996); and Robert O. Crummey, *Aristocrats and Servitors: The Boyar Elite in Russia, 1613–1689* (Princeton, N.J.: Princeton University Press, 1983). On the Imperial period, see, for example, Brenda Meehan-Waters, *Autocracy and Aristocracy: The Russian Service Elite of 1730* (New Brunswick, N.J.: Rutgers University Press, 1982); David Ransel, *The Politics of Catherinian Russia: The Panin Party* (New Haven, Conn.: Yale University Press, 1975); Alfred Rieber, *Merchants and Entrepreneurs in Imperial Russia* (Chapel Hill: University of North Carolina Press, 1982); and Steven Hoch, *Serfdom and Social Control in Russia: Petrovskoe, a Village in Tambov* (Chicago: University of Chicago Press, 1986).

11. See Horace W. Dewey and Ann M. Kleimola, "Suretyship and Collective Responsibility in Pre-Petrine Russia," *Jahrbücher für die Geschichte Osteuropas* 18 (1970): 337–354.

12. Meehan-Waters, *Autocracy and Aristocracy.* For a detailed discussion of the impact of traditional clan and personalized politics on the reign of Peter the Great, see Paul Bushkovitch, *Peter the Great* (Cambridge: Cambridge University Press, 2001).

13. For an example of the impact of court politics on intellectual life, see J. L. Black, *G.-F. Mueller and the Imperial Russian Academy* (Montreal: McGill-Queen's University Press, 1986).

14. For a general overview of Catherine the Great and the expansion of the intellectual realm during her reign, see Isabel de Madariaga, *Russia in the Age of Catherine the Great* (New Haven, Conn.: Yale University Press, 1981), 532–548.

15. On the expansion in publishing, see Gary Marker, *Publishing, Printing, and the Origins of Intellectual Life in Russia, 1700–1800* (Princeton, N.J.: Princeton University Press, 1985). For more detailed insight into the influence of patronage on literary life, see such biographical studies as W. Gareth Jones, *Nikolai Novikov: Enlightener of Russia* (Cambridge: Cambridge University Press, 1984); and Jesse V. Clardy, *G. R. Derzhavin: A Political Biography* (The Hague: Mouton, 1967).

16. Alexander Radishchev, *A Journey from St. Petersburg to Moscow* (Cambridge, Mass.: Harvard University Press, 1958).

17. With regard to secret societies, the impact of Freemasonry, with its Masonic lodges, was considerable. On this topic, see James Billington, *The Icon and the Axe: An Interpretive History of Russian Culture* (New York: Random House, 1966), 242–259. See also A. N. Nikolaevich, *Obshchestvennoe dvizhenie v Rossii pri Aleksandrie I*, 2nd ed. (St. Petersburg: Tipografia M. M. Stasiulevicha, 1885).

18. This circle, which Raeff describes as a study group, was called the "Friendly Literary Society"; note that the term *literary circle*, as Russians used it, could have a very broad meaning. See Marc Raeff, "Russian Youth on the Eve of Romanticism: Andrei I. Turgenev and His Circle," in idem, *Political Ideas and Institutions in Imperial Russia* (Boulder, Colo.: Westview, 1994), 42–64.

19. For a discussion of the intensive cult of friendship in the Turgenev, Herzen-Ogarev, and Stankevich circles, see Lidiia Ginzburg, "The Human Document and the Construction of Personality," in Judson Rosengrant, ed. and trans., *On Psychological Prose* (Princeton, N.J.: Princeton University Press, 1991), 27–106. A seminal work by a U.S. scholar on the Stankevich circle is Edward J. Brown, *Stankevich and His Moscow Circle, 1830–1840* (Stanford, Calif.: Stanford University Press, 1966).

20. Victor Turner, *The Ritual Process: Structure and Anti-Structure* (Chicago: Aldine, 1969), 95, 132–133.

21. Ibid., 109.

22. Ibid., 109–110.

23. Or to put it in Turner's own words, as he sums up some of his ideas on communitas: "The time has now come to make a careful review of a hypothesis that seems to account for the attributes of such seemingly diverse phenomena as neophytes in the liminal phase of ritual, subjugated autochthones, small nations, court jesters, holy mendicants, good Samaritans, millenarian movements, 'dharma bums,' matrilineality in patrilineal systems, patrilineality in matrilineal systems, and monastic orders" (ibid., 125).

24. On intelligentsia exclusion from the traditional *soslovie* system, see Gregory Freeze, "The *Soslovie* (Estate) Paradigm and Russian Social History," *American Historical Review* 91 (1986): 11–36.

25. Turner, *The Ritual Process*, 125.

26. Ibid., 116.

27. Ibid.

28. Turner develops his views on theatrical play as an element of the communitas phenomenon in *From Ritual to Theatre: The Human Seriousness of Play* (New York: Performing Arts Journal Publications, 1982), esp. 7–19. Building on his study of such tribal rituals of social transformation and transition as the installation of a new chief among the Ndembu, as well as on the work of Arnold van Gennep (*Rites of Passage* [London: Routledge and Kegan Paul, 1960]; first published as *Rites de Passage*, 1908), he recognizes a variety of performance experiences that take place in what he calls "dramatic time," including experimental theater, as drawing on the fundamental principle of seeking self-transformation through performance under the condition of liminality.

29. Turner, *From Ritual to Theatre*, 47; see also idem, *The Ritual Process*, 127.

30. See, for example, some of the circles described in N. L. Brodskii, ed., *Literaturnye salony i kruzhki: pervaia polovina XIX veka* (Moscow: Argaf, 2001 [1930]).

31. On this topic more broadly, see Abbott Gleason, *Young Russia: The Genesis of Russian Radicalism in the 1860s* (New York: Viking, 1980). See also Vera Leikina-Svirskaia, *Intelligentsiia v Rossii vo vtoroi polovine XIX veka* (Moscow: Mysl', 1971).

32. For an excellent introduction to the field of network studies, see Barry Wellman and S. D. Berkowitz, *Social Structures: A Network Approach* (Cambridge: Cambridge University Press, 1988).

33. A considerable number of primary and secondary sources support this argument, which I make in the article "Joseph Stalin, 'Our Teacher Dear': Mentorship, Social Transformation, and the Russian Intelligentsia Personality Cult," in Klaus Heller and Jan Plamper, eds., *Personenkulte im Stalinismus/Personality Cults in Stalinism* (Göttingen: Vandenhoeck and Ruprecht, forthcoming). Some of the sources for this argument, as well as for the argument that follows on mentorship, institution building, and circles, are Kendall E. Bailes, *Science and Russian Culture in an Age of Revolutions: V. I. Vernadsky and His Scientific School, 1863–1945* (Bloomington: Indiana University Press, 1990); Harley D. Balzer, "The Engineering Profession in Tsarist Russia," in idem, ed., *Russia's Missing Middle Class: The Professions in Russian History* (Armonk, N.Y.: M. E. Sharpe, 1996); Rosalind Polly Gray, "Questions of Identity at Abramtsevo," in Laura Morowitz and William Vaughan, eds., *Artistic Brotherhoods in the Nineteenth Century* (Burlington, Vt.: Ashgate, 2000); Modeste Tchaikovsky, ed., *The Life and Letters of Peter Tchaikovsky*, trans. Rosa Newmarch (London: John Lane, 1905); V. Bolkhovitinov, *Aleksandr Grigorievich Stoletov (1839–1896)* (Moscow: Molodaia Gvardiia, 1953); Iu. G. Oksman, ed., *N. G. Chernyshevskii v vospominaniiakh sovremennikov* (Saratov: Saratovskoe knizhnoe izdatel'stvo, 1958–1959).

34. Turner does not discuss the theoretical problem of leadership in communitas at any length, though at one point he does discuss particular leaders of communitas in the form of what he calls religions of humility, such as the Buddha, Gandhi, and Lev Tolstoy, arguing that they came from structurally superior social status and therefore often committed themselves to a rejection of status through abandonment of material wealth (Turner, *The Ritual Process*, 195–199). Turner also writes about the important role of elders, doctors, or priests in some proto-communitas tribal rituals of social transformation. He sees such rituals as structurally related to the communitas phenomenon (Turner, *The Ritual Process*, chaps. 1–3).

35. For a thoughtful review of the meaning of literature to the educated elite of Russia, see Jeffrey Brooks, "Readers and Reading at the End of the Tsarist Era," in William Mills Todd III, ed., *Literature and Society in Imperial Russia, 1800–1914* (Stanford, Calif.: Stanford University Press, 1978), 97–150, esp. 99–105.

36. Freeze, "The *Soslovie* (Estate) Paradigm," 11–36.

37. For an analysis of what she calls "Romantic Anticapitalism" among Russian intellectuals of this period, see Katerina Clark, *Petersburg: Crucible of Cultural Revolution* (Cambridge, Mass.: Harvard University Press, 1995), 16–23. Other scholarship on the discomfort of the educated elite (or would-be elite) with capitalist relations includes Laurie Manchester, "The Secularization of the Search for Salvation: The Self-Fashioning of Orthodox Clergymen's Sons in Late Imperial Russia," *Slavic Review* 57 no. 1 (spring 1998): 50–76; and Kendall Bailes, "Reflections on Russian Professions," in Balzer, *Russia's Missing Middle Class*, 39–54. There was a broader European context for this phenomenon; on anticapitalism among intellectuals elsewhere in Europe during this time, see Martin J. Wiener, *English Culture and the Decline of the Industrial Spirit, 1850–1980* (New York: Cambridge University Press, 1981).

38. Cited in B. Eikhenbaum, *Molodoi Tolstoi* (Berlin: Izdatel'stvo Z. I. Grzhebina, 1922), 85. Found in A. I. Reitblat, "Literaturnyi gonorar v Rossii XIX–nachala XX v. (K postanovke problemy)," in *Knizhnoe delo v Rossii vo vtoroi polovine XIX–nachale XX veka,* 3rd printing: *Sobranie nauchnykh trudov,* ed. V. E. Kel'ner (Leningrad: Gosudarstvennaia Publichnaia Biblioteka im. M. E. Saltykova-Shchedrina, 1986), 135.

39. V. Shelgunov, "Literaturnaia sobstvennost'," *Sovremennik* (1862): 3, 238. Found in Reitblat, "Literaturnyi gonorar v Rossii," 135.

40. M. Teleshov, "Vospominaniia o Maksime Gor'kom," in N. L. Brodskii, ed., *M. Gor'kii v vospominaniiakh sovremennikov* (Moscow: Gosudarstvennoe izdatel'stvo khudozhestvennoi literatury, 1955), 189.

41. Anonymous, *Biblioteka dlia chteniia,* (St. Petersburg: L. F. Smirdin, 1835), Vol. 8: Otd. V. C. 1–3. Found in A. G. Tartakovskii, *Russkaia memuaristika XVIII–pervoi poloviny XIX v.: ot rukopisi k knige* (Moscow: Nauka, 1991).

42. This is by no means to argue that there were no market relations in literature; indeed, the anxiety about and hostility toward these relations indicates the threat they represented, especially to those engaged in elite literary production. On the capitalist market primarily for popular literature, see Jeffrey Brooks, *When Russia Learned to Read: Literacy and Popular Literature, 1861–1917* (Princeton, N.J.: Princeton University Press, 1985); and Beth Holmgren, *Rewriting Capitalism: Literature and the Market in Late Tsarist Russia and the Kingdom of Poland* (Pittsburgh: University of Pittsburgh Press, 1998). On this topic from the perspective of the genre of melodrama, see Louise McReynolds and Joan Neuberger, introduction to *Imitations of Life: Two Centuries of Melodrama in Russia,* ed. Louise McReynolds and Joan Neuberger (Durham, N.C.: Duke University Press, 2002), 1–24.

43. As Turner writes: "The inherent contradictions between spontaneous communitas and a markedly structured system are so great . . . that any venture with attempts to combine these modalities will constantly be threatened by structural cleavage or by the suffocation of communitas" (*From Ritual to Theatre,* 49–50).

44. For an extensive discussion of this genre of intelligentsia memoir, see Barbara Walker, "On Reading Soviet Memoirs: A History of the 'Contemporaries' Genre as an Institution of Russian Intelligentsia Culture from the 1790s to the 1970s," *The Russian Review* 59 (July 2000): 327–352. Much of what follows here on this genre is summarized from that article, including some quotations from such memoirs.

45. P. V. Annenkov, *The Extraordinary Decade: Literary Memoirs,* ed. Arthur Mendel, trans. Irwin Titunik (Ann Arbor: University of Michigan Press, 1968).

46. Ibid., 58.

47. On Belinsky's "Hegelian year," during which he isolated himself from his friends over philosophy, see Isaiah Berlin, "Vissarion Belinsky," in Henry Hardy and Aileen Kelly, eds., *Russian Thinkers* (New York: Viking, 1978), 166–171.

48. Annenkov, *The Extraordinary Decade,* 2.

49. Annenkov, *The Extraordinary Decade,* 155. Note the use of the metaphor of family in this passage; it often reveals itself in the discourse over circles during this period.

50. "Iz vospominanii Professora A. V. Nikitenko o K. F. Ryleeve," in V. A. Fedorov, ed., *Dekabristy v vospominaniiakh sovremennikov* (Moscow: Izdatel'stvo Moskovskogo Universiteta, 1988), 87.

51. "Iz vospominanii S. V. Kapnist-Skalon o Dekabristakh," in Fedorov, *Dekabristy v vospominaniiakh sovremennikov,* 115.

52. Alexander Herzen, *My Past and Thoughts,* trans. Constance Garnett, translation revised by Humphrey Higgins (Berkeley: University of California Press, 1982), 230.

53. A. P. Kern, "Vospominaniia o Pushkine, Del'vige i Glinke," in *Vospominaniia, Dnevniki, Perepiska,* ed. Arkadii Moiseevich Gordin (Moscow: Pravda, 1989), 47–49.

54. This discussion of the "contemporaries" memoir genre continues to draw on Walker, "On Reading Soviet Memoirs."

55. Marina Tsvetaeva, *A Captive Spirit: Selected Prose*, trans. J. Marin King (Ann Arbor, Mich.: Ardis, 1980), 64.

56. Marina Tsvetaeva, *Pis'ma k Anne Teskovoi* (St. Petersburg: Vneshtorgizdat, 1991), 87.

57. Marina Tsvetaeva, "A Living Word about a Living Man," in Tsvetaeva, *A Captive Spirit*, 48.

58. Anna Ostroumova-Lebedeva, "Leto v Koktebele," in Kupchenko and Davydov, *Vospominaniia o Maksimiliane Voloshine*, 519.

59. Andrei Bely, *Nachalo Veka* (Moscow: Khudozhestvennaia literatura, 1991), 254.

60. Tsvetaeva, "A Living Word about a Living Man," 81.

61. The articles collected in *Between Tsar and People* reveal many of the alternatives that were available to an educated elite that was expanding rapidly. See Edith Clowes, Samuel Kassow, and James West, eds., *Between Tsar and People: Educated Society and the Quest for Public Identity in Late Imperial Russia, 1800–1914* (Princeton, N.J.: Princeton University Press, 1991).

62. Marshall S. Shatz and Judith E. Zimmerman, eds., *Signposts: A Collection of Articles on the Russian Intelligentsia* (Irvine, Calif.: Charles Schlacks Jr., 1986). For a wide-ranging review of intelligentsia political views and debates at a slightly later period, see Jane Burbank, *Intelligentsia and Revolution: Russian Views of Bolshevism, 1917–1922* (New York: Oxford University Press, 1986).

63. Leopold Haimson, "The Problem of Social Stability in Russia, 1905–1917," in Michael Cherniavsky, ed., *The Structure of Russian History: Interpretative Essays* (New York: Random House, 1970); John Bushnell, *Mutiny amid Repression: Russian Soldiers in the Revolution of 1905–1906* (Bloomington: Indiana University Press, 1985); and Geoffrey Hosking, *The Russian Constitutional Experiment: Government and Duma, 1907–1914* (Cambridge: Cambridge University Press, 1973).

1. VOLOSHIN'S SOCIAL
AND CULTURAL ORIGINS

1. Kupchenko and Davydov, *Vospominaniia o Maksimiliane Voloshine*, photograph on 160.

2. Maximilian Voloshin, *Putnik po vselennym* (Moscow: Sovetskaia rossiia, 1990), 235.

3. Tsvetaeva, "A Living Word about a Living Man," 55.

4. Although Elena Ottobal'dovna reached maturity in an age when a few educated Russian women were beginning to question their role in the family, that she left her husband was nevertheless unusual.

5. Valentina Viazemskaia, "Nashe znakomstvo s Maksom," in Kupchenko and Davydov, *Vospominaniia o Maksimiliane Voloshine*, 73.

6. Margarita Woloschin, *Die Gruene Schlange: Lebenserinnerungen einer Malerin* (Frankfurt am Main: Fischer Taschenbuch Verlag, 1982), 167.

7. On this topic, more broadly, see Laura Engelstein, *The Keys to Happiness: Sex and the Search for Modernity in Fin-de-Siècle Russia* (Ithaca, N.Y.: Cornell University Press, 1992), esp. 396–404.

8. "Serezha" was Tsvetaeva's husband, Sergei Efron, who fought with the Whites in the civil war. She may have recorded (or invented) this dialogue in irony, as, by 1932, when she wrote the memoir, Tsvetaeva herself was practically the sole bread-earner in her family, while her husband pursued obscure political activities.

9. Tsvetaeva, "A Living Word about a Living Man," 61.

10. Viazemskaia, "Nashe znakomstvo s Maksom," 72.

11. Voloshin, *Putnik po vselennym*, 235.

12. Ibid., 242.

13. According to the 1897 census, 21 percent of respondents answered yes to the question: "Can you read?" See Jeffrey Brooks, "Readers and Reading at the End of the Tsarist Era," in Todd, *Literature and Society in Imperial Russia, 1800–1914*, 119. This article is also helpful on the broader question of how the intelligentsia viewed literature.

14. Letter from Voloshin to E. O. Voloshina, February 26, 1897, Theodosia, 2. Typewritten copy in private archive of Vladimir Kupchenko.

15. Letter to Aleksandra Petrova, February 1898, in V. E. Bagno and A. V. Lavrov, eds., *Maksimilian Voloshin: iz literaturnogo naslediia*, vol. 1 (Sankt-Peterburg: Nauka, 1991), 48.

16. Ibid.

17. Vladimir Kupchenko, "Vol'noliubivaia iusnost' poeta," *Novyi mir* 12 (1980): 216–223.

18. For an extensive discussion of student activism and consciousness during this time, see Susan Morrissey, *Heralds of Revolution: Russian Students and the Mythologies of Radicalism* (New York: Oxford University Press, 1998). Voloshin does not entirely fit the more radical pattern she describes, but he appears to have been influenced by its spirit.

19. Bagno and Lavrov, *Maksimilian Voloshin: iz literaturnogo naslediia*, 52 n. 8.

20. Letter from Voloshin to E. O. Voloshina, March 1, 1896. Typewritten copy in private archive of Vladimir Kupchenko.

21. Ibid., October 28, 1897. Typewritten copy in private archive of Vladimir Kupchenko.

22. Ibid.

23. Letter from E. O. Voloshina to Voloshin, October 25, 1901, Institut Russkoi Literatury Akademii Nauk (IRLI), Pushkinskii dom, f. 562, o. 3, d. 649, s. 38.

24. Letter from Voloshin to E. O. Voloshina, October 28, 1897. Typewritten copy in private archive of Vladimir Kupchenko.

25. N. A. Troinitskii, *Pervaia vseobshchaia perepis' naseleniia Rossiskoi imperii*, 89 vols. (St. Petersburg, 1899–1905), vol. 24, Table 2; vol. 37, Table 2.

26. On the culture of elite hospitality, according to whose terms guests could arrive for a party or private visit and stay on for weeks at a time, see Priscilla Roosevelt, *Life on the Russian Country Estate: A Social and Cultural History* (New Haven, Conn.: Yale University Press, 1995), 129–153.

27. Other servants were quite possibly also in this household, but this is not documented.

28. Letter from Voloshin to E. O. Voloshina, October 28, 1897. Typewritten copy in private archive of Vladimir Kupchenko.

29. For more on the *zemliachestvo*, see James C. McLelland, *Autocrats and Academics: Education, Culture, and Society in Tsarist Russia* (Chicago: University of Chicago Press, 1979); Samuel D. Kassow, *Students, Professors, and the State in Tsarist Russia* (Berkeley: University of California Press, 1989); and V. Orlov, *Studencheskoe dvizhenie moskovskogo universiteta v XIX stoletii* (Moscow: Izdatel'stvo vsesoiuznogo obshchestva politkatorzhan i ssyl'no-poselentsev, 1934).

30. IRLI, Pushkinskii dom, f. 562, op. 4, d. 3, s. 16.

31. Letter from Voloshin to E. O. Voloshina, undated (fall of 1900). Typewritten copy in private archive of Vladimir Kupchenko.

32. Ibid., September 20, 1900. Typewritten copy in private archive of Vladimir Kupchenko.

33. Ibid., September 28, 1900. Typewritten copy in private archive of Vladimir Kupchenko.

34. See, for example, George Yaney, *The Systematization of Russian Government: Social Evolution in the Domestic Administration of Imperial Russia, 1711–1905* (Urbana: University of Illinois Press, 1973).

35. Daniel Orlovsky, "Political Clientelism in Russia: the Historical Perspective," in T. H. Rigby and Bohdan Harasyiv, eds., *Leadership Selection and Patron-Client Relations in the USSR and Yugoslavia* (London: Allan and Unwin, 1983), 187.

2. THE RUSSIAN SYMBOLISTS
AND THEIR CIRCLES

1. Briusov wrote in his diary in 1903: "[Voloshin] has letters of recommendation to everyone, to Merezhkovskii, to Minskii, to me" (Valery Bryusov, *The Diary of Valery Bryusov [1893–1905]: With Reminiscences by V. F. Khodasevich and Marina Tsvetaeva*, ed., trans., and with an introduction by Joan Delaney Grossman [Berkeley: University of California Press, 1980], 136).

2. Briusov continued, in typically dry fashion: "In Petersburg he didn't go over so well, but in Moscow everyone fussed over him for three weeks" (ibid., 136).

3. Which of the Russian modernist associations are to be grouped among the Symbolists can be debated; the particular delineation given here draws on Avril Pyman's survey of Symbolism, *A History of Russian Symbolism* (Cambridge: Cambridge University Press, 1994).

4. Letter to Aleksandra Petrova, January 1898, in Bagno and Lavrov, *Maksimilian Voloshin: iz literaturnogo naslediia*, vol. 1, 43.

5. Ibid., 63–65. Voloshin writes to Petrova at length about this problem.

6. Ekaterina Bal'mont, "Redko kto umel tak slushat', kak on," in Kupchenko and Davydov, *Vospominaniia o Maksimiliane Voloshine*, 93.

7. Ibid., 96.

8. On children and the Lenin cult, see Nina Tumarkin, *Lenin Lives! The Lenin Cult in Soviet Russia* (Cambridge, Mass.: Harvard University Press, 1983), 227, 241–242, 260, 265–267. With regard to the Stalin cult, one example of Stalin's much celebrated association with children was the famous photograph of him holding the girl Engelsina Markizova, described in Ludmilla Alexeyeva and Paul Goldberg, *The Thaw Generation: Coming of Age in the Post-Stalin Era* (Pittsburgh: Pittsburgh University Press, 1990), 80–83. A reproduction of this picture, which at one time adorned a Moscow subway station, is included in *The Thaw Generation*.

9. Bal'mont, "Redko kto umel tak slushat', kak on," 94.

10. Ibid., 98, 95, 100.

11. Andrei Bely, *Nachalo veka*, 250.

12. Ibid., 254.

13. Turner discusses this element of communitas, to some extent, in *The Ritual Process*, chap. 5: "Humility and Hierarchy: The Liminality of Status Elevation and Reversal"; and more extensively in his book *From Ritual to Theatre: The Human Seriousness of Play* (New York: Performing Arts Journal Publications, 1982).

14. Vladislav Khodasevich, "Konets Renaty," in idem, *Nekropol' i drugie vospominaniia* (Moscow: Zhurnal 'Nashe nasledie,' 1992), 21–33; Irina Paperno and Joan Delaney Grossman, eds., *Creating Life: The Aesthetic Utopia of Russian Modernism* (Stanford, Calif.: Stanford University Press, 1994).

15. On the Argonauts, see Alexander Lavrov, "Andrei Bely and the Argonauts' Myth-making," trans. Joan Delaney Grossman, in Paperno and Grossman, *Creating Life*, 83–121. On Symbolist theories and experiences of love, see Olga Matich, "The Symbolist Meaning of Love: Theory and Practice," in ibid., 24–50.

16. Irina Paperno, "The Meaning of Art: Symbolist Theories," in Paperno and Grossman, *Creating Life*, 15–23.

17. The importance of networking and patronage relations in the world of modernist publishing was notable; few publications could support themselves solely by means of sales and subscriptions, and therefore depended heavily on the financial patronage of members of the Russian gentry, the merchantry, and the Russian state. It was possible even to rely on the "patronage" of a journal's contributors, by not paying them. Dmitrii Merezhkovskii's journal, *Novyi Put'*, while at first supported by a kind of collective of investor/editors, relied heavily on the generosity of its contributors, paying only the younger ones. It soon collapsed owing to financial trouble. See I. V. Koretskaia, "Novyi put'" and "Voprosy zhizny," in B. A. Bialik, ed., *Literaturnyi protsess i russkaia zhurnalistika kontsa XIX–nachala XX veka* (Moscow: "Nauka," 1982), 181; and Bernice Glatzer Rosenthal, *Dmitrii Sergeevich Merezhkovskii and the Silver Age: The Development of a Revolutionary Mentality* (The Hague: Martinus Nijhoff, 1975), 145. Sergei Diaghilev's glossy journal, *World of Art*, was in part supported by its subscribers, but it also needed funding from Princess Tenisheva and from the state; see I. V. Koretskaia, "Mir Iskusstva," in Bialik, *Literaturnyi protsess i russkaia zhurnalistika kontsa*, 130. *Vesy*, the journal organized and run at times almost single-handedly by Valerii Briusov, would not have survived without the funding of the merchant's son, Poliakov; see K. M. Asadovskii and D. E. Maksimov, "Briusov i *Vesy*," in *Literaturnoe nasledstvo* (Moscow: Nauka, 1976), 85:260. *Apollon* was supported by the tea merchant Ushakov; see John Bowlt, *The Silver Age: Russian Art of the Early Twentieth Century and the "World of Art" Group* (Newtonville, Mass.: Oriental Research Partners, 1979).

18. See Priscilla Roosevelt, "Emerald Thrones and Living Statues: Theater and Theatricality on the Estate," in Roosevelt, *Life on the Russian Country Estate: A Social and Cultural History*, 129–153.

19. The terms *petimetr* and *koketka* refer to members of the Russian elite who adapted all too eagerly to the French models of the dandy (*petit-maitre*) and coquette. See Hans Rogger, *National Consciousness in Eighteenth-Century Russia* (Cambridge, Mass.: Harvard University Press, 1960), 48, 50; and Iurii M. Lotman, "The Poetics of Everyday Behavior in Eighteenth-Century Russian Life," trans. Andrea Beesing, in Alexander Nakhimovsky and Alice Stone Nakhimovsky, eds., *The Semiotics of Russian Cultural History* (Ithaca, N.Y.: Cornell University Press, 1985), 67–94; for Lotman's specific reference to the Symbolist "theater of life," see 94.

20. For more on elite theatricality that enhanced structural (autocratic) power in Imperial Russia, see Richard S. Wortman, *Scenarios of Power: Myth and Ceremony in Russian Monarchy*, 2 vols., (Princeton, N.J.: Princeton University Press, 1995), vol. 1: *From Peter the Great to the Death of Nicholas I*.

21. Maksimilian Voloshin, *Avtobiograficheskaia proza, dnevniki*, ed. Z. D. Davydova and V. P. Kupchenko (Moscow: Kniga, 1991), 193.

22. Ibid., 193.

23. On this concern about gender and sexuality more broadly see Engelstein, *The Keys to Happiness*.

24. Voloshin, *Avtobiograficheskaia proza, dnevniki*, 200–201.

25. Voloshin, *Iz literaturnogo naslediia*, vol. 1, 196 n. 2. On chaste marriages among the Symbolists and the thinking behind them, see Olga Matich, "The Symbolist Meaning of Love: Theory and Practice," in Paperno and Grossman, *Creating Life*, 40–44.

26. Voloshin, *Avtobiograficheskaia proza, dnevniki*, 229.

27. Ibid., 233.

28. Ibid., 231.

29. Woloschin, *Die Gruene Schlange*, 169.

30. L. D. Mikitich, *Literaturnyi Peterburg, Petrograd* (Moscow: Sovetskaia Rossia, 1991), 245–247.

31. Walker, "Joseph Stalin, 'Our Teacher Dear.'"

32. Alexandra Tolstoy, *Tolstoy: A Life of My Father* (New York: Harper and Brothers, 1953), 240, 280–282, 287, 312.

33. Thomas Gaiton Marullo, ed. and trans., *Ivan Bunin: Russian Requiem, 1885–1920* (Chicago: Ivan R. Dee, 1993), 41, 54.

34. Mary Louise Zoe, "Redefining the Intellectual's Role: Maksim Gorky and the *Sreda* Circle," in Clowes, Kassow, and West, *Between Tsar and People*, 295. Unless otherwise noted, the following information on Gorky and *Sreda* comes from that same article, 288–307.

35. See, for example, S. Skitalets, "Maksim Gor'kii," in Brodskii, *M. Gor'kii v vospominaniiakh sovremennikov*, 161.

36. Brodskii, *M. Gor'kii v vospominaniiakh sovremennikov*. See the memoirs in this work by A. Serafimovich (63–68), S. Skitalets (156–167), and M. Teleshov (172–191). All were members of the *Sreda* circle.

37. For Ivan Bunin's memoir about Tolstoy, see his "Lev Tolstoy," in idem, *Memories and Portraits*, trans. Vera Traill and Robin Chancellor, 17–30 (London: John Lehman, 1951); for Valentin Kataev's memoir about Bunin, see his *Sviatoi kolodets: trava zabven'ia* (Moscow: Sovetskii pisatel', 1969).

38. Voloshin, *Avtobiograficheskaia proza, dnevniki*, 202–203.

39. The translated quotation is from Temira Pachmuss, *Women Writers in Russian Modernism* (Urbana: University of Illinois Press, 1978), 192; the original is in Z. N. Gippius, *Zhivye litsa*, 2 vols. (Prague: Plamya, 1925), 2:62.

40. See, for example, Mikitich, *Literaturnyi Peterburg, Petrograd*.

41. A. Turkov, *Aleksandr Blok* (Moscow: Molodaia gvardiia: 1969), 91.

42. Lidiia Ivanova, *Vospominaniia: Kniga ob otse* (Moscow: Rik Kul'tura, 1992), 32. Ivanova also provides a detailed description of the layout of the apartment as it changed over the years.

43. Pachmuss, *Women Writers in Russian Modernism*, 114–173, 191–242; Engelstein, *The Keys to Happiness*, 392, 396–414.

44. Woloschin, *Die Gruene Schlange: Lebenserrinnerungen einer Malerin*, 181.

45. Ibid., 188.

46. For the quotation on Lidiia's interest in a female partner, see Pyman, *A History of Russian Symbolism*, 295.

47. Woloschin, *Die Gruene Schlange*, 190.

48. On this relationship as an expression of *zhiznetvorchestvo*, see Olga Matich, "Symbolist Meaning of Love: Theory and Practice," in Paperno and Grossman, *Creating Life*, 47–49.

49. Ibid., 48.

50. Woloschin, *Die Gruene Schlange*, 170.

51. Voloshin, *Avtobiograficheskaia proza, dnevniki*, 263.

52. Ibid., 265.

53. Ibid., 265–266.

54. The theme of the patriarch who damages household harmony and unity by taking excessive advantage of his domestic power is also found in the Russian literature of the time, indicating its relevance to Russian writers. Lev Tolstoy's famous opening line of *Anna Karenina*—"All happy families are like one another; each unhappy family is unhappy in its

own way"—is followed by a description of how Obolensky injures the peace and happiness of his household by having an affair with the governess (Lev Tolstoy, *Anna Karenina*, trans. David Magarshack [New York: Signet, 1961], 17). Maxim Gorky's memoir, *My Childhood*, depicts Gorky's family and household as ravaged and ultimately destroyed by the brutality and greed of his grandfather (Maxim Gorky, *My Childhood*, trans. and introduction by Ronald Wilks [New York: Penguin, 1966]).

55. Voloshin, *Avtobiograficheskaia proza, dnevniki*, 266–267.

56. Voloshin, *Avtobiograficheskaia proza, dnevniki*, 274.

57. Ibid., 276.

58. On Ivanov's relations with Gorodetskii, see Pyman, *A History of Russian Symbolism*, 293–294; and Matich, "The Symbolist Meaning of Love: Theory, and Practice," 49. Later, demonstrating a further engagement in "sacred incest," Ivanov would marry Lidiia's daughter by a former marriage, Vera.

59. Voloshin, *Avtobiograficheskaia proza, dnevniki*, 268.

3. VOLOSHIN AND THE
MODERNIST PROBLEM OF THE UGLY POETESS

1. An interesting exception to this "rule" was the poet Mirra Lokhvitskaia (1869–1905). See Pachmuss, *Women Writers in Russian Modernism*, 85–92.

2. Svetlana Boym, *Death in Quotation Marks: Cultural Myths of the Modern Poet* (Cambridge, Mass.: Harvard University Press, 1991), 194.

3. Tsvetaeva, "A Living Word about a Living Man," 82–84.

4. Evgeniia Gertsyk, *Vospominaniia* (Paris: YMCA Press, 1973), 79.

5. See Avril Pyman, *The Life of Alexander Blok*, 2 vols. (Oxford: Oxford University Press, 1979), vol. 1: *The Distant Thunder, 1880–1908*, 67–118.

6. In an unsent letter to Blok, Liubov' Mendeleeva wrote: "I can no longer remain in the same friendly relationship to you as before. . . . You look on me as if I were some abstract idea; you have imagined all kinds of wonderful things about me and behind that fantastic fiction which existed only in your imagination you have failed to notice *me*, a live human being with a living soul. . . . I am a live human being and that is what I want to be, even with all my faults" (Pyman, *The Life of Alexander Blok*, 1:96. Original quote in D. E. Maksimov, *Uchenye zapiski Leningradskogo pedagogicheskogo instituta* 18 (1956): 249–250.

7. Gertsyk, *Vospominaniia*, 77.

8. Bogdanovshchina was the home of Sabashnikova's wealthy parents; following the "explosion" of the Ivanov household, she went there to take refuge more or less from both Voloshin and the Ivanovs.

9. Gertsyk, *Vospominaniia*, 77.

10. Tsvetaeva, "A Living Word about a Living Man," 82.

11. Ibid.

12. "'There's enough material in you for ten poets, and all of them remarkable,'" Tsvetaeva records Voloshin as telling her. Ibid., 43.

13. Ibid., 42.

14. Boym, *Death in Quotation Marks*, 200–219. Boym entitles this section of her analysis of Tsvetaeva's work "The Poetess's Self-Defense: Close Reading and Clothes Reading."

15. Anastasiia Tsvetaeva, *Vospominaniia* (Moscow: Sovetskii pisatel', 1983), 320.

16. Ibid., 356.

17. Tsvetaeva, "A Living Word about a Living Man," 28–29.

18. Tsvetaeva, *Pis'ma k Anne Teskovoi*, 87.

19. Maksimilian Voloshin, "Zhenskaia Poeziia," *Utro Rossii*, December 11, 1910.

20. On rituals of status reversal in communitas, see Victor Turner, "Humility and Hierarchy: The Liminality of Status Elevation and Reversal," in Turner, *The Ritual Process*, 166–203.

21. Lidiia Ivanova, *Vospominaniia: Kniga ob otse*, 32.

22. John Malmstad and Nikolay Bogomolov, *Mikhail Kuzmin: A Life in Art* (Cambridge, Mass.: Harvard University Press, 1999), 157–159.

23. Bowlt, *The Silver Age*, 117–121.

24. Art historian John E. Bowlt describes this new journal as an "autumnal flower" of the World of Art movement (ibid., 121).

25. For a reproduction of Leon Bakst's *Portrait of Sergei Diaghilev with His Nurse* (1906; in the possession of the State Russian Museum, Petersburg), see ibid., 47–48. Though female partners in hospitality were often wives or romantic partners to male circle leaders, like Lidiia Ivanova to Viacheslav Ivanov, servants as well as other nonromantic partners could play the dominant female role in circles.

26. Johannes von Guenther, *Ein Leben im Ostwind. Zwischen Petersburg und Muenchen* (Muenchen: Biederstein, 1969), 284.

27. This description of the founding of *Apollon* is taken from three sources: "Istoriia Cherubiny (Rasskaz M. Voloshina v zapisi T. Shan'ko)," in Kupchenko and Davydov, *Vospominaniia o Maksimiliane Voloshine*, 179–194; Johannes von Guenther, *Ein Leben im Ostwind*; and S. Makovskii, *Na Parnasse serebrianogo veka* (Munich: Izdatel'stvo tsentr. ob'edineniia polit. emigrantov iz SSSR, 1961).

28. Letter to Aleksandra Petrova, in Bagno and Lavrov, *Maksimilian Voloshin: Iz literaturnogo naslediia*, 195.

29. Ibid., 196–197.

30. Ibid., 198.

31. For a collection of Voloshin's feuilleton-style journalism in such journals as *Zolotoe Runo* and *Vesy*, and such newspapers as *Rus'*, see Maksimilian Voloshin, *Liki tvorchestva*, ed. V. A. Manuilov, V. P. Kupchenko, and A. V. Lavrov (Leningrad: Nauka, 1989). *Liki tvorchestva* was first published in 1913 in Petersburg.

32. von Guenther, *Ein Leben im Ostwind*, 287.

33. "Istoriia Cherubiny (Rasskaz M. Voloshina v zapisi T. Shan'ko)," 180.

34. Gertsyk, *Vospominaniia*, 86.

35. *Apollo*, no. 2 (1909), trans. Temira Pachmuss; Pachmuss, *Women Writers in Russian Modernism*, 256–257.

36. Sergei Makovskii, *Portrety sovremennikov* (New York: Chekhov, 1955), 337.

37. Ibid., 340.

38. Ibid.

39. Tsvetaeva, "A Living Word about a Living Man," 37–43; Tsvetaeva, *Vospominaniia*, 359.

40. Makovskii, *Portrety sovremennikov*, 342.

41. "Istoriia Cherubiny (Rasskaz M. Voloshina v zapisi T. Shan'ko)," 194.

42. Letters from Voloshin to A. M. Petrova, November 21, 1909, November 26, 1909, November 29, 1909, and December 17, 1909, in Bagno and Lavrov, *Maksimilian Voloshin: Iz literaturnogo naslediia*, vol. 1, 199–205.

43. For the story of Cherubina from the perspective of Mikhail Kuzmin, whose personal and professional relationships were also affected by this event, see Malmstad and Bogomolov, *Mikhail Kuzmin*, 162–166.

44. Voloshin, *Avtobiograficheskaia proza, dnevniki*, 293–301; letters from Voloshin to A. M. Petrova, November 21, 1909, November 26, 1909, November 29, 1909, and December 17, 1909, in Bagno and Lavrov, *Maksimilian Voloshin: Iz literaturnogo naslediia*, vol. 1, 199–205.

45. Voloshin writes "three years ago," but he was in error (letter from Voloshin to A. M. Petrova, November 26, 1909, in Bagno and Lavrov, *Maksimilian Voloshin: Iz literaturnogo naslediia*, vol. 1, 201).

46. This sentence is syntactically awkward in Russian; I have smoothed it somewhat in English. Letter from Voloshin to A. M. Petrova, November 29, 1909, in Bagno and Lavrov, *Maksimilian Voloshin: Iz literaturnogo naslediia*, vol. 1, 201. (See asterisked footnote on page 201 for reference to the awkwardness of the Russian sentence.)

47. Ibid., December 17, 1909, in Bagno and Lavrov, *Maksimilian Voloshin: Iz literaturnogo naslediia*, vol. 1, 204.

48. E. Dmitrieva, "Ispoved'," in Kupchenko and Davydov, *Vospominaniia o Maksimiliane Voloshine*, 198.

4. THE KOKTEBEL' DACHA CIRCLE

1. Or perhaps this just became a convention of their memoirs?

2. Tsvetaeva, *Vospominaniia*, 372–373.

3. Tsvetaeva, "A Living Word about a Living Man," 64.

4. Steven Lovell, "Between Arcadia and Suburbia: Dachas in Late Imperial Russia," *Slavic Review* 61, no. 1 (spring 2002): 66–87.

5. Tsvetaeva, "A Living Word about a Living Man," 48.

6. See the conclusion of chapter 2, above.

7. Three letters from Voloshin to E. O. Voloshina, tentatively dated 1908, after the month of May. Typewritten copies in private archive of Vladimir Kupchenko.

8. Letter from Voloshin to E. O. Voloshina, November 21, 1911. Typewritten copy in private archive of Vladimir Kupchenko.

9. Tsvetaeva claims that the "Bruederschaft" was drunk "*uzhe pri mne*"; if she means literally in her presence, this would put the event at least three years later, since Tsvetaeva did not meet mother and son together until 1911 at the very earliest (Tsvetaeva, "A Living Word about a Living Man," 58). Yet Voloshin began in his letters to address his mother with the familiar form after May 1907. Letter (using formal address) from Voloshin to E. O. Voloshina, May 5, 1907; letter (using familiar address) from Voloshin to E. O. Voloshina, tentatively dated 1908. Typewritten copies in archive of Vladimir Kupchenko.

10. Letter from Voloshin to E. O. Voloshina, tentatively dated between 1907 and 1909. Typewritten copy in private archive of Vladimir Kupchenko.

11. Ibid., December 9, 1913. Typewritten copy in archive of Vladimir Kupchenko.

12. Ibid., January 2, 1909. Typewritten copy in private archive of Vladimir Kupchenko.

13. Leonid Fainberg, "Iz knigi 'Tri leta v gostiakh u Maksimiliana Voloshina,'" in Kupchenko and Davydov, *Vospominaniia o Maksimiliane Voloshine*, 268–293, 269, 270, 270–271.

14. Ibid., 271.

15. The word *plavnost'* is used here several times, which I have translated either as "evenness" or "smoothness."

16. Fainberg, "Iz knigi 'Tri leta v gostiakh u Maksimiliana Voloshina,'" 283. Marina Tsvetaeva writes several pages on Voloshin as peacemaker (Tsvetaeva, "A Living Word about a Living Man," 61–63).

17. Tsvetaeva, "A Living Word about a Living Man," 275.

18. Ibid., 286.

19. I use the term *carnivalesque* with reference to the Bakhtinian theory of carnival as folk mockery of traditional hierarchies and rituals; Bakhtin developed this theory in his 1940 study of the French author Rabelais. For Bakhtin's introduction to this idea, see

Mikhail Bakhtin, *Rabelais and His World,* trans. Helene Iswolsky (Bloomington: Indiana University Press, 1984), 7–12. For a historically contextualized discussion of Bakhtin's theory of carnival, see Katerina Clark and Michael Holquist, *Mikhail Bakhtin* (Cambridge, Mass.: Harvard University Press, 1984), 295–320. There are some interesting parallels between Turner's theory of status reversal and Bakhtin's theory of the carnivalesque; Bakhtin's theory seemed more illuminating for my purposes here.

20. The story that follows is from Tsvetaeva, *Vospominaniia,* 374–382.

21. Ibid., 378, 375, 377–378.

22. Ibid., 380.

23. Tsvetaeva, "A Living Word about a Living Man," 82–84.

24. Tsvetaeva, *Vospominaniia,* 382.

25. The story of this *mistifikatsiia* is in Fainberg, "Iz knigi 'Tri leta v gostiakh u Maksimiliana Voloshina,'" 276–277.

26. Ibid., 668 n.

27. Ibid., 277, 277.

28. Ibid., 276.

29. Ibid., 279. "The Pathfinder" is the nickname of a summer visitor staying nearby.

30. Ibid., 275.

31. Voloshin's first collection of poetry, entitled *Poetry. 1900–1910,* had been published in February 1910 at the Moscow publishing house "Grif." During the spring of 1911 he wrote the cycle of poems "Sonety o Koktebele."

32. Elizaveta Krivoshapkina, "Veseloe plemia 'obormotov,'" in Kupchenko and Davydov, *Vospominaniia o Maksimiliane Voloshine,* 314.

33. Ibid.

5. INSIDERS AND OUTSIDERS, GOSSIP AND MYTHOLOGY

1. Although it may seem of lesser importance, Voloshin's growing library of books and journals from throughout Europe represented another of the attractions that traditional mentors had long been offering their clients for intellectual and professional development.

2. Voloshin, though, did not particularly approve of the marriage: "I would imagine the marriage of Marina and Sergei is only an 'episode,' and a short one at that," he wrote his mother (letter from Voloshin to E. O. Voloshina, undated, sometime between November 12, 1911, and November 25, 1911. Typewritten copy in private archive of Vladimir Kupchenko.

3. Iuliia Obolenskaia, "Iz dnevnika 1913 goda," in Kupchenko and Davydov, *Vospominaniia,* 302.

4. Ibid., 303.

5. Voloshin, *Putnik po vselennym,* 299.

6. Vladimir Kupchenko, "Osip Mandelshtam v Kimmerii," *Voprosy literatury* 7 (1987): 188.

7. On Khodasevich, see David Bethea, *Khodasevich: His Life and Art* (Princeton, N.J.: Princeton University Press, 1983).

8. Tsentral'nyi Gosudarstvennyi Arkhiv Literatury i Iskusstva (TsGALI), f. 537, op. 1, d. 45, s. 5.

9. Ibid., ss. 10, 14, 35.

10. Ibid., ss. 42, 53.

11. Krivoshapkina, "Vesoloe plemia 'obormotov,'" 315.

12. A humorous song about members of the Koktebel' community.

13. The change presumably would make disputed lines read: "She appeared at the 'Diamond,' / To the sounds of many trumpets, / She ran into Mandelshtam."

14. Krivoshapkina, "Vesoloe plemia 'obormotov,'" 316.

15. Ibid.

16. Ibid., 317.

17. On the important role of gossip (which this "oral tradition" may be called) in network and small group social organization, see Max Gluckman, "Gossip and Scandal," *Current Anthropology* 4, no. 3 (1963): 307–315.

18. Iuliia Obolenskaia, "Iz dnevnika 1913 goda," in Kupchenko and Davydov, *Vospominaniia o Maksimiliane Voloshine*, 303.

19. Krivoshapkina, "Vesoloe plemia 'obormotov,'" 313.

20. Vikentii Veresaev, *Vospominaniia* (Moscow: Pravda, 1982), 527.

21. Tsvetaeva, "A Living Word about a Living Man," 81. This quotation is drawn from a far longer and brilliantly illuminating discussion of mythmaking and Voloshin's talent for this art, subtitled "Max and the Folktale," 79–97.

22. See, for example, Fainberg, "Iz knigi 'Tri leta v gostiakh u Maksimiliana Voloshina,'" 277; Obolenskaia, "Iz dnevnika 1913 goda," 305.

6. VOLOSHIN CARVES
POWER OUT OF FEAR

1. On prerevolutionary bureaucracy and personal ties, see Orlovsky, "Political Clientelism in Russia: The Historical Perspective," 174–199.

2. This debate is rooted in an early struggle in Soviet historiography between those who believed that the origins of the Soviet system lay in the Civil War period of War Communism under Lenin (Leonard Shapiro, *The Communist Party of the Soviet Union* [New York: Random House, 1959]) and those who argued that Stalin was responsible for distorting the essentially good socialist system that Lenin had established (Isaac Deutscher, *Stalin: A Political Biography* [Oxford: Oxford University Press, 1949]). A recent work of scholarship that takes up this issue in more nuanced fashion is Donald Raleigh, *Experiencing Russia's Civil War: Politics, Society, and Revolutionary Culture in Saratov, 1917–1922* (Princeton, N.J.: Princeton University Press, 2002). Raleigh sees the beginnings of the system in War Communism; for a summary of his argument on this topic, see *Experiencing Russia's Civil War*, 416. A recent book that offers another solution to the problem of periodization is Peter Holquist's *Making War, Forging Revolution: Russia's Continuum of Crisis, 1914–1921* (Cambridge, Mass.: Harvard University Press, 2002). Holquist argues for seeing a continuum in violence and the processes of mobilization that began with World War I.

3. Roland Stromberg, *Redemption by War: The Intellectuals and 1914* (Lawrence: Regents Press of Kansas, 1982).

4. Letter from Voloshin to E. O. Voloshina, August 19, 1915. Typewritten copy in private archive of Vladimir Kupchenko.

5. An ellipsis appears here in Kupchenko's typewritten copy of the letter, but what it represents (Voloshin's own punctuation or military censorship) is unclear.

6. Letter from Maximilian Voloshin to E. O. Voloshina, January 22, 1915. Typewritten copy in private archive of Vladimir Kupchenko.

7. Maximilian Voloshin, *Stikhotvoreniia, stat'i, vospominaniia sovremennikov* (Moscow: Pravda, 1991), 98.

8. Letter from Voloshin to E. O. Voloshina, August 19, 1915. Typewritten copy in private archive of Vladimir Kupchenko.

9. Ibid.

10. Travel itinerary in "Khronologicheskaia kanva zhizni i tvorchestva M. A. Voloshina," in Kupchenko and Davydov, *Vospominaniia o Maksimiliane Voloshine*, 58.

11. Ibid.

12. Peter Kenez, *Civil War in South Russia, 1919–1920* (Berkeley: University of California Press, 1977), 191.

13. The following summary of the Russian civil war in the Crimea comes from ibid., 191–202.

14. Vikentii Veresaev, *V tupike* (Petersburg: Lenizdat, 1989).

15. Kenez, *Civil War in South Russia*, 91–202.

16. See his essay of 1917, "*Proroki i mstiteli,*" in Voloshin, *Stikhotvoreniia, stat'i, vospominaniia sovremennikov*, 267–294.

17. To read some of this poetry, see Voloshin, *Puti Rossii*, esp. 20–98.

18. On the relationship between Tolstoy and Bunin, see chapter 2 of this book.

19. Bunin's most famous "pupil" was Soviet author-to-be Valentin Kataev, who wrote a memoir about Bunin in later years. See chapter 2 of this book.

20. Like many a disciple, Voloshin truly needed access to Bunin's table. After one meal, Vera Muromtseva-Bunina wrote: "Voloshin ate very well—he is always starving. He even ate up our rationed pea-like bread which we cannot swallow" (Marullo, *Ivan Bunin*, 296).

21. Ibid., 297, 297.

22. Ibid., 322.

23. N. A. Teffi, *Nostal'giia: Rasskazy, Vospominaniia* (Leningrad: Khudozhestvennaia literatura, 1989), 355.

24. Ibid., 356.

25. For other self-narratives of the civil war experience, especially with a focus on the theme of survival, see Raleigh, *Experiencing Russia's Civil War*, 246–281. The title of Raleigh's chapter on this topic is "Narratives of the Self and Other: Saratov's Bourgeoisie."

26. Ivan Bunin, *Memories and Portraits*, trans. Vera Traill and Robin Chancellor (London: John Lehmann, 1951), 143.

27. Ibid., 144.

28. Ibid.

29. Voloshin, *Putnik po vselennym*, 269.

30. Ibid., 271.

31. Ibid. The man was Innokentii Kozhevnikov, commander of the Thirteenth Army until March 1919.

32. Ibid., 272.

33. Ibid., 273.

34. The words "*vne ocheredi*" are a peculiarly Russian/Soviet expression indicating that horses, passes, tickets, and living space were to be obtained without having to wait one's turn or wait in line for them.

35. Institut Russkoi Literatury Akademii Nauk (IRLI), Pushkinskii dom, f. 562, op. 4, d. 3, s. 8.

36. Voloshin, *Putnik po vselennym*, 273.

37. Note that in his memoir Voloshin recalls the "Art Section" as a "Department of Art."

38. Voloshin, *Putnik po vselennym*, 274.

39. Ibid., 275.

40. Ibid., 276.

41. For an extensive discussion of the question of locality, local politics, and center-periphery relations in Soviet state-society relations, see J. Arch Getty, *Origins of the Great Purges: The Soviet Communist Party Reconsidered, 1933–1938* (Cambridge: Cambridge University Press, 1985).

42. Veresaev, *Vospominaniia*, 530.

43. On Soviet use of theatrical media in the civil war, see Peter Kenez, *The Birth of the Propaganda State: Soviet Methods of Mass Mobilization, 1917–1929* (Cambridge: Cambridge University Press, 1985).

44. Veresaev, *Vospominaniia*, 530.

45. Voloshin, *Putnik po vselennym*, 276.

46. Ibid., 277.

47. Ibid., 279.

48. Ibid., 284, 285.

49. Ibid., 285.

50. Ibid., 286.

51. Ibid., 289.

52. Ibid., 293.

53. Ibid., 294.

54. Il'ia Erenburg, "Iz knigi 'Liudy, gody, zhizn',"" in Kupchenko and Davydov, *Vospominaniia o Maksimiliane Voloshine*, 346.

55. Raissa Ginzburg, "Chasy neizgladimye," in Kupchenko and Davydov, *Vospominaniia o Maksimiliane Voloshine*, 376.

56. Interview with Andrei Borisovich Trukhachev, son of Anastasiia Tsvetaeva, March 18, 1992.

57. Voloshin, *Putnik po vselennym*, 301.

58. Ibid.

59. Emilii Mindlin, "Iz 'Neobyknovenye sobesedniki,'" in Kupchenko and Davydov, *Vospominaniia o Maksimiliane Voloshine*, 426.

60. Ibid., 427.

61. Ibid., 429–430.

62. Ibid., 430.

7. VOLOSHIN CARVES POWER, CONT'D

1. Voloshin, *Puti Rossii*, 93.

2. Mariia Izvergina, "V te gody," in Kupchenko and Davydov, *Vospominaniia o Maksimiliane Voloshine*, 457.

3. IRLI, Pushkinskii dom, f. 562, op. 4, d. 3, s. 12.

4. Ibid., s. 13. This document is slightly unclear; it is a "ticket," not an *udostoverenie*, actually a form from the Administration of Registration and Allocation of Workers' Forces, in which Voloshin's name, profession, institution (Crimean Bureau of People's Enlightenment), and duties (head of the [illegible] Department of the Literary Section) have been filled in. Perhaps this served as a document identifying Voloshin's status for the sake of his rationing rank.

5. Ibid., s. 19.

6. Ibid., f. 562, op. 3, d. 39, s. 1.

7. For a contemporary analysis (by Russian liberal Mark Vishniak) of this phenomenon, see Jane Burbank, *Intelligentsia and Revolution: Russian Views of Bolshevism, 1917–1922*, 85–99.

8. IRLI, Pushkinskii dom, f.562, op. 4, d. 14, 15.

9. Ibid., d. 41.

10. Ibid., op. 3, d. 72.

11. "Khronologicheskaia kanva zhizni i tvorchestva M. A. Voloshina," in Kupchenko and Davydov, *Vospominaniia o Maksimiliane Voloshine*, 61.

12. IRLI, Pushkinskii dom, f. 562, op. 3, d. 18, s. 4.

13. Ibid.

14. Ibid., op. 2, d. 3, s. 6.

15. "Khronologicheskaia kanva zhizni i tvorchestva M. A. Voloshina," 61.

16. IRLI, Pushkinskii dom, f. 562, op. 2, d. 3, s. 29.

17. Bunin, *Memories and Portraits*, 139.

18. IRLI, Pushkinskii dom, f. 562, op. 4, d. 42.

19. Ibid.

20. Ibid.

21. Information about the proposed "Experimental Artistic-Scientific Studio" is taken from a typewritten proposal tentatively dated 1921 (ibid., as well as from an application to TsUKK dated April 21, 1921 [ibid., d. 62, s. 2]).

22. Ibid., op. 2, d. 3, s. 21.

23. "Khronologicheskaia kanva zhizni i tvorchestva M. A. Voloshina," in Kupchenko and Davydov, Vospominaniia o Maksimiliane Voloshine, 62.

24. See Alec Nove, *An Economic History of the USSR* (New York: Penguin, 1969), 83–118.

25. Tsvetaeva, "A Living Word about a Living Man," 48.

26. N. Lesina, *Planerskoe/Koktebel'* (Simferopol': Izdatel'stvo Krym, 1969), 19.

27. IRLI, Pushkinskii dom, f. 562, op. 3, d. 51.

28. Ibid., op. 4, d. 62, s. 3.

29. Ibid., ss. 9, 15.

30. For insight into of some of those debates, see Sheila Fitzpatrick, "The Soft Line on Culture and Its Enemies," in idem, *The Cultural Front: Power and Culture in Revolutionary Russia* (Ithaca, N.Y.: Cornell, 1992), 91–114.

31. As discussed in chapter 6, *khlopotat'* means to solicit something by petitioning, by bustling about, often petitioning one bureaucratic office after another.

32. Khodasevich, *"Nekropol'" i drugie vospominaniia*, 121–122.

33. Ibid., 121.

34. P. A. Nikolaev, ed., *Russkie pisateli, 1800–1917: Biograficheskii slovar'* (Moscow: NVP FIANIT, 1992), 557.

35. Ibid., 337.

36. Valerii Briusov, *Neizdannoe i nesobrannoe* (Moscow: Kliuch, 1998), 215–223.

37. Gosudarstvennyi Arkhiv Russkoi Federatsii (GARF), f. 2306, op. 22, d. 27.

38. Ibid.

39. Ibid., f. 393, op. 43, dd. 24, 77, 256, 257.

40. For a detailed discussion of Gorky's activities as "the great intercessor," see Tovah Yedlin, *Maxim Gorky: A Political Biography* (Westport, Conn.: Praeger, 1999), esp. chap. 6. See also Bertram Wolfe, *The Bridge and the Abyss: The Troubled Friendship of Maxim Gorky and V. I. Lenin* (New York: Praeger, 1967), esp. chaps. 7–10. This work was published for the Hoover Institution on War, Revolution, and Peace, Stanford University, Stanford, California.

41. For examples of the many pleas addressed to Gorky for help in preserving or rescuing individuals from arrest and potential death, see Gippius, *Zhivye litsa*, 1:181; see also Institut Mirovoi Literatury Akademii Nauk (IMLI), Arkhiv Gor'kogo, KG-P/33/1/8 (letter from Veniamin Kaverin about Kaverin's brother). For other rescues, see Yedlin, *Maxim Gorky*, 126. For references in memoirs to some of the other types of state-based aid from Gorky, see, for example, Galina Belaya, ed., *Gorky and His Contemporaries: Memoirs and Letters*, trans. Cynthia Carlyle (Moscow: Progress, 1989), 100–103, 126–127, 152. For a specific reference to his aid in solving the problems of communal living, see a partly hu-

morous, partly painful exchange of letters between Gorky and Mikhail Zoshchenko in 1930, when Zoshchenko was having difficulties with his apartment mates in a collective living situation. Gorky did all he could to help and the problem was alleviated (IMLI, Ar. Gor'kogo, KG-P/29/4/2).

42. For a description of how Gorky *khlopotal* for Blok's right to travel abroad, see Wolfe, *The Bridge and the Abyss*, 121.

43. See Gorky's letters to Yagoda, which contain requests for aid to writers, especially for permission to travel abroad (from, for example, Boris Pasternak on behalf of himself and his wife and child; N. Kamenskii; and Mikhail Sholokhov) (IMLI, Ar. Gor'kogo PG-rl/58/29/4, 5).

44. For a description of life at "World Literature," see Kornei Chukovsky's depiction in Belaya, *Gorky and His Contemporaries*, 92–98. See also Yedlin, *Maxim Gorky*, 125.

45. Sheila Fitzpatrick, *The Commissariat of Enlightenment: Soviet Organization of Education and the Arts under Lunacharsky, October 1917–1921* (Cambridge: Cambridge University Press, 1970), 133.

46. For a detailed description of the House of the Arts, see Khodasevich, *"Nekropol'" i drugie vospominaniia*, 275–285.

47. Belaya, *Gorky and His Contemporaries*, 100–103, 126–127, 152.

48. See, for example, the January–February 1923 letter from Gorky to Serapion V. Ivanov asking him to contribute a story to the Berlin-based journal *Beseda* (IMLI, Ar. Gor'kogo, PG-rl/17/3/7); 1926 letter from Serapion I. Gruzdev to Gorky saying "*goriachee spasibo* [heartfelt thanks] from all of us [apparently other Serapions]" for your help in getting manuscripts published (IMLI, Ar. Gor'kogo, KG-P/23/1/17); and December 1926 letter from Gorky to P. Kriuchkov urging him to include V. Ivanov in an anthology because he was a good writer (IMLI, Ar. Gor'kogo, KG-P/41a/1/119).

49. Quotation and details in Dan Levin, *Stormy Petrel: The Life and Work of Maxim Gorky* (New York: Schocken, 1986), 214–215. For further details on the internal politics and foreign diplomacy of both the Soviets and the Americans in this matter, see N. Sh. Tsikhalashvili and David Engerman, "Amerikanskaia pomoshch' Rossii v 1921–1923 godakh: konflikty i sotrudnichestvo," *Amerikanskii ezhegodnik* (1995): 191–212. See also Benjamin Weissman, *Herbert Hoover and Famine Relief to Soviet Russia* (Stanford, Calif.: Hoover Institution Press, 1974).

50. For a fascinating view into the more formal aspects of ARA distribution (i.e., more formal than Voloshin's simple method of dividing up what arrived for him), see Alexis Babine, *A Civil War Diary: Alexis Babine in Saratov, 1917–1922*, ed. Donald Raleigh (Durham, N.C.: Duke University Press, 1988).

51. *Letopis' zhizni i tvorchestva A. M. Gor'kogo* (Moscow: Izdatel'stvo Akademii Nauk SSSR, 1958–60).

52. It is not entirely clear, however, whether TsKUBU itself made these choices. The Kontrol'naia Komissiia, as appointed by the Petrosoviet, was the deciding organ; and in this same protocol (signed by Gorky) it is resolved that the Special Commission of Sovnarkom makes the final decision on the list of ration recipients (IMLI, Ar. Gor'kogo, Bio 15/37; n.d.).

53. Ibid., Bio 15/11, Bio 15/7.

54. Ibid., Bio 15/11.

55. Ibid., Bio 15/2.

56. Letter from Maxim Gorky to Artemii Bargatovich (last name unknown), dated October 10, 1927, Sorrento. This letter is located in Nikolai Bukharin's file in the Central Party Archive, which contains many letters from Gorky directly to Bukharin (Tsentral'nyi Partinyi Arkhiv [RKhIDNI], f. 329, op. 2, d. 4, s. 51).

57. Teleshov, "Vospominaniia o Maksime Gor'kom," in Brodskii, ed., *M. Gor'kii v vospominaniiakh sovremennikov*, 189.

58. Fitzpatrick, *The Commissariat of Enlightenment*, 19.

59. Ibid.

60. Ibid., 163.

61. IMLI, Ar. Gor'kogo, Bio 15.

62. TsGALI, f. 1824.

63. Ibid., f. 591, op. 1.

64. Ibid., f. 1824.

65. Ibid., op. 1, d. 1, s. 6.

66. IRLI, Pushkinskii dom, f. 562, op. 4, d. 21, s. 13.

67. Ibid.

68. Note Zoshchenko's struggle with roommates, as described above (IMLI, Ar. Gor'-kogo, KG-P/29/4/2).

69. Interview with Ida Moiseevna Nappelbaum, May 1, 1992.

70. For a development of this argument, see Barbara Walker, "*Kruzhok* Culture and the Meaning of Patronage in the Early Soviet Literary World," *Contemporary European History*, Special Issue: *Patronage, Personal Networks, and the Party-State*, 2, no. 1 (2002): 107–123.

71. See Steven Cohen, *Bukharin and the Bolshevik Revolution* (New York: Knopf, 1973), 216–223.

72. Mandelshtam, *Hope against Hope*, 113.

73. For the poem, see ibid., 13.

74. Ibid., 21–22.

75. For more on the transformation of the "contemporaries" memoir genre during the Soviet period, see Walker, "On Reading Soviet Memoirs," esp. 343–351.

76. Marina Tsvetaeva, "Geroi truda (zapisi o Valerii Briusove)," in *Proza* (New York: Iz-datel'stvo imeni Chekhova, 1953), 270. Translation: *The Diary of Valery Bryusov (1893–1905): With Reminiscences by V. F. Khodasevich and Marina Tsvetaeva*, ed., trans., and with an introduction by Joan Delaney Grossman (Berkeley: University of California Press, 1980), 173. For another anti-cult memoir complaining of pernicious neglect by a locus of power, see Gippius, *Zhivye litsa*, 1:181.

77. Gosudarstvennyi Literaturnyi Muzei (GLM), f. 123, op. 1.

8. INSIDE VOLOSHIN'S SOVIET CIRCLE

1. Voloshin, *Puti Rossii*, 166.

2. On early Soviet attempts to transform the roles of women in society, see Gail Lapidus, *Women in Soviet Society: Equality, Development and Social Change* (Berkeley: University of California Press, 1978), esp. chap. 2, "Toward Sexual Equality: Revolutionary Transformation and Its Limits, 1917–1930"; Richard Stites, *The Women's Liberation Movement in Russia: Feminism, Nihilism, and Bolshevism, 1860–1930* (Princeton, N.J.: Princeton University Press, 1978); Wendy Goldman, *Women, the State, and Revolution: Soviet Family Policy and Social Life, 1917–1936* (Cambridge: Cambridge University Press, 1993); and Choi Chatterjee, *Celebrating Women: Gender, Festival Culture, and Bolshevik Ideology, 1910–1939* (Pittsburgh: University of Pittsburgh Press, 2002).

3. Lidiia Arens, "O Maksimiliane Aleksandroviche Voloshine i ego zhene Marii Ste-panovne," in Kupchenko and Davydov, *Vospominaniia o Maksimiliane Voloshine*, 611.

4. Letter from Voloshin to Mariia Stepanovna Zabolotskaia, November 18, 1922 (IRLI, Pushkinskii dom, f. 562, op. 3, d. 18).

5. Ibid.

6. Ibid.

7. He had published the poetry collection *Demony Glukhonemye* in 1919 in Kharkov; this book would be republished in Berlin in 1923: Maximilian Voloshin, *Demony Glukhonemye* (London: Flegon, 1965; Berlin: Kni-vo pisatelei, 1923).

8. Letter from Voloshin to Maria Stepanovna Zabolotskaia, December 31, 1922. (IRLI, Pushkinskii dom, f. 562, op. 3, d. 18).

9. Ibid.

10. No longer exactly servants but rather independent contractors—see below.

11. For an introduction to the Soviet gift economy, see Vladimir Shlapentokh, *Love, Marriage, and Friendship in the Soviet Union: Ideals and Practices* (New York: Praeger, 1984), 237–240.

12. Elizaveta Polonskaya, "Tysiacha deviat'sot dvadtsat' chetvertyi god: Petrograd—Leningrad—Koktebel'," Archive of Elizaveta Polonskaya in the possession of her son, Mikhail Polonskii, 7.

13. Ibid., 9–10.

14. Konstantin Polivanov, "Koktebel' (leto 1924 goda)," Archive of Konstantin Polivanov, in the possession of his grandson, Konstantin Polivanov, 11.

15. Ibid., 17.

16. Ibid. 14.

17. Ibid., 17.

18. Nove, *An Economic History of the USSR*, 63–74, 90–93.

19. IRLI, Pushkinskii dom, f. 562, op. 4, d. 21, ss. 1–8; d. 13, s. 4.

20. Ibid., d. 24.

21. Ibid. d. 13. The topic of bread rations comes up during 1929, 1930, and 1931; potatoes are discussed only in 1931. This may have been because Voloshin was having troubles (which I discuss in the next chapter) with local authorities with regard to obtaining his rations; but it should also be noted that forced grain collections from the Soviet peasants began early in 1928, and forced collectivization early in 1929. Agricultural products were flowing toward the city, as Stalin attempted to take control of peasant production and lay the economic foundations of Soviet industry. This may have caused shortages in an area as remote as Koktebel' (Nove, *An Economic History of the USSR*, 160–179).

22. Vikentii Veresaev, "Koktebel'," in Kupchenko and Davydov, *Vospominaniia o Maksimiliane Voloshine*, 451.

23. Polivanov, "Koktebel' (leto 1924 goda), 17.

24. James R. Millar, "The Little Deal: Brezhnev's Contribution to Acquisitive Socialism," in *Soviet Society and Culture: Essays in Honor of Vera S. Dunham*, ed. Terry Thompson and Richard Sheldon (Boulder, Colo.: Westview, 1988), 3–19.

25. Scholarship on the use of theater for the purposes of social transformation by the Soviet state includes Kenez, *The Birth of the Propaganda State*; Lynn Mally, *Revolutionary Acts: Amateur Theater and the Soviet State, 1917–1938* (Ithaca, N.Y.: Cornell University Press, 2000); and Chatterjee, *Celebrating Women*. On confession in the context of the Soviet collective, see Oleg Kharkhordin, *The Collective and the Individual in Russia: A Study of Practices* (Berkeley: University of California Press, 1999).

26. Irina Paperno, *Chernyshevsky and the Age of Realism: A Study in the Semiotics of Behavior* (Stanford, Calif.: Stanford University Press, 1988), esp. 1–38.

27. Turner, *From Ritual to Theatre*, 49.

28. Richard Stites, *Revolutionary Dreams: Utopian Vision and Experimental Life in the Russian Revolution* (New York: Oxford University Press, 1989).

29. Ibid., 98–100.

30. Clark, *Petersburg*, 133, 147, 154; quote at 133. For an alternative view of Soviet ceremony in a slightly later period, see Karen Petrone, *Life Has Become More Joyous, Comrades: Celebrations in the Time of Stalin* (Bloomington: Indiana University Press, 2000). Petrone argues that such mass ceremonies and spectacles can be seen as negotiations between citizens and state leaders for control of Soviet culture. For insight into the continued possibilities for genuine and sincere revolutionary self-transformation under Stalin, see Jochen Hellbeck, "Fashioning the Stalinist Soul: The Diary of Stepan Podlubnyi, 1931–9," in *Stalinism: New Directions*, ed. Sheila Fitzpatrick (London: Routledge, 2000), 77–116.

31. Nadezhda Rykova, "Moi vstrechi," in Kupchenko and Davydov, *Vospominaniia o Maksimiliane Voloshine*, 514, 516.

32. Gleb Smirnov, "Na ekskursii," in Kupchenko and Davydov, *Vospominaniia o Maksimiliane Voloshine*, 547–550. It should be noted that Voloshin received his state stipend in part for welcoming such excursions into his home and reading his poetry to these visitors. But, according to Smirnov, other Koktebel' writers on the tour received these awkward guests with far less kindness than Voloshin.

33. Anna Ostroumova-Lebedeva, "Leto v Koktebele," in Kupchenko and Davydov, *Vospominaniia o Maksimiliane Voloshine*, 519.

34. Rykova, "Moi vstrechi," in Kupchenko and Davydov, *Vospominaniia o Maksimiliane Voloshine*, 513.

35. Erikh Gollerbakh, "On byl bolee znamenit, chem izvesten," in Kupchenko and Davydov, *Vospominaniia o Maksimiliane Voloshine*, 502–503.

9. COLLAPSE OF A PATRONAGE NETWORK AND VOLOSHIN'S DEATH

1. Kornei Chukovskii, *Dnevnik, 1901–1929* (Moscow: Sovetskii pisatel', 1991), 248.

2. IRLI, Pushkinskii dom, f. 562, op. 3, d. 51, s. 15.

3. Ibid.

4. Ibid., op. 4, d. 62, ss. 10–12.

5. Ibid., f. 562, op. 4, d. 62.

6. See Sheila Fitzpatrick, "Cultural Revolution as Class War," in idem, ed., *Cultural Revolution in Russia, 1928–1931* (Bloomington: Indiana University Press, 1984), 8–40. For a recent review of the topic, see Michael David-Fox, "What Is Cultural Revolution," *The Russian Review* 58, no. 2 (1999): 181–201; Sheila Fitzpatrick, "Cultural Revolution Revisited," *The Russian Review* 58, no. 2 (1999): 202–209; and Michael David-Fox, "*Mentalité* or Cultural System," *The Russian Review* 58, no. 2 (1999): 210.

7. Moshe Lewin, "Society, State and Ideology during the First Five-Year Plan," in Fitzpatrick, *Cultural Revolution in Russia*, 41–77.

8. IRLI, Pushkinskii dom, f. 562, op. 4, d. 13, s. 7.

9. Ibid., s. 2.

10. Fitzpatrick, "Cultural Revolution as Class War," 15.

11. IRLI, Pushkinskii dom, f. 562, op. 3, d. 72.

12. In those last words, we learn of the origins of the remarkable personal archive that makes this study of Voloshin's life and circle possible (ibid., ss. 4–6).

13. Ibid., f. 562, op. 3, d. 72.

14. Ibid.

15. Lidiia Arens, "O Maksimiliane Aleksandrovne Voloshine i ego zhene Marii Stepanovne," in Kupchenko and Davydov, *Vospominaniia o Maksimiliane Voloshine*, 609.

16. Ibid., 619.

17. Nikolai Chukovskii, "Iz knigi 'Literaturnye vospominaniia,'" in Kupchenko and Davydov, *Vospominaniia o Maksimiliane Voloshine*, 621.

CONCLUSION

1. Party Resolution, April 23, 1932, "O perestroike literaturno-khudozhestvennykh organizatsii" (On the reorganization of literary-artistic organizations), *Osnovnye direktivy i zakonodatel'stvo o pechati: sistematicheskii sbornik*, 50.

2. Protocols of three meetings of the Presidium of the Organizing Committee of the All-Russian Union of Writers, May 25, June 7, and June 10, 1932 (IRLI, Pushkinskii dom, f. 521, op. 42).

3. Ibid. Protocol of the meeting of the Presidium of the Organizing Committee of the All-Russian Union of Writers, June 10, 1932.

4. See letter from Alexei Tolstoy to Konstantin Fedin, April 16, 1932, in *Perepiska A. N. Tolstogo*, ed. A. M. Kriukova, 2 vols. (Moscow: Khudozhestvennaia Literatura, 1989), 2:140.

5. For a literary description of such a building (though, in this case, not for writers but for government officials, scholars, and other members of the elite), see Iurii Trifonov, *The House on the Embankment*, trans. Michael Glenny (New York: Simon and Schuster, 1983).

6. Jeffrey Brooks, *Thank-you Comrade Stalin! Soviet Public Culture from Revolution to Cold War* (Princeton, N.J.: Princeton University Press, 2000), see, esp., chap. 4, "The Economy of the Gift: 'Thank-you Comrade Stalin, for a Happy Childhood,'" 83–105. For a general review of recent scholarship on patronage and networking relations in the Soviet period, see Barbara Walker, "(Still) Searching for a Soviet Society: A Review of Recent Scholarship on Personal Ties in Soviet Political and Economic Life," *Comparative Studies in Society and History* 43 no. 3 (July 2001): 631–642.

7. Hugo Cunningham's 1998 website, "Da zdravstvuet I. V. Stalin!" (Long live I. V. Stalin!) (http://www.cyberussr.com/rus/st-flat.html; accessed February 12, 2004) collects many expressions of praise of Stalin as a teacher, including such translations as "Great leader and teacher," cited from *Voprosy istorii*, November 18, 1951. One can also listen to the song "Pesnya o Staline" (Song about Stalin) written by M. Blanter and S. Surkov, as well as to read the words at http://www.cyberussr.com/rus/sg-st-bla.html (accessed February 12, 2004), including the refrain citing Stalin as "our wise leader and dear teacher." Other songs lauding Stalin as a great teacher can be found through the same website, including "Spasibo veliki uchitel'" (Thank you, great teacher).

8. Edward J. Brown, *The Proletarian Episode in Russian Literature, 1928–1932* (New York: Columbia University Press, 1953), 217.

9. Alexeyeva and Goldberg, *The Thaw Generation*, 83, 97, 97.

10. Interviews with Vladimir Kupchenko, March 27, 1992; Mikhail Polivanov, March 19, 1991; Anastasiia Polivanova, May 20, 1992; and Mirel Shaginian, June 12, 1992; and also e-mail message to Barbara Walker from Konstantin Polivanov, April 5, 2003.

11. For example, her letter to Elizaveta Borisovna Auerbakh, dated 20/IX, and contained in a folder for letters from 1937 (Dom-Muzei Maksimiliana Voloshina [D-MMV]).

12. Letter from Maria Stepanovna Voloshina, December 15, 1949 (ibid.).

13. Rough draft of letter from Maria Stepanovna Voloshina to P. N. Rozanov, 1962 (ibid.).

14. Letter to Maria Stepanovna Voloshina from unknown correspondent, September 19, 1963 (Leningrad) (ibid.).

15. Interview with Vladimir Kupchenko, March 27, 1992.

16. Tamara Shmeleva, "Navechno v Pamiati i Zhizni," in Kupchenko and Davydov, *Vospominaniia o Maksimiliane Voloshine*, 488.

17. Letter from Marina Mikhailovna Polivanova to Vladimir Kupchenko, n.d. (Archive of Konstantin Polivanov, in the possession of his grandson, Konstantin Polivanov).

BIBLIOGRAPHY

PUBLIC ARCHIVES

Dom-Muzei Maksimiliana Voloshina (D-MMV)
Gosudarstvennyi Arkhiv Russkoi Federatsii (GARF)
Gosudarstvennyi Literaturnyi Muzei (GLM)
Institut Mirovoi Literatury (IMLI), Arkhiv Gor'kogo
Institut Russkoi Literatury (IRLI), Pushkinskii dom
Tsentral'nyi Gosudarstvennyi Arkhiv Literatury i Iskusstva (TsGALI), now Rossiiskii Gosudarstvennyi Arkhiv Literatury i Iskusstva (RGALI)
Rossiiskii Tsentr Khraneniia i Izucheniia Dokumentor Noveishei Istorii (RTsKhIDNI), now Rossiiskii Arkhiv Sotsial'no-Politicheskoi Istorii (RGASPI)

PRIVATE ARCHIVES

Vladimir Kupchenko
Konstantin Polivanov, in possession of his grandson, Konstantin Mikhailovich Polivanov
Elizaveta Polonskaya, in possession of her son, Mikhail Polonskii

INTERVIEWS

Vladimir Kupchenko, March 27, 1992
Ida Nappelbaum, March 29, 1992
Mikhail Polivanov, March 19, 1991
Anastasiia Polivanova, May 20, 1992.
Mirel Shaginian, June 12, 1992
Andrei Trukhachev, March 18, 1992
Anastasiia Tsvetaeva, March 2, 1992

SELECT MATERIALS DOCUMENTING
MAXIMILIAN VOLOSHIN'S LIFE AND WORK

Bagno, V. E., V. P. Kupchenko, A. V. Lavrov, and N. N. Skatov, eds. *Maksimilian Voloshin: iz literaturnogo naslediia*. Vol. 2. St. Petersburg: Nauka, 1999.
Davydov, Z. D., and V. P. Kupchenko, eds. *Krym Maksimiliana Voloshina: Avtografy, risunki, fotografii, dokumenty, otkrytki iz gosudarstvennykh i chastnykh sobranii: fotoal'bom*. Kiev: Mistetsvo, 1994.
Kupchenko, V. P. *Trudy i dni Maksimiliana Voloshina: letopis' zhizni i tvorchestva*. St. Petersburg: Aleteiia, 2002.

Kupchenko, V. P., and Z. D. Davydov, eds. *Vospominaniia o Maksimiliane Voloshine.* Moscow: Sovetskii pisatel', 1990.

Voloshin, Maksimilian. *Demony Glukhonemye.* Edited by V. P. Kupchenko and Z. D. Davydov. 2nd ed. London: Flegon, 1965 [1923].

———. *Stikhotvoreniia i poemy v dvukh tomakh.* Edited by B. A. Fillipov, Gleb Struve, and N. A. Struve. Paris: YMCA Press, 1982–84.

———. *Liki Tvorchestva.* Edited by V. A. Manuilov, V. P. Kupchenko, and A. V. Lavrov. Leningrad: Nauka, 1988.

———. *Putnik po vselennym.* Moscow: Sovetskaia Rossiia, 1990.

———. *Maksimilian Voloshin: iz literaturnogo naslediia.* Edited by V. E. Bagno and A. V. Lavrov. Vol. 1. St. Petersburg: Nauka, 1991.

———. *Avtobiograficheskaia proza, dnevniki.* Edited by Z. D. Davydova and V. P. Kupchenko. Moscow: Kniga, 1991.

———. *Stikhotvoreniia, stat'i, vospominaniia sovremennikov.* Edited by Z. D. Davydov and V. P. Kupchenko. Moscow: Pravda, 1991.

———. *Puti Rossii.* Edited by A. Zorin. Moscow: Sovremennik, 1992.

———. *Izbrannoe: stikhotvoreniia, vospominaniia, perepiska.* Edited by Z. D. Davydov and V. P. Kupchenko. Minsk: Mastatskaia literatura, 1993.

OTHER MATERIALS

Ahearn, Laura. "Language and Agency." *Annual Review of Anthropology* 30 (2001): 109–137.

Alexeyeva, Ludmilla, and Paul Goldberg. *The Thaw Generation: Coming of Age in the Post-Stalin Era.* Pittsburgh: University of Pittsburgh Press, 1990.

Annenkov, P. V. *The Extraordinary Decade: Literary Memoirs.* Edited by Arthur Mendel. Translated by Irwin Titunik. Ann Arbor: University of Michigan Press, 1968.

Asadovskii, K. M., and D. E. Maksimov. "Briusov i *Vesy.*" In *Literaturnoe Nasledstvo,* Vol. 85. Moscow: Nauka, 1976.

Babine, Alexis. *A Civil War Diary: Alexis Babine in Saratov, 1917–1922.* Edited by Donald Raleigh. Durham: Duke University Press, 1988.

Bailes, Kendall E. *Science and Russian Culture in an Age of Revolutions: V. I. Vernadsky and His Scientific School, 1863–1945.* Bloomington: Indiana University Press, 1990.

———. "Reflections on Russian Professions." In Harley D. Balzer, ed., *Russia's Missing Middle Class: The Professions in Russian History,* 39–54. Armonk, N.Y.: M. E. Sharpe, 1996.

Bakhtin, Mikhail. *Rabelais and His World.* Translated by Helene Iswolsky. Bloomington: Indiana University Press, 1984.

Balzer, Harley D. "The Engineering Profession in Tsarist Russia." In Harley D. Balzer, ed., *Russia's Missing Middle Class: The Professions in Russian History.* Armonk, N.Y.: M. E. Sharpe, 1996.

———, ed. *Russia's Missing Middle Class: The Professions in Russian History.* Armonk, N.Y.: M. E. Sharpe, 1996.

Belaya, Galina. *Gorky and His Contemporaries: Memoirs and Letters.* Translated by Cynthia Carlyle. Moscow: Progress, 1989.

Bely, Andrei. "Vospominaniia ob A.A. Bloke." *Epopeia* 4 (June 1923): 156–157.

———. *Nachalo veka.* Moscow: Khudozhestvennaia literatura, 1991. For earlier publication, see *Nachalo veka.* Moscow: Gosudarstvennoe izdatel'stvo khudozhestvennoi literatury, 1933.

Berlin, Isaiah. *Russian Thinkers.* Edited and with an introduction by Henry Hardy and Aileen Kelly. New York: Viking, 1978.

Bethea, David. *Khodasevich, His Life and Art.* Princeton, N.J.: Princeton University Press, 1983.

Billington, James. *The Icon and the Axe: An Interpretive History of Russian Culture.* New York: Random House, 1966.

Black, J. L. *G.-F. Mueller and the Imperial Russian Academy.* Montreal: McGill-Queen's University Press, 1986.

Bolkhovitinov, V. *Aleksandr Grigorievich Stoletov (1839–1896).* Moscow: Molodaia Gvardiia, 1953.

Bowlt, John. *The Silver Age: Russian Art of the Early Twentieth Century and the "World of Art" Group.* Newtonville, Mass.: Oriental Research Partners, 1979.

Boym, Svetlana. *Death in Quotation Marks: Cultural Myths of the Modern Poet.* Cambridge, Mass.: Harvard University Press, 1991.

Brodskii, N. L., ed. *Literaturnye salony i kruzhki: pervaia polovina XIX veka.* Moscow: Argaf, 2001 [1930].

———. *M. Gor'kii v vospominaniiakh sovremennikov.* Moscow: Gosudarstvennoe izdatel'stvo khudozhestvennoi literatury, 1955.

Brooks, Jeffrey. "Readers and Reading at the End of the Tsarist Era." In William Mills Todd III, ed., *Literature and Society in Imperial Russia, 1800–1914,* 97–150. Stanford, Calif.: Stanford University Press, 1978.

———. *When Russia Learned to Read: Literacy and Popular Literature, 1861–1917.* Princeton, N.J.: Princeton University Press, 1985.

———. *Thank-you Comrade Stalin! Soviet Public Culture from Revolution to Cold War.* Princeton, N.J.: Princeton University Press, 2000.

Brower, Daniel. "The Problem of the Russian Intelligentsia." *Slavic Review* 26 (1967): 638–639.

Brown, Edward J. *The Proletarian Episode in Russian Literature, 1928–1932.* New York: Columbia University Press, 1953.

———. *Stankevich and His Moscow Circle, 1830–1840.* Stanford, Calif.: Stanford University Press, 1966.

Bryusov, Valery. *The Diary of Valery Bryusov (1893–1905): With Reminiscences by V. F. Khodasevich and Marina Tsvetaeva.* Edited, translated, and with an introduction by Joan Delaney Grossman. Berkeley: University of California Press, 1980.

———. *Neizdannoe i nesobrannoe.* Moscow: Kliuch, 1998.

Bunin, Ivan. *Memories and Portraits.* Translated by Vera Traill and Robin Chancellor. London: John Lehmann, 1951.

Burbank, Jane. *Intelligentsia and Revolution: Russian Views of Bolshevism, 1917–1922.* New York: Oxford University Press, 1986.

———. "Were the Russian *Intelligenty* Organic Intellectuals?" In Judith Farquhar, Leon Fink, Stephen Leonard, and Donald Reid, eds., *Intellectuals and Political Life.* Ithaca, N.Y.: Cornell University Press, 1994.

Bushkovitch, Paul. *Peter the Great.* Cambridge: Cambridge University Press, 2001.

Bushnell, John. *Mutiny amid Repression: Russian Soldiers in the Revolution of 1905–1906.* Bloomington: Indiana University Press, 1985.

Chatterjee, Choi. *Celebrating Women: Gender, Festival Culture, and Bolshevik Ideology, 1910–1939.* Pittsburgh: University of Pittsburgh Press, 2002.

Chichkine, Andrei. "Le Banquet platonicien a la 'Tour' petersbourgeoisie." *Cahier du Monde Russe* 30, nos. 1–2 (1994): 15–18.

Chukovskii, Kornei. *Dnevnik, 1901–1929.* Moscow: Sovetskii pisatel', 1991.

Clardy, Jesse V. *G. R. Derzhavin: A Political Biography.* The Hague: Mouton, 1967.

Clark, Katerina. *Petersburg: Crucible of Cultural Revolution.* Cambridge, Mass.: Harvard University Press, 1995.

Clark, Katerina, and Michael Holquist. *Mikhail Bakhtin*. Cambridge, Mass.: Harvard University Press, 1984.

Clowes, Edith, Samuel Kassow, and James West, eds. *Between Tsar and People: Educated Society and the Quest for Public Identity in Late Imperial Russia, 1800–1914*. Princeton, N.J.: Princeton University Press, 1991.

Cohen, Steven. *Bukharin and the Bolshevik Revolution*. New York: Knopf, 1973.

Confino, Michael. "On Intellectuals and Intellectual Traditions in Eighteenth- and Nineteenth-Century Russia." *Daedalus* 101 (1972): 117–149.

David-Fox, Michael. "What Is Cultural Revolution?" *Russian Review* 58, no. 2 (1999): 181–201.

———. "*Mentalité* or Cultural System." *Russian Review* 58, no. 2 (1999): 210.

de Madariaga, Isabel. *Russia in the Age of Catherine the Great*. New Haven, Conn.: Yale University Press, 1981.

Deutscher, Isaac. *Stalin: A Political Biography*. Oxford: Oxford University Press, 1949.

Dewey, Horace W., and Ann M. Kleimola. "Suretyship and Collective Responsibility in Pre-Petrine Russia." *Jahrbücher für die Geschichte Osteuropas* 18 (1970): 337–354.

Durova, Nadezhda. *The Cavalry Maiden: Journals of a Russian Officer in the Napoleonic Wars*. Edited and translated by Mary Fleming Zirin. Bloomington: Indiana University Press, 1991.

Eastman, Max. *Artists in Uniform: A Study of Literature and Bureaucratism*. New York: Octagon, 1972 [1934].

Engel, Barbara. *Mothers and Daughters: Women of the Intelligentsia in Nineteenth Century Russia*. Cambridge: Cambridge University Press, 1983.

Engelstein, Laura. *The Keys to Happiness: Sex and the Search for Modernity in Fin-de-Siècle Russia*. Ithaca, N.Y.: Cornell University Press, 1992.

Fedorov, V. A. *Dekabristy v vospominaniiakh sovremennikov*. Moscow: Izdatel'stvo Moskovkogo Universiteta, 1988.

Fitzpatrick, Sheila. *The Commissariat of Enlightenment: Soviet Organization of Education and the Arts under Lunacharsky, October 1917–1921*. Cambridge: Cambridge University Press, 1970.

———. "Cultural Revolution as Class War." In Sheila Fitzpatrick, ed., *Cultural Revolution in Russia, 1928–1931*, 8–40. Bloomington: Indiana University Press, 1984.

———. "Cultural Orthodoxies under Stalin." In idem, *The Cultural Front: Power and Culture in Revolutionary Russia*, 238–256. Ithaca, N.Y.: Cornell University Press, 1992.

———. "The Soft Line on Culture and Its Enemies." In idem, *The Cultural Front: Power and Culture in Revolutionary Russia*, 91–114. Ithaca, N.Y.: Cornell University Press, 1992.

———. "Cultural Revolution Revisited." *The Russian Review* 58, no. 2 (1999): 202–209.

Fogelevich, L. G. *Osnovnye direktivy i zakonodatel'stvo o pechati: sistematicheskii sbornik*. Moscow: Sovetskoe zakonodatel'stvo, 1936.

Freeze, Gregory. "The *Soslovie* (Estate) Paradigm and Russian Social History." *American Historical Review* 91 (1986): 11–36.

Garrard, John, and Carol Garrard. *Inside the Soviet Writers' Union*. New York: Free Press, 1990.

Gertsyk, Evgeniia. *Vospominaniia*. Paris: YMCA Press, 1973.

Getty, J. Arch. *Origins of the Great Purges: The Soviet Communist Party Reconsidered, 1933–1938*. Cambridge: Cambridge University Press, 1985.

Ginzburg, Lidiia. *On Psychological Prose*. Edited and translated by Judson Rosengrant. Princeton, N.J.: Princeton University Press, 1991.

Gippius, Zinaida. *Zhivye litsa*. Vol. 1. Tbilisi: Merani, 1991.

Gleason, Abbott. *Young Russia: The Genesis of Russian Radicalism in the 1860s.* New York: Viking, 1980.

Gluckman, Max. "Gossip and Scandal." *Current Anthropology* 4, no. 3 (1963): 307–315.

Goldman, Wendy. *Women, the State, and Revolution: Soviet Family Policy and Social Life, 1917–1936.* Cambridge: Cambridge University Press, 1993.

Gray, Rosalind Polly. "Qestions of Identity at Abramtsevo." In Laura Morowitz and William Vaughan, eds., *Artistic Brotherhoods in the Nineteenth Century.* Burlington, Vt.: Ashgate, 2000.

Haimson, Leopold. "The Problem of Social Stability in Russia, 1905–1917." In Michael Cherniavsky, ed., *The Structure of Russian History: Interpretative Essays.* New York: Random House, 1970.

Hellbeck, Jochen. "Fashioning the Stalinist Soul: The Diary of Stepan Podlubnyi, 1931–9." In *Stalinism: New Directions*, ed. Sheila Fitzpatrick, 77–116. London: Routledge, 2000.

Herzen, Alexander. *My Past and Thoughts.* Translated by Constance Garnett, rev. ed. Humphrey Higgins. Berkeley: University of California Press, 1982.

Hittle, J. Michael. *The Service City: State and Townsmen in Russia, 1600–1800.* Cambridge, Mass.: Harvard University Press, 1979.

Hoch, Steven. *Serfdom and Social Control in Russia: Petrovskoe, a Village in Tambov.* Chicago: University of Chicago Press, 1986.

Holmgren, Beth. *Rewriting Capitalism: Literature and the Market in Late Tsarist Russia and the Kingdom of Poland.* Pittsburgh: University of Pittsburgh Press, 1998.

Holquist, Peter. *Making War, Forging Revolution: Russia's Continuum of Crisis, 1914–1921.* Cambridge, Mass.: Harvard University Press, 2002.

Hosking, Geoffrey. *The Russian Constitutional Experiment: Government and Duma, 1907–1914.* Cambridge: Cambridge University Press, 1973.

Institut mirovoi literatury imeni A.M. Gor'kogo. *Letopis' zhizni i tvorchestva A. M. Gor'kogo.* Moscow: Izdatel'stvo Akademii Nauk SSSR, 1958–1960.

Ivanova, Lidiia. *Vospominaniia: Kniga ob otse.* Moscow: Rik Kul'tura, 1992.

Jones, W. Gareth. *Nikolai Novikov: Enlightener of Russia.* Cambridge: Cambridge University Press, 1984.

Kassow, Samuel D. *Students, Professors, and the State in Tsarist Russia.* Berkeley: University of California Press, 1989.

Keenan, Edward. "Muscovite Political Folkways." *Russian Review* 45, no. 2 (April 1986): 115–182.

Kenez, Peter. *Civil War in South Russia, 1919–1920.* Berkeley: University of California Press, 1977.

———. *The Birth of the Propaganda State: Soviet Methods of Mass Mobilization, 1917–1929.* Cambridge: Cambridge University Press, 1985.

Kern, A. P. "Vospominaniia o Pushkine, Del'vige i Glinke." In idem (Markova-Vinogradskaia), *Vospominaniia, dnevniki, perepiska.* Moscow: Pravda, 1989.

Kharkhordin, Oleg. *The Collective and the Individual in Russia: A Study of Practices.* Berkeley: University of California Press, 1999.

Khodasevich, Vladislav. *"Nekropol'" i drugie vospominaniia.* Moscow: Zhurnal 'Nashe nasledie,' 1992.

Kivelson, Valerie. *Autocracy in the Provinces: The Muscovite Gentry and Political Culture in the Seventeenth Century.* Stanford, Calif.: Stanford University Press, 1996.

Kollmann, Nancy Shields. *Kinship and Politics: The Making of the Muscovite Political System, 1345–1547.* Stanford, Calif.: Stanford University Press, 1987.

Koretskaia, I. V. "Mir Iskusstva." In B. A. Bialik, ed., *Literaturnyi protsess i russkaia zhurnalistika kontsa XIX–nachala XX veka.* Moscow: "Nauka." 1982.

Kriukova, A. M., ed. *Perepiska A. N. Tolstogo v dvukh tomakh.* Moscow: Khudozhestven-naia Literatura, 1989.

Kupchenko, V. P. "Vol'noliubivaia iunost' poeta." *Novyi mir* 12 (1980): 216–223.

———. "Osip Mandelshtam v Kimmerii." *Voprosy literatury* 7 (1987): 188.

———. "Maksimilian Voloshin as a Memoirist." In John Elsworth, ed., *The Silver Age in Russian Literature: Selected Papers from the Fourth World Congress for Soviet and East European Studies, Harrogate, 1990.* New York: St. Martin's, 1992.

———. *Stranstvie Maksimiliana Voloshina.* St. Petersburg: Logos, 1996.

———. "Maksimilian Voloshin in London: An Unknown Episode of His Biography." *Slavonica* 7, no. 1 (2001): 42–49.

Kuzmin, M. A. *Sobranie stikhov III.* Edited by John E. Malmstad and Vladimir Markov. Munich: Centrifuga [Wilhelm Fink Verlag], 1977.

Lapidus, Gail. *Women in Soviet Society: Equality, Development, and Social Change.* Berkeley: University of California Press, 1978.

Levin, Dan. *Stormy Petrel: The Life and Work of Maxim Gorky.* New York: Schocken, 1986.

Leikina-Svirskaia, Vera. *Intelligentsiia v Rossii vo vtoroi polovine XIX veka.* Moscow: Mysl', 1971.

Lesina, N. *Planerskoe-Koktebel'.* Simferopol': Izdatel'stvo Krym, 1969.

Lewin, Moshe. "Society, State, and Ideology during the First Five-Year Plan." In Sheila Fitzpatrick, ed., *Cultural Revolution in Russia, 1928–1931,* 41–77. Bloomington: Indiana University Press, 1984.

Lotman, Iurii M. "The Poetics of Everyday Behavior in Eighteenth-Century Russian Life." Translated by Andrea Beesing. In Alexander Nakhimovsky and Alice Stone Nakhimovsky, eds., *The Semiotics of Russian Cultural History,* 67–94. Ithaca, N.Y.: Cornell University Press, 1985.

Lovell, Steven. "Between Arcadia and Suburbia: Dachas in Late Imperial Russia." *Slavic Review* 61, no. 1 (spring 2002): 66–87.

Lovell, Steven, Alena Ledeneva, and Andrei Rogachevskii, eds. *Bribery and Blat in Russia: Negotiating Reciprocity from the Middle Ages to the Present.* New York: St. Martin's, 2000.

Makovskii, Sergei. *Portrety sovremennikov.* New York: Chekhov, 1955.

———. *Na Parnasse serebrianogo veka.* Munich: Izdatel'stvo tsentral'naia ob'edineniia politicheskikh emigrantov iz SSSR, 1961.

Malia, Martin. "What Is the Intelligentsia." In Richard Pipes, ed., *The Russian Intelligentsia,* 1–18. New York: Columbia University Press, 1961.

———. *Alexander Herzen and the Birth of Russian Socialism.* New York: Grosset and Dunlap, 1965.

Mally, Lynn. *Revolutionary Acts: Amateur Theater and the Soviet State, 1917–1938.* Ithaca, N.Y.: Cornell University Press, 2000.

Manchester, Laurie. "The Secularization of the Search for Salvation: The Self-Fashioning of Orthodox Clergymen's Sons in Late Imperial Russia." *Slavic Review* 57, no. 1 (spring 1998): 50–76.

Mandelshtam, Nadezhda. *Hope against Hope: a Memoir.* New York: Atheneum, 1970.

Marullo, Thomas Gaiton, ed. and trans. *Ivan Bunin: Russian Requiem, 1885–1920.* Chicago: Ivan R. Dee, 1993.

Mauss, Marcel. *The Gift: Forms and Functions of Exchange in Archaic Societies.* London: Cohen and West, 1954.

McClelland, James C. *Autocrats and Academics, Education, Culture, and Society in Tsarist Russia.* Chicago: University of Chicago Press, 1979.

McReynolds, Louise, and Joan Neuberger, eds. *Imitations of Life: Two Centuries of Melo-drama in Russia.* Durham, N.C.: Duke University Press, 2002.

Meehan-Waters, Brenda. *Autocracy and Aristocracy: The Russian Service Elite of 1730.* New Brunswick, N.J.: Rutgers University Press, 1982.

Mikitich, L. D. *Literaturnyi Peterburg, Petrograd.* Moscow: Sovetskaia Rossia, 1991.

Millar, James R. "The Little Deal: Brezhnev's Contribution to Acquisitive Socialism." In Terry Thompson and Richard Sheldon, eds., *Soviet Society and Culture: Essays in Honor of Vera S. Dunham,* 3–19. Boulder, Colo.: Westview, 1988).

Morrissey, Susan. *Heralds of Revolution: Russian Students and the Mythologies of Radi-calism.* New York: Oxford University Press, 1998.

Mueller, Otto. *Intelligencija: Untersuchungen zur Geschichte eines politischen Schlag-wortes.* Frankfurt: Athenaem, 1971.

Nikolaev, P. A., ed. *Russkie pisateli, 1800–1917: Biograficheskii slovar'.* Moscow: NVP FIANIT, 1992.

Nikolaevich, A. N. *Obshchestvennoe dvizhenie v Rossii pri Aleksandrie I.* 2nd ed. St. Pe-tersburg: M. M. Stasiulevicha, 1885.

Nove, Alec. *An Economic History of the USSR.* New York: Penguin, 1969.

Oksman, Iu. G., ed. *N. G. Chernyshevskii v vospominaniiakh sovremennikov.* Saratov: Sara-tovskoe knizhnoe izdatel'stvo, 1958–1959.

Orlov, V. *Studencheskoe dvizhenie moskovskogo universiteta v XIX stoletii.* Moscow: Iz-datel'stvo vsesoiuznogo obshchestva politkatorzhan i ssyl'no-poselentsev, 1934.

Orlovsky, Daniel. "Political Clientelism in Russia: The Historical Perspective." In T. H. Rigby and Bohdan Harasyiv, eds., *Leadership Selection and Patron-Client Relations in the USSR and Yugoslavia,* 174–199. London: Allen and Unwin, 1983.

Ortner, Sherry. "Theory in Anthropology since the Sixties." *Comparative Studies in Soci-ety and History* 26, no. 1 (1984): 126–166.

———. *Making Gender: The Politics and Erotics of Culture.* Boston: Beacon, 1996.

Pachmuss, Temira, ed. and trans. *Women Writers in Russian Modernism: An Anthology.* Urbana: University of Illinois Press, 1978.

Paperno, Irina. *Chernyshevsky and the Age of Realism: A Study in the Semiotics of Behav-ior.* Stanford, Calif.: Stanford University Press, 1988.

Paperno, Irina, and Joan Delaney Grossman, eds. *Creating Life: The Aesthetic Utopia of Russian Modernism.* Stanford, Calif.: Stanford University Press, 1994.

Petrone, Karen. *Life Has Become More Joyous, Comrades: Celebrations in the Time of Stalin.* Bloomington: Indiana University Press, 2000.

Piast, V. *Vstrechi.* Moscow: Federatsiia, 1929.

Pyman, Avril. The Life of Alexander Blok. 2 vols. Vol. 1: The Distant Thunder, 1880–1908. Oxford: Oxford University Press, 1979.

———. *A History of Russian Symbolism.* Cambridge: Cambridge University Press, 1994.

Radishchev, Alexander. *A Journey from St. Petersburg to Moscow.* Cambridge, Mass.: Har-vard University Press, 1958.

Raeff, Marc. "Russian Youth on the Eve of Romanticism: Andrei I. Turgenev and His Cir-cle." In idem, *Political Ideas and Institutions in Imperial Russia,* 42–64. Boulder, Colo.: Westview, 1994.

Raleigh, Donald. *Experiencing Russia's Civil War: Politics, Society, and Revolutionary Cul-ture in Saratov, 1917–1922.* Princeton, N.J.: Princeton University Press, 2002.

Ransel, David. *The Politics of Catherinian Russia: The Panin Party.* New Haven, Conn.: Yale University Press, 1975.

Read, Christopher. *Culture and Power in Revolutionary Russia: The Intelligentsia and the Transition from Tsarism to Communism.* New York: St. Martin's, 1990.

Reitblat, A. I. "Literaturnyi gonorar v Rossii XIX–nachala XX v. (K postanovke problemy)." In *Knizhnoe delo v Rossii vo vtoroi polovine XIX–nachale XX veka*, Vol. 3: *Sobranie nauchnykh trudov*, ed. V. E. Kel'ner. Leningrad: Gosudarstvennaia Publichnaia Biblioteka imeni M. E. Saltykova-Shchedrina, 1986.

Rieber, Alfred. *Merchants and Entrepreneurs in Imperial Russia*. Chapel Hill: University of North Carolina Press, 1982.

Rogger, Hans. *National Consciousness in Eighteenth-Century Russia*. Cambridge, Mass.: Harvard University Press, 1960.

Roosevelt, Priscilla. *Life on the Russian Country Estate: A Social and Cultural History*. New Haven, Conn.: Yale University Press, 1995.

Rosenthal, Bernice Glatzer. *Dmitrii Sergeevich Merezhkovskii and the Silver Age: The Development of a Revolutionary Mentality*. The Hague: Martinus Nijhoff, 1975.

Rudd, Charles A. *Russian Entrepreneur: Publisher Ivan Sytin of Moscow, 1851–1934*. Montreal: McGill-Queen's University Press, 1990.

Schatz, Marshall S., and Judith E. Zimmerman, eds. and trans. *Signposts: A Collection of Articles on the Russian Intelligentsia*. Irvine, Calif.: Charles Schlacks Jr., 1986.

Shapiro, Leonard. *The Communist Party of the Soviet Union*. New York: Random House, 1959.

Shlapentokh, Vladimir. *Love, Marriage, and Friendship in the Soviet Union: Ideals and Practices*. New York: Praeger, 1984.

Stites, Richard. *The Women's Liberation Movement in Russia: Feminism, Nihilism, and Bolshevism, 1860–1930*. Princeton, N.J.: Princeton University Press, 1978.

———. *Revolutionary Dreams: Utopian Vision and Experimental Life in the Russian Revolution*. New York: Oxford University Press, 1989.

Stromberg, Roland. *Redemption by War: The Intellectuals and 1914*. Lawrence: The Regents Press of Kansas, 1982.

Tartakovskii, A. G. *Russkaia memuaristika XVIII–pervoi poloviny XIX v.: ot rukopisi k knige*. Moscow: Nauka, 1991.

Tchaikovsky, Modeste, ed. *The Life and Letters of Peter Tchaikovsky*. Translated by Rosa Newmarch. London: John Lane, 1905.

Teffi, N. A. *Nostal'giia: Rasskazy, vospominaniia*. Leningrad: Khudozhestvennaia literatura, 1989.

Tolstoy, Alexandra. *Tolstoy: A Life of My Father*. New York: Harper and Brothers, 1953.

Trifonov, Iurii. *The House on the Embankment*. Translated by Michael Glenny. New York: Simon and Schuster, 1983.

Troinitskii, N. A. *Pervaia vseobshchaia perepis' naseleniia Rossiiskoi imperii*. Vol. 24. St. Petersburg: Tsentral'nyi statisticheskii komitet, 1899–1905.

Tsikhalashvili, N. Sh., and David Engerman. "Amerikanskaia pomoshch' Rossii v 1921–1923 godakh: konflikty i sotrudnichestvo." *Amerikanskii ezhegodnik* (1995): 191–212.

Tsvetaeva, Anastasiia. *Vospominaniia*. Moscow: Sovetskii pisatel', 1983.

Tsvetaeva, Marina. "Geroi truda (zapisi o Valerii Briusove)." In idem, *Proza*. New York: Izdatel'stvo imeni Chekhova, 1953.

———. *A Captive Spirit: Selected Prose*. Translated by J. Marin King. Ann Arbor, Mich.: Ardis, 1980.

———. "A Living Word about a Living Man." In Marina Tsvetaeva, *A Captive Spirit: Selected Prose*. Translated by J. Marin King. Ann Arbor, Mich.: Ardis, 1980.

———. *Pis'ma k Anne Teskovoi*. St. Petersburg: Vneshtorgizdat, 1991.

Tumarkin, Nina. *Lenin Lives! The Lenin Cult in Soviet Russia*. Cambridge, Mass.: Harvard University Press, 1983.

Turkov, A. *Aleksandr Blok*. Moscow: Molodaia gvardiia, 1969.

Turner, Victor. *The Ritual Process: Structure and Anti-Structure.* Chicago: Aldine, 1969.
———. *From Ritual to Theatre: The Human Seriousness of Play.* New York: Performing Arts Journal Publications, 1982.
van Gennep, Arnold. *Rites of Passage.* London: Routledge and Kegan Paul, 1960.
Venturi, Franco. *Roots of Revolution: A History of the Populist and Socialist Movements in Nineteenth Century Russia.* New York: Grosset and Dunlap, 1960.
Veresaev, Vikentii. *Vospominaniia.* Moscow: Pravda, 1982.
———. *V tupike.* Petersburg: Lenizdat, 1989.
von Guenther, Johannes. *Ein Leben im Ostwind. Zwischen Petersburg und Muenchen.* Munich: Biederstein, 1969.
Walker, Barbara. "On Reading Soviet Memoirs: A History of the 'Contemporaries' Genre as an Institution of Russian Intelligentsia Culture from the 1790s to the 1970s." *Russian Review* 59 (July 2000): 327–352.
———. "(Still) Searching for a Soviet Society: A Review of Recent Scholarship on Personal Ties in Soviet Political and Economic Life." *Comparative Studies in Society and History* 43, no. 3 (July 2001): 631–42.
———. "*Kruzhok* Culture and the Meaning of Patronage in the Early Soviet Literary World." In *Contemporary European History* 2, no. 1 (2002): 107–123. Special Issue: *Patronage, Personal Networks and the Party-State.*
———. "Joseph Stalin, 'Our Teacher Dear': Mentorship, Social Transformation, and the Russian Intelligentsia Personality Cult." In Klaus Heller and Jan Plamper, eds., *Personenkulte im Stalinismus/Personality Cults in Stalinism.* Göttingen: Vandenhoeck and Ruprecht, forthcoming.
Walicki, Andrej. *The Slavophile Controversy: History of a Conservative Utopia in Nineteenth-Century Russian Thought.* Translated by Hilda Andrews Rusiecka. Oxford: Clarendon, 1975.
Weissman, Benjamin. *Herbert Hoover and Famine Relief to Soviet Russia.* Stanford, Calif.: Hoover Institution Press, 1974.
Wellman, Barry, and S. D. Berkowitz. *Social Structures: A Network Approach.* Cambridge: Cambridge University Press, 1988.
Wiener, Martin J. *English Culture and the Decline of the Industrial Spirit, 1850–1980.* New York: Cambridge University Press, 1981.
Wirtschafter, Elise Kimerling. *Social Identity in Imperial Russia.* Dekalb: Northern Illinois University Press, 1997.
Wolfe, Bertram. *The Bridge and the Abyss: The Troubled Friendship of Maxim Gorky and V. I. Lenin.* New York: Praeger, 1967. Published for the Hoover Institution on War, Revolution, and Peace, Stanford University, California.
Woloschin, Margarita. *Die Gruene Schlange: Lebenserinnerungen einer Malerin.* Frankfurt am Main: Fischer Taschenbuch Verlag, 1982.
Wortman, Richard S. *Scenarios of Power: Myth and Ceremony in Russian Monarchy.* 2 vols. Vol. 1: *From Peter the Great to the Death of Nicholas I.* Princeton, N.J.: Princeton University Press, 1995.
Yaney, George. *The Systematization of Russian Government: Social Evolution in the Domestic Administration of Imperial Russia, 1711–1905.* Urbana: University of Illinois Press, 1973.
Yedlin, Tovah. *Maxim Gorky: A Political Biography.* Westport, Conn.: Praeger, 1999.
Zoe, Mary Louise. "Redefining the Intellectual's Role: Maksim Gorky and the *Sreda* Circle." In *Between Tsar and People: Educated Society and the Quest for Public Identity in Late Imperial Russia,* 288–307. Princeton, N.J.: Princeton University Press, 1991.

INDEX

Page numbers in italics refer to illustrations.

Barbara Walker is Associate Professor of History at the University of Nevada, Reno.